# The Messenger

# The Messenger

## THE IMPROBABLE STORY
## OF A GRIEVING MOTHER
## AND A SPIRIT GUIDE

Helen Delaney

White Bird Enterprises, Cambridge, MD

White Bird Enterprises
5 Glenburn Avenue
Cambridge, MD 21613

Scripture quotations are taken from the Holy Bible, King James Version.

ISBN-13: 978-0692355237
ISBN-10: 0692355235

Cover Design by Edward A. Butler
Library of Congress Control Number: 2014922767
White Bird Enterprises, Cambridge, MD

# ACKNOWLEDGEMENTS

———— ❧ ————

OVER THE COURSE OF SOME twenty years, I have been blessed with friends who read portions of this book. They were kind, and patient, and encouraging. I wish to thank them now for keeping the faith with me. I am grateful to two wonderful writers, Dianne Houston, who was the first to tell me that my story was a book, and Dorothy Randall Gray, who taught me that the Source would always be there.

To Jim Thomas goes my deepest appreciation. Thank you, Jim, for keeping me writing. Thank you, Julia Lightfoot, my fellow believer, fellow traveler, reader of many versions, and source of inspiration.

Thank you to all who read the final version from start to finish, especially my daughters, my brother, Ed Butler, my sister-in-law, Jane Butler, Barbara Wasserman, and my friends Janna Craze and Jackie Noller. A special thank you to Jesse Hoffman for the enormous job of editing a raw manuscript.

I owe my greatest debt of gratitude to the Working Writers Forum of Easton, Maryland: Thank you Laura Ambler, Linda Fritz Bell, Bill Brashares, Mala Burt, Brent Lewis, Anne McNulty, Marcia Moore, Beth Schucker, Gerald Sweeney, and Wilson Wyatt. You taught me, supported me, and inspired me. Without you, there would be no book.

To Reverend F. Reed Brown: You saved my life. May joy and peace be yours in abundance and may your gift continue to give hope to others like me.

To my husband Bill: You were a tireless reader, patient editor, faithful partner, and friend. You read more iterations of this book than either of us could count, and always gave me more credit than I deserved. Thank you, Billy, for the gift of true love.

To my daughters Debbie, Niki, and Michaela: You are my pillars—always hopeful, always encouraging, always believing. Without your faith and love I would have given up long ago. Thank you for living this life with me. To my granddaughters Céline and Elenni: You have filled every space in the heart that was broken. Thank you, too, for being here now.

And to my son Eddie, who has gone before and who still shines like the sun: This book is for you.

*"O death, where is thy sting? O grave, where is thy victory?"*
*~ I Corinthians 15:55*

# CHAPTER 1

—–⊛⊛⊛—–

*You do not have to believe this story. It happened all the same.*

—–⊛⊛⊛—–

What I remember about the bedroom in my apartment on Massachusetts Avenue is the window that looked out onto the street and the digital clock that sat on a table at the foot of the bed. On the morning of September 23, 1979, I sat up abruptly and saw its red numbers glaring at me: 7:30 a.m.

"I'm going to be late for work," I thought. Panic began to rise in my stomach. Then I remembered: It was Sunday. And another bonus: I was not hung over. I laid back, relieved, and closed my eyes.

I was drifting into sleep when I felt a *presence* in the bed beside me. It was comforting and sweet. *Who is this?* I wondered. Then it came to me that I was alone. Eddie was spending the weekend with his friend, Geoffrey. And then, I fell asleep.

—–⊛⊛⊛—–

The telephone jarred me awake and I looked at the clock again: 8:30 a.m.

"Hello?" I said in my sleep voice.

It was Geoffrey's father, Gil. I sat up. My heart leapt in my body.

"Helen. I have bad news," he said. I hardly recognized his voice.

My mind flitted to Geoffrey's motorcycle and quickly concocted a scenario: a little accident. *The worst it could be is a broken leg. But Eddie's okay*, I told myself. *Don't worry. He's all right.*

"Is Eddie all right?" I said.

"No," he answered.

"Is he hurt?"

"It's worse."

I froze.

And then, his voice broke. "He's dead."

A yawning black hole opened wide and closed around me.

"The police will be there to see you in a few minutes." Through the blackness I could hear him sobbing.

"I'll have to call you back. I can't talk now," I said, as if we were having a normal conversation, as if my saying that would make the black hole go away. I sat there on the side of my bed, as still as death, until the policeman was at my door.

❦

He enters, tall and solemn. We sit on the couch. He tells me that Eddie fell from Gil's balcony, nine stories up.

I sit there, uncomprehending, in a spell.

"Did Eddie have any enemies?" His words are slow and careful.

"No. Everybody loved Eddie."

The policeman is writing into a small notebook.

"He was with his best friend and his father. They've known him since he was born." I am mouthing words. They don't mean anything.

"The father was out when it happened."

He tells me that it was probably an accident. It seems that the boys were fooling around, he says, and Eddie fell.

"You'll have to come to the Washington Hospital Center to identify the body."

"What?"

"You'll have to come to the Washington Hospital Center to identify the body, ma'am. I'm sorry. Is there someone who can drive you?"

"His father will drive me." *I've got to call Harold. Maybe this isn't true.*

"I am sorry for your loss, ma'am," he says.

I see him to the door, turn around, and face the window. Pink azalea plants are on the windowsill, blooming. Someone is insane.

I am aware of someone screaming. I am standing at the window, looking at the sky, searching for God, and the screaming is coming from me.

"Take *me*, you Son of a Bitch! Take *me*!" Over and over I beg Him, I *dare* Him, I entreat Him. I shake both my fists at Him. The sky disappears. Rage has made me blind.

The telephone rings, jars me into the present. A timid voice from the reception desk says that my neighbors in the adjoining apartments are complaining about the noise.

"Tell them my *son* died," I scream into the phone. I am tight and cold. But I will the screaming to stop, because I have to call his father.

At the Hospital Center, they will not allow me to identify the body. They are afraid I will faint, and they appoint my ex-husband, Harold. He will view him on a television screen. They have already performed an autopsy. The coroner tells us that the cause of death was trauma to the head. Harold is escorted away to his dreadful duty, and I am left with the coroner.

"Did he suffer?" I ask, trembling violently.

"No," he says. "He died instantly." He puts the time of death at 7:30 a.m.

Harold drives me home. My daughter Niki, who has come with her father, is in the back seat of the car, stone-like, staring out the window.

We reach my apartment and Harold says, "You should pack a few things and come to the house." He means our house, his house now. "We'll make arrangements from there."

My apartment is still and lifeless. I pile clothes into a bag. At the door I turn around. In the window, the azalea blossoms have turned to brown tissue paper. They have died from fright, from the screaming.

---

I am in the old house, but I am not at home. The years of betrayed love and hurt are in the walls. It is difficult to breathe there. The only thing that makes it bearable is alcohol.

I drink with purpose: to escape, to obtain oblivion. It doesn't work. No matter how much I drink, I stay trapped in the epicenter of a bad dream. And awake.

My three daughters, Debbie, Niki, and Michaela, are in the house, in their old rooms, but for the first time in their lives, I do not know if they eat, or when they sleep. Neighbors bring food. Friends console them. I am frozen.

---

I lay down on the old, sad bed. I let tears come for the first time. They escalate quickly into choking sobs, and I know immediately that I have made a dangerous mistake. I have opened a floodgate that I will not be able to close. Like the blow of an axe, the first wave of grief slams into me. I cannot move or breathe, but I can see through the window that the sun is low in the sky, and a line from the movie *War and Peace* flits across my mind: *It is so hard to stay alive at sunset.*

I feel my heart begin to break. I can feel it; I can see it, small fissures opening up here and there in that red muscle, like the first cracks at the beginning of an earthquake. I call out for Harold, beg him to call the psychiatrist I am seeing. I need a tranquilizer, a pill, something to stop my heart from breaking. The alcohol isn't working. I am in full panic. The cracks open wider. I can hear him on the telephone, talking to the doctor in a slow, unhurried voice. *He doesn't care if I die,* I think. *He thinks it was all my fault anyway.* He comes back into the room and looks down at me. "Dr. Wyatt says there is no pill for grief. It will not kill you." He's wrong. It's only a matter of time.

Years later, I learned the name of this internal earthquake. It is called *cardiomyopathy*, or Broken Heart Syndrome. It is triggered by a severe emotional trauma, and in its throes, the heart's main pumping chamber is stretched and weakened. People die from it all the time. Grief *can* kill you. That would have been fine with me. I was frightened by the intensity of it, but I wanted to die. The sooner the better.

---

The week of funeral arrangements is foggy, with visits to the funeral home in the day and drinking at night, alone, upstairs in Harold's grim house, with one memory.

Eddie and I were good friends. We talked about everything. One rainy, cozy night, we sat on the couch in my apartment, talking about funerals, I have no idea why. We agreed that extravagant funerals were a waste, a profit-making disgrace, foisted on the grieving.

"When it's my time," Eddie said, "I'm going in a pine box."

"Me, too!" I said. We high-fived and laughed.

The funeral director doesn't have a pine box. I tell him that we will move heaven and earth until one is found. In two days, a pine box is procured from a Jewish funeral director in New York. He will ship it to Washington, D.C.

---

Friends and family are pressed together in the funeral home for the brief evening service. The room is packed to capacity, the crowd spilling into the hall and out into the street. The pine box sits inside a closed casket. I will not allow myself or my daughters to see him; I will not have that memory haunt us forever.

My daughters are poised and dry-eyed except the youngest, Michaela, who weeps pitifully through the service, like the child she is. Niki is the only one of us who can speak, and she does so with dignity and a steady voice, tracing Eddie's brief, bright life and our love for him.

When the adults have passed through our receiving line with their embraces and goodbyes, I stand there, waiting for them: the army of Eddie's friends and classmates. Stunned and wordless, they come to me with single roses and poems, pressing them into my hand. Only a few short months ago, they were applauding and cheering as Eddie walked across the stage to receive his high school diploma.

———

At Mass the next morning, my mother sits next to me, holding my hand. It is almost over when I feel myself leaning toward her, losing consciousness. Someone puts smelling salts under my nose, a sharp, humiliating jolt.

Outside, a friend bends down to look at me through the closed funeral car window. "God loves you," she mouths silently, as the driver pulls away. *And how would you know that?* I want to scream at her.

My daughters and I and my ex-husband stand together in the dignified old Rock Creek Cemetery on an overcast day. Crepe myrtle trees are everywhere, their pink and fuchsia blossoms blots of color in the gloom.

"Ashes to ashes, dust to dust. I am the Resurrection and the Life," the priest intones.

The grave faces a lily pond.

———

In a few days, Debbie will depart for Europe, leaving her years at Princeton behind. Niki will return to the Philadelphia College of Art. Michaela will remain here, but with her father. After the divorce, she stayed with him because the house was close to her middle school in Takoma Park, but mainly to keep and take care of her dog, a spotted pointer named Clyde, whom Harold had threatened to send to the pound.

It didn't occur to me that he, better armed in every way, would take everything in the divorce. But later, when Eddie opted to live with me, I didn't care. Harold, the lawyer, had a house. I had a son.

———◦∞∞◦———

On a cold, dark day in November, I enter my apartment after work, reach for a glass, fill it with ice and cover it with bourbon. Still wearing my coat, I drink it down and pour another. I am the death lady, possessed by grief and primordial failure. A child died on my watch. I need to die too.

# CHAPTER 2

—⦚—

IT IS TWO A.M., AND I am sitting on the floor of my living room, clasping Eddie's sneakers to my chest, rocking back and forth. And I hear a prayer in my head: *"Oh God, please help me to get sober."*

For the past twenty-two years, from the moment I learned of the first of my husband's many betrayals, alcohol has been my friend, my constant companion, my cure-all, snake oil magical potion for heartache and loneliness. If ever I needed it, I need it now. Yet this prayer arises unbidden, from a source and a depth I cannot fathom. I have asked God, whom I hate, for something I don't want. I dismiss it and finish the bottle at my side.

—⦚—

"Get right back to work," my boss said. "It's the best thing to do." But I cannot read. I cannot concentrate. I sit in my office, dim and hung over. No one sees me. I am the Washington representative for an organization that is based in Philadelphia. They call us lone professionals.

In the city of Washington, D.C., there are four other women working in my field—Sandy, Martha, Ann, and Barbara. They watch over me, try to save my job. They fill me in on the hearings I do not attend and the issues I am supposed to cover. I will lose my job eventually.

I have only one fear—that I will end up on the street in the wintertime. I can see myself: *a street lady with swollen feet*. I see them every day, lost souls in the cold, carrying dirty plastic bags filled with their earthly belongings. I wonder where they sleep. I need to figure out how to die before that happens.

———⊙⊙⊙———

My friend Ann enters my office, a determined look on her face. "There is a man you have to see," she says. "He's a psychic, a medium." I'm too weary to argue with her. I acquiesce, but regret it within minutes. I try to back out. Ann persists. "*You*," she tells me, "have nothing to lose."

———⊙⊙⊙———

The medium, Reverend Reed Brown, is a nice-looking young man in a navy blue suit, white shirt, and silk tie. Ann introduces me. He's holding a cup and saucer of fine china. He asks if I'd like to have a cup of coffee.

"No, thank you," I say. I just want to get this over with.

It is 10:30 a.m. The church is in Georgetown, an upscale section of Washington, D.C. The sanctuary is sunny and lovely through leaded glass windows. It is not the setting I expected.

Reverend Brown hands me a three-by-five card. "Write down the names of three people who have crossed over," he says in a clear, pleasant voice, "and three questions. I'll wait for you in my office."

Ann has gone off somewhere. I sit in one of the pews and scan the ceiling, looking for mirrors. I don't see any, but I shield my card anyway. Bending over it, I write three names: Eddie, Jim, my friend who died recently, and Butsie, my favorite uncle, who died in a fire. Ann doesn't know the last two people on my list. I'm sure she has coached Reverend Brown and that he already knows about Eddie. *This is ridiculous. But it'll get Ann off my back.*

I write one question. I want to know if Eddie is happy. I fold the card several times as instructed, enter Reverend Brown's office, which is just off the sanctuary, and sit down in front of his desk. A *desk*.

I put the folded card in his hand as he asks me to, and place my hand over it. He closes his eyes, asks Spirit to assist us and protect us as we open the door to the two worlds. In a minute, he asks me if I know someone named Mary. "She is here," he says, and she wishes me well. I don't know anyone named Mary. Then he asks if someone in my family used to "*know things,* you know, was psychic." "She's here, too," he says. I don't know anyone in my family who was psychic. I squirm in my chair. *What a waste of time.* All of a sudden, he opens clear, corn-flower-blue eyes, looks directly at me and says, "Who's Eddie?"

He has my attention. "My son," I say. My legs are weak. "He's here," the Reverend Mr. Brown says, "and he's laughing." *So like Eddie,* I think. *He laughed all the time.* "He says he's happy and he wants you to be happy too." I am stunned. He has answered my question.

"Someone is here whose name begins with a J," he says. *Jim.* "He says to tell you that he still loves you and that he is sorry, but he was confused." *Jim committed suicide. We used to drink together.*

And then, he calls my uncle's name—his nickname, the one I called him as a child: Uncle Butsie, the name I wrote on the card. Only Reverend Brown pronounces it "Bootsie." Uncle "Bootsie" is glad to see me and tells me that everything is going to be all right. Reverend Brown looks at me with those clear blue eyes again and says, "They are telling me that doors are going to open for you, doors are going to open for you. Everything is going to be all right." When I come out wobbly and dazed, Ann is waiting for me.

"How was it?" she says. Her smile is just a bit smug.

---

I call my mother to tell her my incredulous story. "Mama," I say, "First of all, I want you to know that I'm cold sober."

The only things he didn't get right, I tell her, was somebody named Mary, and somebody in the family who was "psychic." "Oh," my mother replies, "how could you forget your best friend when you were a little girl—*Miss Mary who lived next door?* Oh yes, and my sister Gertrude was psychic. You didn't know her. She died before you were born."

# CHAPTER 3

———❦———

CHRISTMAS IS CRUEL. IT COMES three months after Eddie's death. It will be here in a week. Harold calls to discuss Christmas for the girls, who will be home for the holidays.

"It should be as normal as possible," he is saying. "We ought to have dinner here, with a tree and decorations."

"A tree?" I scream. This is unbelievable. "A *tree?*" I lose it. I am crying and angry. "Are you crazy?" The pain shoots out of my voice. "There will be no more Christmases. Not in this lifetime. I can't believe you're thinking about *decorations!*" I scream at him. And I say it again: "Are you *crazy?*"

The thought of Christmas is like a kick in the stomach: a table with no place for Eddie. *No gifts for Eddie.* Christmas is a fresh, new brand of pain. God saw to that. The little glimmer of light from my encounter with Reverend Brown goes out, extinguished by decorations.

Harold starts to say something when I hear a loud crash in the hallway.

"Wait," I say. "I heard a noise in the hallway."

"Go look," he says, "I'll stay on the line."

There is nothing in the hallway. I open the coat closet. Several boxes have fallen from the shelf onto the floor. Last year's Christmas decorations. There aren't many boxes, just a few: a single person's Christmas decorations. I open one box of glass ornaments, then another. Nothing is broken.

*"I hear you, Eddie,"* I whisper, *"I hear you."*

I am shaking when I return to the phone. Harold tries to rationalize what has happened. Rumbling trucks going by on my downtown street must have shaken the boxes off the shelf, he tells me.

"Then why has nothing else fallen?" I say.

We will have a tree.

---

Christmas Day is dark and rainy. The tree looks old and sad. Harold's handi-work. I am cooking dinner alone in my old kitchen, drinking too quickly. By dinnertime I am drunk, and the over-ambitious duck *à l'orange* is burned black and reduced to a cinder.

The girls leave and go to a neighboring house, where their friend's mother will have prepared a Christmas dinner that will be warm and plentiful. I am guilty and drowning in pain. I want my daughters to come back. I want to start all over again. I want to make it up to them. I want us to have a real Christmas.

The house is empty and hollow. Harold sits at the table alone, drunk, his anger echoing around the room.

I drive to the cemetery and lie down on Eddie's grave, an empty wine bottle in my hand. No grass has grown here. The grave is mud, a wound in the ground. It is pouring rain. I do not know how long I lie there. I do not remember the drive back to my apartment.

---

I am still alive when summer comes and my four friends take me to see Sarah Vaughn, who is singing in the park. My contribution to the picnic supper is a half-gallon of wine. Sitting on a blanket under the stars, I am the only one drunk. Ann takes me home with her, and when I wake up the next morning on her couch, toxic, dirty, sick and ashamed, I know that a line has been crossed. And I am relieved. Maybe it is, at last, time to die.

I have forgotten my desperate prayer to get sober, but it is then, at the low-est, darkest hour of my sorrow, that it is answered. It happens without my help, without my will, without the doctors, therapists, and clergymen I have visited throughout the years. It happens with Sandy.

---

It was the Monday morning after the concert in the park that Sandy asked me to come with her to a church that was a block away from my office. I'd barely noticed that Sandy had stopped drinking with me. I agreed to go with her. Why, I do not know.

Barbara, Ann, and Martha met us there. At noon, two blocks away from the White House, in the basement of an old historic church, the five of us took seats in the back of the kindergarten room. I knew that I had come to the end of something. Martha held my hand.

I sat pressed against the back wall, shaking, barely comprehending what was said. I was too sick to concentrate. A word or two penetrated the sharp pain in my head. But when the man who was speaking asked if there was anyone there for the first time, I felt my hand rise of its own accord. I never intended to speak, but the words spilled out of my mouth. I said my name and the one, vital truth that had escaped me for so long: *I am an alcoholic.* The people in the room turned and smiled at me, their eyes saying, *we know, we know, we know.* My friends smiled, their eyes wet with relief and love.

---

I am sober for a whole day, than another, and another. I go to the church basement every day at noon. Most of us bring our lunch in paper bags. We drink coffee from Styrofoam cups. The room is filled with laughter at times, at times with tears.

I count the days without alcohol: two, three. Thirty. The fog begins to lift.

Clarity of mind is slow to come, but it makes its appearance in small, sad flashes. I am not prepared for the remorse that comes with consciousness. I am guilty of so much. I ask my younger daughters, Niki and Michaela, to forgive me for the mess I made of Christmas, for the mess I made of my life, and theirs, and six months later, I make a shaky trip to Paris, to see my oldest daughter, Debbie. She meets my flight, and I ask her to have a cup of coffee with me before we leave the airport. If she does not forgive me, I will turn around and go home, and not blame her. I tell her that I know that I am an alcoholic, and that I have not had a drink for six months. There are happy tears in her eyes. We take a taxi to her apartment in the lovely Sixteenth *Arrondissement* of Paris.

It has taken some time, but it dawns on me that I am not the only one who has lost Eddie. My children have grieved alone, with no comfort from me, no wise words, no mother's arms to hold them. Still, they are loving and forgiving. How did they get that way? I have heard parents in that basement room speak of children who will not see them, not speak to them. I am one of the lucky ones.

I am with Debbie for a week. We talk about Eddie—good, sweet things we remember. We cry. We are not healed, but we are together.

I sit in the magnificence of Notre Dame without rancor. I make a vow to be a mother to my daughters. But I am not ready to reconcile with God.

# CHAPTER 4

———⚬⚬⚬———

I AM NOT NORMAL. I am not like other people. I know no one who has lost a child, but I know *you never get over the death of a child*. I am alive and sober, but defective. Broken.

Every young man I see reminds me of Eddie. Sometimes I think I see him. One day I follow a boy for blocks, hoping he will turn around and it will be Eddie. *Maybe some other boy died.*

The question, "Why?" haunts me. It tortures me—that *Why*. It is at the core of my resentment, the basis of the hate I feel toward God. Eddie was such a good boy, such a sweet boy. He was too young to die. *You did this*, I rage at God. I will hate Him forever and never know peace.

———⚬⚬⚬———

I am called to Philadelphia, to my home office, to attend a Board meeting. It is there that I find myself afterwards, wandering around a bookstore in the 30th Street Station, waiting for the train to take me home to Washington, D.C. I walk up and down the aisles, until a little book—at eye level—stops me. It is called "*Opening to Channel: How to Connect with Your Guide*." The authors are Sanaya Roman and Duane Packer. I touch it, and it falls off the shelf, into my hand.

———⚬⚬⚬———

Swaying in my seat on the jostling train, I read, spellbound. Anyone who is willing, the little book says, can channel information from the spirit world. Channeling, it says, is a skill that allows one to connect with a high-level Spirit Guide. All that is necessary to access higher realms of consciousness is the willingness to become open and connect. *A skill.* Something like an electric shock passes through my body.

I look out the train window. Rain rolls in rivulets down the glass. I wonder if Eddie has given this to me.

---

Day after day, I follow the instructions in the book. I try to empty my mind, *open it to channel,* but it is preoccupied with despair.

I try to meditate. My apartment is too small. Stifling. I try sitting in the park nearby. I read books on meditation methods. I try focusing on a candle flame. I repeat a mantra. I walk for miles. I sit with a yellow pad and pen as the book instructs, hoping to make contact. Again and again I make the effort, striving for stillness, the bridge to my Spirit Guide. It will not come.

As the weeks go by, I grow weary of the struggle. Sitting by my window one day, awash in a somber gray sky, I give up. I lean my head against the back of the chair, close my eyes, and give up.

I am almost asleep when I feel a tingling behind my left shoulder, and then I feel a presence— *a very large presence*—next to my chair.

I jump, and it vanishes. I ask it to return. *Where is the pad and pen?* Frantically, I fumble beneath my chair and retrieve them. I sit upright, ready. Pen poised. My hand moves—by itself—and writes one letter: "L," scrawled large across the page with a great flourish.

Every day it is the same: L, L, L, nothing more. But one day, an entire name is spelled out: *Lukhamen.* And again, every day it is the same: Lukhamen, Lukhamen, Lukhamen— nothing more.

I consult the little book again, and it says that the Guide has to get used to your energy system, and make fine, subtle adjustments. And so we practice every day: Lukhamen, Lukhamen, Lukhamen.

And then one day, quite suddenly, other words appear on the pad:

*L*

*Beloved. Did you think our love had ceased to be, that we were gone forever because of the funeral pyres? Oh, no, Beloved. The fire did not consume us, nor could the desert wind and a thousand years keep us apart. Love is greater than fire, and wind, and time.*

---

I sit in my chair every day, as still as I can be, waiting for more. I meditate. Nothing happens. Did I imagine it? No, there it is on the pad. One morning, out of the blue, the tingling begins again and instead of words, I am impressed with a scene.

My eyes are closed, but I can *see*, in my mind's eye, a tall man walking down a river road. A breeze is blowing against his robe. It comes to my mind that he is a high priest. A leper scuttles toward him.

"Alms, alms!" cries the leper.

The high priest stops, takes a coin from a bag he wears around his waist, and drops it into the trembling hand that is stretched toward him. It is gnarled and devoid of all but two fingers.

"Amon's blessings on you, Lord!" says the leper, cowering.

He looks after the tall man who walks on down the road, then glances down into his hand. Sunlight strikes the coin, blinding him. He blinks and blinks again. "Jesus," he whispers, "*Jesus*." He has never before held gold in his hand. He begins to tremble.

The priest walks on. He turns his head to look across the river, to where the ancients sleep in the Valley of the Kings. His profile suggests a face that bears a great beauty, a face born of ages and sorrows I do not know. There is a tear in his eye. I know that it is the year 214 AD, and that we are in Egypt, in the city of Luxor.

In a few minutes, the image is gone. I write it all down quickly, before I forget what I have seen. I decide that I will wait for him at my computer. Whatever this is, I must record it.

I do not have to wait long.

# CHAPTER 5

———⬡⬡⬡———

*L*

*Egypt. Beloved of my heart, my soul. Even now I can hear her people's cries, smell the desert-blossom perfumes, and feel the hot streams of sunlight burning my back. Even now, long after I have gone into Spirit, her voices and rhythms come to me and rush through my soul like strains of a love song. Egypt, Egypt!*

*Oh, to be a child again, and to see my mother. So long, and still I miss her. She was everything that Egypt is, that Egypt was. She painted her eyelids and brows in the style of the ancients; and when she walked, her robes rustled softly, like water rushes in the breeze. She was warm and smelled of oranges and cardamom.*

*I remember the coffee and sweet, pungent odors that came from our kitchen, and I long for the days of my childhood in Luxor. Oh, to feel again the touch of my mother's hand on my brow. Oh, to hear her voice, calling my name!*

*She would come to me when I was with my nurse, and bring me a slice of fruit, or a sweet. Like a little bird, I'd open my mouth, and she would put something delicious on my tongue, smile at me, and smooth my hair. I could see the love in her eyes. I would sit in her lap and she would whisper, Lukhamen, my Little Love. That was long, long ago, before I became a man, when she still held me.*

# CHAPTER 6

WHATEVER THIS IS, I KNOW it is a gift. I made a request, and a spirit guide, Lukhamen, answered it. I wait at my computer each day, to write down what I see, what I *picture* in my mind. When my guide is with me, when he is in my consciousness, my mind is quiet and still, free from its usual noise. I am in an altered state, and there I am privy to another world, another lifetime, unfolding behind my closed eyes.

When I am in his lifetime, I am not in mine. I am neither tortured by questions with no answers, nor languishing in despair. That is, for now, quite enough.

I see her, his mother. She is on a low sofa in the garden, large with child, asleep. The boy tiptoes up to her.

"Mother," he whispers, "Mother." She opens her eyes. "May I feed the birds now, Mother? I think they must be hungry for breakfast," he says, narrowing his great brown eyes. "They have been waiting since sunup, you know."

Soft, brown curls crown his head, spill over onto his brow and down the back of his neck. He looks like his father.

"Good morning, Lukhamen," she says.

"Good morning, Mother."

Her first inclination is to reach out and gather him into her arms. But her husband has forbidden it. She looks at the little face whose brows are furrowed into a frown. She reaches out, then pulls back. *I can't hold him anymore. The temple priests have made him too old, too serious. But if this next one is a boy, he will not belong to them. He will belong to me. I swear it.*

"I must feed the birds, Mother!"

"Very well. But ask Semnut to help you."

He runs off, and in a flash he is back, dragging the old nurse by the hand.

"Semnut, do hurry!"

He pulls her toward a birdcage that is sitting in the middle of the garden.

"Semnut, *pleeease!*"

A bag of seeds swings from his free hand. His mother watches as the old woman lifts him onto a stool and steadies him as he opens the tiny cage door. He sprinkles the seeds, and the cage comes to life. Tiny turquoise and yellow birds drop like flashes to the cage floor. Lukhamen jumps back and almost falls, but Semnut has him. The birds pick at the little feast. In the blink of an eye, the picking becomes a mêlée, an unruly, squawking blur of feathers. He cannot restore order.

The boy turns to the old woman. "I will come down, now, Semnut," he says with dignity. His mother's hand is over her mouth. She is trying not to laugh.

"You see, Mother? They had to wait *entirely* too long for breakfast."

She bursts into laughter, and he laughs with her. All is well. She turns to the old woman.

"Semnut, send Cook to me," she says. "I will plan tonight's dinner."

"Yes, Mistress," says the old woman.

The boy settles at his mother's feet. He is arranging rows of wooden soldiers along the tiled path. A breeze sweeps through, sprinkling lavender petals onto his battlefield. He brushes them away.

# CHAPTER 7

$$\text{〰}$$

$$☥$$

THE HIGH PRIEST PAUSES BEFORE the pylons, as if waiting for some sign to enter. He is dreaming of his childhood, the days when he stood here with *his* father. The temple stretches out into the distance, its giant stone blocks the color of desert sand.

Colossal statues of Ramses II, in kilts and double crown, sit at the entrance. They are blind; their eyes are without irises, without pupils. Their hands rest quietly on their laps. The high priest looks beyond, far down the corridor. From here he can see another statue of Ramses in the courtyard, waiting.

He walks through the great pylons. The shadowy corridor is cool. Then he is in the sun again, in the courtyard. Statues of Ramses rim the perimeter.

From behind one of these, a tall, thin priest appears. He has been waiting in the shade. His skin is the color of ebony, his hair a halo of white. Resplendent in a white robe, he walks forward to meet the high priest. He is Khenti, Chief of the Temple.

They walk without speaking through the courtyard, and into a second corridor, then turn right between two great papyrus-shaped columns, and into an anteroom, the bath chamber. Khenti snaps his fingers, and two boy priests, who have been waiting in the shadows, jump forward. The boys relieve the high priest of his dusty gown and guide him down into a sunken tiled bath. He slides into warm, scented water. The air in the darkened chamber is cool. Smoke from incense curls upward into a small opening in the ceiling, sweetening the air.

"Ah ..." says the high priest, closing his eyes. "The heat is oppressive today."

Khenti is busy, seeing to towels, soap, sponges. The high priest continues.

"There was no one on the road but a leper." He frowns. His head hurts.

Khenti stops what he is doing, and kneels at the edge of the sunken tub. With the tips of his long, slender fingers, he presses small circles into the temples of the high priest, then presses into the base of the skull with his thumbs.

"Thank you," whispers the high priest.

The boys step forward, but Khenti nods them away.

"You used to do this for my father," says the high priest, his eyes still closed.

"Yes, Sire," says the older priest.

"Things were different then," says the high priest. "I miss him."

Khenti's eyes mist, but he quickly recovers. "As do I, Sire," he says.

He waves the boys forward with soap and sponges. Afterwards, wrapped in a towel, the high priest sits on the edge of the tub with a cup of red tea, studying the old man. He has known him since he was a boy. Khenti is in a straight-backed chair, his long, lanky legs crossed. His feet are bony in his sandals, his robe immaculate. His hair is a mass of airy, white fluff that seems to float around his head. There is a bald spot on top. His nose is long, fine-boned. His eyes are lined with kohl and he is wearing small gold earrings.

"You should ride the river road, Your Excellency. The sun is far too brutal this time of year." His speech is clipped, precise. "And it is not seemly that you should walk about among common people and lepers."

"The people expect to *see* us, my friend, especially now. No, now is not the time to hide behind the curtains of a sedan chair."

The old priest changes tack.

"And the young Lukhamen? How goes he?"

The sound of marching outside the temple wall halts their conversation. The sound grows nearer and louder, and enters the temple, defiling it. Through a crack in the wall, it appears: the brown-red plumage of Roman helmets on parade. Long after they have passed, the men remain still and motionless. The echo of marching feet lingers in the long corridors.

When the temple is quiet again, Khenti speaks. "Come, Sire," he says, his hand on the high priest's shoulder. "The sanctuary awaits you."

—— ∞∞∞ ——

It is sunset, and the leper is still on the river road, trembling against the trunk of a tree, the gold piece still in his hand. Dragging himself upright, he glances right and left, and hides the coin in the folds of a ragged sleeve. The sign of the cross is on the inside of his wrist. A tattoo. He stumbles off down the road and through a field, toward a little group of reed shacks. His legs tremble violently from the exertion. Tall shafts of wild wheat strike him in the face. At the edge of the clearing, he falls. Other lepers come running, stumbling. They carry him into the little compound and prop him against a tree. Someone brings water in a gourd, and the old man takes a few sips.

"Rich!" he whispers, holding out the gold coin. He can barely breathe. "We are rich!"

More lepers pour out of the little hovels and crowd around him. He calls for Joseph, his son, whose face does not yet bear the dreaded lesions, and tells him to go into town and buy meat, fish, fruit, and wine.

"Beer and sweet dates," he shouts, "and plenty. Enough for all!"

The old man begins to laugh, and cough. Someone fans him with reeds. The old man closes his eyes, the coin still clutched tightly in his hand, and prays.

"Jesus." Tears stream down his dusty old face.

# CHAPTER 8

HER NAME IS ALENNA. SHE steps out of the tub, hugely pregnant, holding onto her old nurse, Semnut. She arches her back and presses tiny fists into her sides. Semnut drapes a towel around her. Alenna holds onto her swollen belly as if it will fall. Semnut helps her onto the massage table.

"Careful, old woman," she says. The old nurse rubs perfumed oil onto her neck and shoulders. But Alenna cannot lie still. It is hot in the room, and she is irritable.

"That's enough. Stop. Stop!" she shouts. Semnut helps her off the table and leads her to a small chair in front of a dressing table. "A mirror, Semnut."

The old woman hands her a polished metal mirror. It is framed in wood; the handle is long, slender, beautifully carved. Alenna peers at the reflection of her swollen face and dashes it to the floor. The old woman picks it up and places it on the dressing table, takes a brush and begins to brush her hair, gently.

She wraps Alenna in a lavender robe. It is woven loosely, tied beneath the breasts. Her hair is fastened in back with a barrette made of gold and lapis lazuli, and she is wearing a single piece of jewelry: a gold cuff bracelet.

Semnut leads her mistress down steep stairs, holding onto one hand. Alenna steadies herself, sliding the other hand against the wall.

On the ground floor, they pass into a reception hall with columns of green, delicately veined marble. A few couches line the whitewashed walls, which are bare except for a few sconces. The hall leads to a dining room whose archways open onto the garden. Sheer white curtains hang from the archways, puffing gently from the breeze.

Alenna keeps to a mosaic-tiled path bordered by bougainvillea. Her gaze is fixed on the back garden wall, where a sofa sits under a large sycamore tree. A bronze pot sits on a small table next to the sofa. A demitasse of clear glass set into a silver-filigreed holder sits beside it. Someone has placed a red hibiscus flower next to it. A small papyrus scroll is on the sofa, where Alenna last left it. Locusts buzz in the tree overhead. The air is filled with their din. Alenna looks up, annoyed.

"Quiet! Quiet!" she shouts, her voice echoing off the garden wall. The din ceases.

"There now," she says, settling heavily onto the settee. "That's better."

Semnut pours coffee, offers it to her. Alenna takes a sip and spills the cup of hot liquid onto her lap. She cries out. She is covered in sweat and struggling for breath. "The doctor, Semnut! Quickly!" Her voice is hoarse.

The boy Lukhamen, in a far corner of the garden, looks up from his toy soldiers, suddenly aware of a change in the air.

"Mother?"

Alenna screams. A servant girl comes running. She and the old nurse lift Alenna to her feet and walk her quickly toward the house. At the foot of the stairs, she doubles over in pain.

"Mother, Mother!" cries Lukhamen. He has followed them into the house.

"Mother! What is it?"

"They are coming too fast, Semnut," she says, trying to breathe.

Water gushes from between her legs, pools on the floor. They make it up the stairs and into her bed chamber.

"Mother! What is it?" The boy is right behind, his eyes wide, alarmed, looking backward at the pool on the floor. He follows them into her bedchamber.

Alenna looks at the old nurse. Her eyes are desperate.

She hisses, "Semnut! Take him from this room! Now!"

Semnut approaches the boy but he steps around her deftly and moves toward the bed.

"Mother, please. What is it?"

She is gasping, her chest heaving.

"The baby is coming, that is all, Lukhamen. Father will be here shortly. You are to wait for him in the garden." She turns to the nurse. "Semnut!"

Semnut nods to the other servant. Together they drag the struggling boy from the room.

"No! Mother!" He can be heard screaming down the stairs, through the great hall, the dining room, and out into the garden.

An older man appears in the doorway of the bedchamber. His face is ashen.

"We have sent for the physician, mistress, and someone has gone to fetch the high priest."

He is Manut, the head steward.

---

In the garden, Lukhamen is fighting with all his strength. He sinks his teeth into Semnut's arm. She screams and lets go of him. In an instant he is back, in the great hall. The steward is standing at the center, barking orders to servants who are running here and there, into one another. Lukhamen spies a break in the traffic and bolts. He turns his head and sees Semnut coming up behind, turns back, and too late to stop, runs headlong into a pillar, and then lies on the ground, motionless.

Semnut screams, "Manut, help!"

The steward runs to where the boy lies, lifts him from the floor, and carries him to a couch.

"Quickly!" says Semnut, "A cloth and some crushed olive boughs in water. Hurry! O ye gods!"

---

The high priest kneels before the stone altar, eyes closed. He is in the sanctuary, the holy of holies, the farthermost room of the temple. It is dark, the only light coming from a few torches in wall sconces. Above him, in a niche in the far wall, a mammoth black granite statue looms, polished and gleaming. It is adorned in a kilt, high feathered crown, and ceremonial beard. The left foot is extended. He is Amon, the God of all Creation.

Khenti enters from behind, noiselessly ... waits a minute.

"Sire," he whispers. The high priest does not hear him.

"Sire, it is time."

The high priest opens his eyes.

"It is time you were home, Sire."

Khenti's eyes are unusually bright, like dark coals afire. The high priest is on his feet. In a few minutes, he is on the river road, walking quickly. On the way, he meets the servant who has been sent to fetch him.

---

The high priest enters his house like a rush of wind. He is with the physician, who has arrived at the same moment. He slams the door behind him. The servants in the large reception hall freeze.

"What is this *madness!*" roars the high priest, looking around. "What has happened to my son? And where is my wife?"

He looks around at the crowd of servants ... pointedly at Semnut.

"Is she alone, then? A house full of servants and my wife is *alone* in her labor? Manut!" His voice echoes from the walls. The head steward steps forward, trembling.

"Your Excellency." Not taking his eyes from the high priest, he gestures toward the boy lying on the couch. "He ran and he fell, Your Excellency."

The physician Sechmetna walks over to the boy, examines the knot that is beginning to rise on Lukhamen's head. He opens one eyelid, then the other.

"The boy is merely stunned." He turns to Manut. "Make a poultice. Soak it in crushed olive boughs and water. Keep it cool and on the boy's head until he revives." A blood-curdling scream from the second floor jolts them. Sechmetna turns to the nurse. "Will you assist me, then, Semnut?"

She leads the physician up the stairs. The high priest follows. Sechmetna turns at the landing to face him.

"If you please, Your Excellency." He smiles. "I will let her come to no harm."

Another cry from the bedchamber, and the doctor turns and hurries up the stairs. The high priest looks after him, waits a moment, then turns and descends.

Lukhamen whimpers as his father lifts him from the couch. He lays his head on his father's chest. They go into the garden that way, to Alenna's couch under the sycamore tree. A young manservant follows with cups on a tray.

"Mother is safe now, Lukhamen," says the high priest. "The doctor is helping her."

He puts his hand on the boy's brow. The child's face is flushed, his little body drenched. The priest puts a cup to his mouth.

"It's your favorite, Lukhamen. Pomegranate."

The boy takes a sip, refuses more. He stretches out on the couch, puts his head in his father's lap, and falls asleep. The knot on his head is fully raised and is now an ugly purple. The servant puts the tray on the table.

"Wine," the high priest whispers.

The servant bows, hurries into the house. In a minute he is back, pouring purple-black wine into a silver cup.

"Leave me, please."

The young man leaves the pitcher on the table, bows, and leaves. The priest drains the cup, pours another and drains it, pours a third but puts it down. He leans his head against the headrest, but cannot sleep. He notices a small papyrus scroll that has fallen to the ground. He reaches over the sleeping boy and picks it up. It is a collection of love poems.

A tear spills down his cheek.

"I beseech thee, O Lord Amon," he whispers, "Keep her safe."

# CHAPTER 9

THE GARDEN IS DARK; THERE are storm clouds overhead. The birdcage is silent and still. A few feet away, on a small sofa under the sycamore tree, the high priest is asleep.

A gust of cool air sweeps past his face. Lightening crackles, lights the garden. A clap of thunder wakes the boy on his lap and he bolts upright, trembling. Great elongated drops of water splatter into the dust. Faster and faster they fall till they become a sheet beating down palm fronds, bending bougainvillea to the ground, pouring through the shelter of the sycamore tree. The boy tries to cover his head with his arms.

"Come, Lukhamen," says the high priest.

He lifts the boy into his arms and walks quickly toward the house. Manut is standing in the archway with a large towel. Sechmetna the physician is standing beside him. The priest ignores the towel, fixes his eyes on the physician.

"All is well, Sire," says the physician. "You have a son."

"My wife?"

"She is well."

He takes a deep breath, lowers the boy to the floor, and takes the old physician's hands.

"Thank you, Sechmetna."

"I did very little, Your Excellency. They did quite well on their own."

"May I see them?"

"She is sedated, but your son is wide awake and awaits you. I shall look in on both of them tomorrow."

"Well done, Sechmetna. Manut will see to a sedan chair for you. Until tomorrow, then." The high priest bounds up the stairs, the boy after him.

"Father, wait! Wait for me!" he cries.

The old man looks after them and smiles.

Sheer white curtains hang from the bedposts and billow gently in the rainy breeze. A light flickers in a small oil lamp. The scent of myrrh is in the air. Semnut is sitting in a chair by Alenna's bed. She rises and steps noiselessly into the shadows. The high priest moves into her chair and stares at his wife. Her eyes are closed.

He leans over to peek into the bundle at her side. She opens her eyes.

"Beloved," she whispers.

"Do not talk, Alenna. Rest."

He sits on the bed, takes her hand. She smiles.

"Your hair is wet," she says.

"It's raining."

She frowns. "Raining?"

"Yes."

She closes her eyes. "Is that a sign?"

"A most propitious sign, my love."

"We have a son," she says. Her speech is slow, drowsy.

"Yes, I know." A bit of stray hair has fallen onto her brow. He brushes it away.

"Mother?"

They have forgotten the boy. She opens her eyes, focuses on him.

"Lukhamen, my little love, what has happened to your head?"

"It is nothing, Mother," he says. "I fell."

He comes closer, leans over her.

"Is that the baby?"

She nods and he comes around to the other side of the bed, eyes widening as he nears.

# CHAPTER 10

———— ⊶⊶ ————

I GO TO WORK EVERY day. I ride the subway; I read the newspaper. It takes all my energy to appear normal, to talk, to walk about with other human beings, normal people whose world has not flattened out. I watch them on the subway reading their newspapers. The young ones chatter away like magpies, mindlessly drowning in oceans of trivia, and I think: *they don't know Eddie died.* They don't know about that gaping hole in the ground.

Survival is a long, lonely business. I employ one tactic: I do not think too much about how Eddie died. I live one day at a time. And every morning, I sit in front of a blank computer screen and wait for the story to continue. It always comes, and it never lasts long. I write it down because maybe there is a point to this telling. Maybe it will explain why Eddie is gone and I am here.

———— ⊶⊶ ————

When his father and I separated and Eddie chose to live with me, I asked him to wait until I could get a pullout couch.

"I'll sleep on the floor," he said.

He was only seventeen, and already my protector. Before the separation, he was the light in that sad home, and most of the time, the only male presence in our feminine coterie. His heart was light, his spirit joyful. He made us laugh. He could dispel the gloom.

He had come to my office on Friday afternoon, and asked if he could spend the weekend with his best friend, Geoffrey. He and Geoffrey had known each other since they were infants together on a grim army base in Germany.

"Sure," I said. I handed him some money.

"Thanks, Mom. See ya'."

"See ya'," I said.

It was just like that. I never saw him again.

Bits and pieces of the nightmare flash before me when I least expect it. We are at the table, staring at the ruinous Christmas dinner. No one knows what to do with it. In front of my daughters, my ex-husband blurts out drunkenly, in the throes of his own pain, it's *your fault, your fault, your fault*. I retreat into a boozy refuge and a rain-soaked blackout on Eddie's grave.

# CHAPTER 11

WHEN I CALL FOR AN appointment, I am told that Reverend Brown is not available, but there is an opening with his associate, Mr. John Bordeaux. I take it.

John Bordeaux is like Reverend Brown: young, good-looking, and dressed in a dark suit and tie. We go through the same ritual: he hands me a three-by-five card and leaves me alone. I write Eddie's name on it, and Uncle Butsie's. I, who am riddled with questions, can't think of one. I leave the rest of the card blank and fold it eight times as I am told.

The room is warm and sunny. I place the card in his hand, put my hand over it.

"Protect us, O Lord," he prays, "and guide us as we open the door to the two worlds. Give us only that which is uplifting and for our higher good."

I remove my hand, and he closes the folded card into his own. His eyes are closed. We are quiet together, waiting. He opens his eyes and says, "There's been a healing in you."

A healing? I'm never going to heal. He's wrong.

"Yes," he says, "there has been a healing, and you've done it yourself. I don't understand. Can you explain it to me?"

I don't know what to say to this, so I tell him the one thing that has changed. "I'm not drinking anymore."

"Well, that must be it," he says. "Your soul was like this," he lifts his hands and intertwines the fingers pointing downward, knuckles up, "and now it's like this," he says, and he turns his hands inside out so that palms and fingers are pointing upward. Like a lotus blossom.

"There are uncles here and grandfathers who are so proud of you," he says, "because they tried to do this and couldn't."

Jesus. Alcoholism did kill my two favorite uncles. But grandfathers who drank? This is news to me.

He turns blue eyes to me again and says, "There is an anniversary, isn't there?"

"Yes," I say.

"But it isn't today is it?"

"No."

"It was three days ago."

"Yes."

It was a year and three days since Eddie died.

He continues. "They are all celebrating, bringing you flowers. Eddie is bringing you flowers. The whole family is here, grandfathers, grandmothers, aunts, uncles. They are celebrating Eddie's crossing over. It's one big party. Who is Eddie?" he says.

"Eddie is my son," I tell him.

Just before I leave, he tells me that Eddie and I lived together in a former life, in Spain. He was an artist then and the name Raphael is coming to him.

"Eddie was an artist in this life too," I tell him.

I stumble out in a daze, as I did the first time with Reverend Brown. I need to let this sit a while. Absorb it. All I can think of is that they, all my relatives, all the people we loved and lost, all the people we *thought* we lost, were *celebrating*.

A few months after my reading with him, I learned that John Bordeaux died of a massive heart attack. But I can't think of it that way anymore. I have to think of it in his words: He crossed over. Someone is celebrating with him now.

———— ✇ ————

Weeks later, I am listening to the radio. A well-known talk show host, Diane Rehm, is interviewing a newspaper journalist who has written several books on her experience with channeling. She speaks of her guides, a collective group that has taken the name "Lily." They advise her, impart their wisdom, and lend her their observations on reincarnation. The journalist's name is Ruth Montgomery.

On National Public Radio, a well-known writer is saying that it was important for her to have credibility as a serious journalist before the books on channeling were published, lest people dismiss her work as that of an ... oddity, to put it kindly. That's why her guides chose this time in her life to appear.

I read Ruth Montgomery's books and every spiritual book I can get my hands on. I find myself immersed in the metaphysical experiences of others. There are legions.

Metaphysics, I learn, is the investigation of principles of reality that transcend science. The word is from the Medieval Latin *Metaphysica,* the title of Aristotle's treatise on the subject, and is derived from the Greek words *meta (transcending)* and *physika (physics, the science of matter and energy).* It is a division of philosophy that is concerned with the fundamental nature of reality and being: a study of what is *outside* objective experience.

It is also a field ripe for opportunists, for frauds—unscrupulous charlatans who prey upon people in grief: fortune tellers, telephone psychics, storefront mediums, con artists. No wonder people are skeptical. But that is not what is happening with me. My fee to Reverend Brown for saving my life was twenty-five dollars, and for an additional twenty-five dollars, John Bordeaux gave me a gift that was far above and beyond anything money could buy: the idea that nobody dies.

I think of the lines from Shakespeare's *Hamlet,* as Horatio declares, "O day and night, but this is wondrous strange!" And Hamlet answering, "And therefore as a stranger, give it welcome. There are more things in heaven and earth, Horatio, than are dreamt of in your philosophy."

———— ⚬⚬⚬ ————

A few months later, Reverend Brown establishes the Metaphysical Chapel of Arlington, Virginia. I am delighted at the utter simplicity of the place, with its little garden out front and its old-fashioned wooden siding.

I sit in the small chapel beneath a stained-glass window, the sun streaming through, warming the wound in my heart. Here there is calm, and peace. I go early on Sunday mornings before the services to sit. Others are there, in meditation. I sit quietly with them.

The teachings are simple: God is Infinite Intelligence. Nature, both physical and spiritual, is the expression of Infinite Intelligence. The existence and personal identity of the individual continues after leaving the physical world, and *communication with Spirit is a natural experience.*

We sing the old hymns, hymns from my childhood in the Presbyterian Church where I sat Sunday mornings beside my mother. They bring tears to my eyes and memories of a warmer, more innocent life and time.

They speak often of the Golden Rule: *Do unto others as you would have them do unto you.* Reverend Brown's sermons sometimes expound on another belief, that of personal responsibility: that we create our own happiness or unhappiness as we live in harmony or discord with natural physical and spiritual laws. I am not sold on that one yet, but for now, this is the only place in my world where anything makes sense.

In my mind, still clouded by grief, there begins the faintest glimmer of hope, that if all of these people—my aunts, my uncles, my grandfathers, *Lukhamen*— are still alive, then *so is Eddie.* I don't think too much about it. I just do what keeps me alive. I "tune in." If I am insane, I don't care.

# CHAPTER 12

♀

A STONEMASON SITS BY THE temple wall, his hands covering his face. His stomach is churning. The sun is almost directly overhead. It is burning the top of his head, trapping fiery heat in his clothes. The only shade on this side of the road is in the corridor of the temple's pylons, but he is not allowed to wait inside the corridor or walk unescorted into the temple.

"Bastard," he says out loud.

He lurches to his feet, crosses the road, and under a lane of palm and sycamore trees, makes his way into town. He turns onto a narrow street and slips into a dark tavern.

A short time later, he is drunk. "The cursed priest leaves me to fry in the sun, and this is rancid wine, you fat pile of *shit!*" he screams at the proprietor.

A figure appears in the doorway and blocks the light. "Simon, Simon." He is a large man wearing a carpenter's tool belt. "You're scaring the poor man to death."

He takes a stool and turns to the shaking tavern owner.

"When Simon asks for wine, give him *wine*. Don't give him the piss you keep for desert trash."

"But…"

"Get wine. Go on, get it."

"But sir, Simon never pays."

The man puts down a coin.

"Get it."

"I don't need charity from a god-damned *carpenter,* now do I?" says Simon. "I have *credit* here, don't I, Piss Proprietor?"

"Simon," says the carpenter, "come work for me."

Simon is wavering on the stool. His eyes are unfocused.

"Doing what?" he answers. "Building another Roman dog another house?"

The wine arrives, and Simon drinks it in one gulp. He motions to the proprietor to refill his cup.

"Help me finish the church," John says.

"I have a job," says Simon, "rebuilding the god-damned temple wall. It's about to fall down on the god-damned high priest." He laughs. "But the god-damned high priest wasn't there today." He laughs again. "So I have decided to celebrate."

"Simon, come help me finish the church," John says.

"The church," Simon slurs. "What do I care about the church?"

John stands and sighs. "Very well. We will build it without you."

The large man walks out the door to a clap of thunder.

⸺⛉⸺

Downriver, workmen are putting the finishing touches on the roof of the little mud church. Three men are balanced around the rim of the dome, lowering a wooden cross into the apex. When the cross is settled and righted in its hole, they fill it with mud, tamp it tightly, and climb down to survey their work, inching their way into the crowd which has been watching from the road.

All eyes are on the cross as a chariot rounds the corner at top speed. The crowd reacts late, scattering helter-skelter. One of the workmen is knocked to the ground and is caught beneath the wheels. At length, the driver pulls to a stop.

The Roman deputy superintendent of the granaries steps out of his chariot, fleshy and pale.

"Get this idiot from beneath my chariot," he hisses to the driver between clenched teeth, "and be quick about it."

He removes his helmet, and with plump, manicured hands, attempts to replace the long, pomaded strands of hair that have recently covered his bald spot. Stubbornly, they stick out over his right ear. He swipes at the sweat which is making rivulets through the powder on his face.

"Hurry!"

"The man is dead, sir."

He looks to the crowd, which has regrouped and is now advancing toward him. He puffs himself up with indignation, whirls on the driver, and snatches the whip from his hand.

"*Idiot!*" he shrieks, striking him across the face, opening the skin. Whirling around again, he reaches into a pouch hanging from his middle and tosses a handful of coins onto the ground.

"This is more than enough to bury the man. Give what is left to his widow, if he has one. And tell her that he was careless. Very, very careless," he says, bounding into the chariot.

It creaks under his weight. The driver hops aboard, snaps the reins, and the horses are off again at top speed. In his haste, the deputy superintendent of the granaries has failed to replace his helmet, but holds onto the chariot tightly with his free hand, errant bits of hair notwithstanding.

An old priest kneels beside the body, as a woman pushes her way through the crowd. At the edge of the clearing, her knees give way and she crawls toward the body, whimpering pitifully. The face is bloody, unrecognizable. She lifts a hand, sees the ring she had given him on their wedding day. Her scream causes the crowd to step back a little, as if she needed more space to rend the air.

One of the workmen stands in the middle of the road, apart from the crowd, glaring through red-rimmed eyes at the dust in the chariot's wake: Simon.

"One day, Antonious, you godless, faithless scum, Holy Providence will deliver you into my hands," he whispers to himself.

He turns back, elbows his way through the crowd, and lifts the woman from her husband's body. She faints in his arms, bloodied and covered in dust.

# CHAPTER 13

$$\frac{\varphi}{}$$

THE HIGH PRIEST STOOPS IN the low archway of the bath chamber. Alenna is in a small marble tub near the window, her head resting against the rim. Her arms are draped over the sides, her eyes are closed. Her hair, which has been carefully lifted over the rim, hangs dark as night against the white marble. He stares at it for a moment, then enters noiselessly.

Iridescent trails of oil on the water outline the tops of her breasts. Sunlight slants in through shutters, highlighting her hair. It glints off glass jars of perfumed oil that line a shelf on the far wall. A peacock-blue silk robe hangs over a chair.

Semnut is quietly folding towels in the corner, her back to the intruder. He is a spy, savoring their secret, feminine world. Alenna raises a leg and props it on the rim of the tub. Her toenails are lacquered dark red. Water drips from her foot onto the floor.

"Now, then!" he says in his deepest voice.

He smiles as both women, startled, jump.

"Sorcery! Surely sorcery is practiced here!"

Alenna, quickly regaining her composure, lowers her foot into the tub and sits up in one slow, sensuous movement, displaying the tiny, dark nipples that were hidden beneath the water.

"Greetings, my lord," she says with a coy little smile.

Semnut slips from the room.

"And to what do I owe the honor of this visit?" Her voice is a purr.

He lifts her hair, which has fallen into the water, kisses her lightly on the back of her neck, then takes a sponge and squeezes water down her back.

"Alenna," he whispers into her hair.

She ignores his little advance, punishing him for interrupting her quiet retreat.

"A towel, if you please."

She stands, giving him a full view of the lithe, taut young body dripping with oil and bath water, skin gleaming in the half-light like bronzed silk. There is no swelling in her body. Her little breasts are firm.

"Sorcery," he whispers. "Nothing less than sorcery."

"The *sorcery*, my lord, is Semnut's massages and barley tea."

He holds out his hand. She steps from the tub and he winds her in a large towel. From behind he wraps her into his arms, nuzzles his face into her neck. She leans her head back against him and closes her eyes.

"How do you do it?" she murmurs.

"How do I do what?"

"How do you fill a room, just by entering it?"

"This is hardly a room, Alenna."

She smiles, keeping her eyes closed.

"I miss you, my love."

"I miss you, too. I am not sleeping well."

She moves against him. "Come back to my bed."

He moves away. She moves closer again. He steps away, takes her hands.

"Sechmetna has not yet given us permission."

"Sechmetna is an old man. What does he know?"

"He is a good doctor, Alenna."

"*I* know when I am *healed*, Lukhamen."

"We will speak no more of it. I would not have you die of an infection. It would be foolish."

He hands her the peacock robe.

"And where is my namesake?"

"In the nursery, where he spends every waking moment."

"Lukhamen!" His voice echoes throughout the house. "LUKHAMEN!"

The boy comes running.

"Ah, so here you are, then. Let us leave the baby to the women today, shall we? I want you to come to the temple with me."

His eyes are big and round. "Oh, Father, is it true?"

"Tell Semnut to get you ready. Wait for me in the great hall. I have a surprise for you."

"A surprise!"

"Go now, and be quick!"

The boy turns to bolt from the room.

"Lukhamen." His mother's voice stops him. "Will you not say goodbye to your mother, then?"

He runs back and crushes her in a little embrace.

"Goodbye, Mother!"

She holds him a moment. Then he is off.

"You mustn't allow him to do that, Alenna. He is about to become a man."

"He is but a *boy!*"

"He is *about* to become a *man*, Alenna."

She is stunned for a moment. Her eyes fill with fear, then anger.

"Alenna, listen. Listen."

He reaches for her hands. She pulls away.

"You knew this day would come."

"Like this? With no warning?"

He speaks slowly, carefully. "I was told only this morning." He takes her hands again. This time he will not let her pull away.

"The astrologers wanted to be certain. There is no mistake."

Tears well in her eyes.

"Today is the Feast of Amon, Alenna! Never before in all the recorded births of all the high priests has a day of ordination coincided with the Feast of

Amon. It is a sign, don't you see? Lukhamen was born to this. His reign will see the restoration of our faith."

"Day of ordination? Restoration of our *faith*? He is just a boy. He is still a baby. He plays with *toys*, yet." Her voice breaks.

"I was nine years old, Alenna, the same age as Lukhamen is now, when I was taken into the temple."

"Because your mother was not there to prevent it!" Her voice is bitter.

He feels the sting, the awful loneliness after his mother's death.

"Let him be a child a little longer! Don't take him from me, I beg of you!"

But he persists. "He will have a good life, a privileged life, Alenna. He will be educated beyond your wildest dreams for him. He will travel to the great temples of Egypt, be taught by doctors, theologians, historians. He will learn Greek and Latin. He will be a high priest, Alenna."

He is finished. He has done his best, and he must go. They are waiting for him. He walks to the window. Below, Haraa, Alenna's childhood friend, is stepping from her sedan chair. He turns to Alenna.

"Haraa is here. I have asked her to come. She will stay with you."

There is fire in her eyes.

"So. Haraa knows of this before me?"

"No. I only asked her to come."

She turns her back to him.

"He will be a light unto his people, Alenna." He turns to leave.

She picks up a bottle of bath oil that is close by and throws it with all her might at his back. But he is gone. It crashes against the wall. An oily stain drips to the floor. The scent of orange blossoms fills the room.

Mindless of the broken glass, she runs barefoot out of the room, down the hall and into the nursery where the infant is sleeping, quiet and peaceful, unaware of the oil dripping down the wall and the broken glass and angry words that linger in the next room. She looks down at him. Tears are making bitter little trails down her cheek.

"Take him, then," she says, looking toward the window, "Make him your prisoner! Make him an old man before his time! Forge him into a savior for your dying faith and your dying faithless! But I swear, you shall not have this one! Not this one!"

She walks to the window, wiping her eyes angrily. She sees the young Lukhamen skipping alongside his father, chattering like a little bird. Then she hears Haraa's steps on the stairs, heavy under her own burden of child.

# CHAPTER 14

&#10086;

☥

A MARSH BIRD IS STUCK fast in the mud that lines the bank. He struggles to free his stalk-like legs, stretches his long neck. A foot away in the shallow water, a crocodile leers at him through old, rheumy eyes. The birds are silent and dull in the still trees, mindless of the hapless heron and the drama of death about to unfold beneath them.

"The surprise, Father. What is the surprise?"

"You will know soon enough, Lukhamen. Now, recite for me, please, the names of Amon."

The boy stops skipping and takes a deep breath.

"Amon. Amon, God of the Air, God of Wind, and Breath. God of Sun, and...oh look, Father, a crocodile!"

The old crocodile, which had crawled onto the bank toward the marsh bird, turns and slides into the water. The bird, sensing its reprieve, pulls and lunges and flies off downriver, shrieking loudly.

"I used to be afraid of them when I was little, you know," says the boy in a manful voice.

He is still looking at the spot where the crocodile slipped into the water.

"They are very dangerous, Lukhamen. Never go near them."

"I won't, Father."

The High Priest looks across the river and is soon lost in dreams—dreams of the boy in a great light, dreams of the temple, restored and resplendent, and the face of his father, smiling.

# CHAPTER 15

—◦◦◦—

*L*

*AH, YES. I BORE HIS name and we walked the river road together, inhabiting his dreams. And they were with us, the Divine Ones who slept in their tombs across the river. They haunted our air, taunted us with beauty and beguiled us with love. And were they not divine, after all? Did they not lead Egypt to glory while those in the cold dark lands gave birth to their young in caves, the same ones who later came to take away our treasures?*

*But on that day, on that splendid day, Beloved, we were together on the Feast of Amon. I was balm for his wounds, ransom for our lost splendor! We were beloved captives, Father and I. I was his, and he was theirs.*

# CHAPTER 16

Lepers call to him from the side of the road and wake him from his reverie.

"Hail, most High Priest of Amon! Blessings upon you, and upon your son!"

He nods to them.

"What is wrong with them, Father?"

"They are sick, Lukhamen."

The boy stares at them as he passes, and turns his head to look again after they have gone a way down the road.

"Do not stare, Lukhamen."

"Will they die, Father?"

"Yes, they will die, Lukhamen."

"Will we die, Father?"

"Yes, Lukhamen. But we will not die from leprosy, and only when we are very, very old."

"Leprosy?"

"Yes. That is what the physicians call their sickness."

"How did they get it, Father?"

"They got it from being poor, Lukhamen."

"When you are poor you get this…leprosy?"

"It's…easier to get it when you are poor, Lukhamen. They don't have enough food to eat, and they cannot bathe like we do. Their bodies are weak."

"We have enough to eat, Father."

"Yes. We are fortunate."

"Why don't we give them some of our food, then, Father?"

They reach the temple, and the boy forgets his line of questioning. He stops to stare at the two obelisks that loom above and the colossal twin statues of Ramses the Second.

"Not today, Lukhamen. There is no time."

"But Father…"

"You will take the bath with me today. Come."

The boy is stunned into silence. He follows behind, running to keep up.

Lukhamen stands beside his father in the deep tub and is lathered with soap and prayers. The silence—the dark dignity and solemnity of the ritual—quiets him. He stands very still. They are toweled dry and rubbed with oil. Under the watchful eye of Khenti, two boy priests step forward with robes of amethyst silk. Lukhamen watches wide-eyed as Khenti drops the robe over his father's head and winds a sash of gold around his waist. He reaches for the smaller robe, but the high priest takes it from his hands.

"Thank you, Khenti. I will dress him." The high priest slips the robe over his son's head.

"Your arms, Lukhamen."

The boy puts his arms through sleeves trimmed in gold, and stands stiffly as his father places gold bracelets on each wrist and a beaded collarette around his neck. The high priest looks down at the boy whose eyes are riveted to his own, and whose body is now trembling. He leans down, takes the small, frightened face into his hands and whispers, "There is nothing to fear, Lukhamen. You are the Beloved of Amon."

He places a small amulet in the boy's hand, then says in a deliberate, stentorian voice,

"You are Lukhamen Sa'at, eldest son and namesake of this Lukhamen Sa'at, the High Priest of the Temple of Amon in Thebes, twenty-eighth in the unbroken line of Sa'at high priests, the line that has existed since ancient times, the same who served the great pharaohs. You are the next High Priest of Amon, and today you are to be ordained in this sacred temple, as was your father, and his father, and all the fathers who lie sleeping across the river. Today, you are the hope of your people. You are *Egypt*."

He turns and walks out into the corridor. Lukhamen stands rooted and dumfounded, staring after him.

---

"Master Lukhamen."

Lukhamen does not move.

"After you, Master Lukhamen."

Khenti turns him around, toward the doorway. Lukhamen steps into the corridor and stumbles over a raised stone. Khenti steadies him, and they move forward to where a procession of priests awaits.

The boy moves down the corridor as in a dream, and as he passes through the great hypostyle hall, the lonely sound of a reed flute and a small clash of brass finger cymbals sound close by. Lukhamen does not look toward the sound, nor does he turn around when the priests' chant begins to drone behind him. His eyes are fixed on the cloud of incense that is rising between him and the white *khat* headdress that is folded in the shape of the female cobra tense with rage: the headdress of his father, the High Priest of Amon.

The boy is seated directly in front of the altar in a small chair. His eyes are fixed straight ahead. He is vaguely conscious of murmurings and chants, and the bleating of a small lamb that is partially hidden from his sight, but whose blood he can see when it spills over the altar stone and onto the floor. His father's voice floats in and out of his consciousness, and he understands little of what is said.

From time to time, his eyes rise to the black granite figure of the Lord Amon above him, at the top of the stairs behind the altar. Gleaming and regal, in a high-feathered crown, plaited beard, and pleated kilt, the statue of the Lord Amon stares ahead blankly, through eyes without irises or pupils.

The boy is aware of his father coming toward him, standing before him, placing something upon his head. And then, suddenly, his father's words echo in his ears with startling clarity:

"In the name of Amon, Lord of Heaven and Earth, I make you priest and first prophet in his service, to be his representative in the Earth, to be his servant, and the servant of his people, all the days of your life."

He feels the oil, warm from his father's fingers, on his forehead and on his temples.

The high priest ascends the stairs and places a wreath of papyrus flowers at the feet of the Lord of Heaven and Earth. It is precisely midday. As the sun passes directly overhead, it slants through an opening in the ceiling, sheathing the boy in light. The high priest turns. His eyes fall on the boy, who is now in a white shimmer, as in a mirage. Slowly, one by one, *they* come into the light, bathed in radiance: Amenophis; Queen Tiye; Isis, mother of Tuthmosis; the Princess Khnumit; Sety and his son, Ramses. They touch the boy's head and smile, and in one voice they proclaim: *Egypt. You are Egypt.*

As suddenly as it had come, the sun passes over, and the room is darkened again. The boy is alone, staring at his father with wide eyes. He trembles, like his father. The ceremony is over.

Khenti leads the boy out into the courtyard, followed by the procession of priests. The high priest remains at the foot of the altar, lost in the dream.

In the blinding sunlight and heat of the courtyard, Khenti suddenly shivers and looks toward the sanctuary. It begins as a low rumble, like faraway thunder. He looks up in time to see the first great stone fall; then, as if in slow motion, another follows. Whole sections of the outside wall give way. The ceiling caves in with a series of sickening thuds, and the sanctuary is a mountain of broken stones. A cloud of dust rises to the sky. Khenti instinctively grabs the boy in his arms, shielding him with his body. But it is over. Dust and dirt rain down upon them, and then, all is quiet.

The amulet his father has given him slips from the boy's hand and falls onto the dirt floor of the courtyard.

# CHAPTER 17

I HEARD A RINGING IN my ears, and then a low rumble, like thunder in the distance. I thought the temple was going to fall again, but it changed into a whirring sound that spoke my name. Lukhamen. Lukhamen, it said, do not be afraid.

# CHAPTER 18

I SAW THE TEMPLE WALL collapse, one great stone after another thudding to the ground. I stood beside the boy and felt his shock, his fear. I felt the dirt and dust rain down, and with it, the awful anticipation of grief.

I don't want to feel his grief. I have enough of my own.

I am someone else now, transmuted by loss, no longer comprised of the same components. Am I still Eddie's mother?

I cannot think in terms of *never*, as in he will *never* be back, I shall *never* see him again. I force these thoughts away. Sobriety has steadied me somewhat, but only enough to understand the enormity of my loss, the shaky hold I have on life. I am adrift, operating without a precedent, without a compass, and I have lost the north.

I am not drinking, but I cannot connect with my new sober friends. They speak of the joy of living. They laugh at suffering, at death. I am still aligned with it. I do not want to forsake my grief; to lose it is to lose Eddie. He was my love. Now he is my suffering. And in that, he has life. He is still with me. He lives in my pain.

I wake one morning in a panic. I cannot remember his face. The old sickening pain sends me to my knees. Later, his face comes back, but now I am afraid. I am afraid that I will go on losing him until I have lost him forever.

One image of him is still clear. He is a toddler, and I am home from the hospital, having had an ectopic pregnancy and a near-death experience: a rupture; mind-numbing pain; a hemorrhage; and the amazing, draining process of bleeding out. I ask for a priest. The surgeon barks an order: "Get her one. Quick!" *I must be dying*, I think to myself. A priest appears, gives me a hasty blessing; there is no time for last rites. I am in and out of consciousness as the blood leaves my brain.

"Am I going to be all right?" I ask the doctor in a lucid moment.

He answers as I am rolled down a corridor at top speed, "If we can get you to the operating room in time."

He has told me the truth, and I am not afraid. I ask the nurse if I can keep the rosary in my hand. She breaks the rules and whispers to me to keep it hidden under the sheets. This is not how I thought it would be. I am vomiting blood, and I am not alarmed. The last moments of consciousness are sweet and peace-ful. *Dying isn't so bad*, I think. *It's lovely.* The doctor is standing over me. I cannot see his face. The bright lights of the operating theater are in my eyes.

"I'm ready," I say in his direction.

"We're ready for you," he says.

No. That's not what I mean. I mean I'm *ready*. But all goes black before I can tell him.

---

I wake to red roses. I stare at them in ecstasy. *I made it*, I think. I'm in *heaven*. Two blurred white figures are at my feet.

One of them says, "She's cute. Is she married?"

And the other answers, "Yes. Her husband brought her those roses."

*I'm still here.* I feel a great let-down. I want to go back, back to the peace!

Three days later, my body goes into shock. Shivering and miserable, I am fully returned to the world of pain and fear, the world of physical reality and near-misses.

The surgeon has saved me and ten days later, I am back in our quarters on an army base in Germany. My little girls, Debbie and Niki, are waiting for me, smiling and shy, but Eddie is still with friends. I want to see my baby. I sit up in bed, waiting for him. I am afraid he will not remember me. But he sees me and smiles. He holds out chubby little arms and wraps them around my neck. He is so beautiful. Great, brown curls fall onto his forehead, and his big brown eyes are shaded by long, silky lashes. But it is the joy in him that permeates me. He is so happy. He is happiness in my arms. I feel it in his little body. I have cheated death, and Eddie reminds me that life is delicious. To this day, I can feel his little arms around my neck, his feet on my lap, jumping up and down. He is laughing.

Reverend Brown's first words to me about Eddie were, *He's here, and he's laughing.*

# CHAPTER 19

THE GOVERNOR IS ALONE IN his office on the second floor. It's a spacious room, sparsely furnished and painted white. The ceiling is high, and the room opens onto a balcony that winds around three sides and looks out over the river. The wooden-slatted shutters are open, but there is no breeze. The governor steps onto the balcony, wipes the perspiration from his brow with a handkerchief, tucks it into his belt, returns to the room, and claps his hands. A servant girl appears in the doorway.

"I will take tea in the garden," he says.

"Yes, Sire."

She backs out of the room. He hears her running down the stairs.

He follows her down the wide staircase, taking his time. Outside, he settles into a chair that is shaded by a large sycamore.

*I could retire here and live well on my pension,* he thinks. *I can't live in Rome any more. Too noisy and crowded. There is too much ambition there, too many clawing, grasping climbers. Turtles. That's what they're like, turtles, scrambling over one another to get to the emperor. Like Antonious. What a shifty, hateful little man. I don't trust him.*

He gazes at the river; a breeze is now giving rise to small waves that are lapping at the shore. The leaves above him rustle. A pelican flies overhead. He follows its flight downriver until it is out of sight.

The girl appears with a tray and places it on a small table.

*I'm happy here and I like the people.* He watches her pour the tea. She holds back her sleeve with her free hand as she pours, revealing a small tattoo on the inside of her wrist: a cross. She drops a dollop of honey into the cup, stirs it, then bows and walks away.

She pauses before a tiny hummingbird that has fluttered into her path. It darts here and there, hovers for a moment above a crimson hibiscus, and flies away. She plucks the blossom, tucks it into her hair, and disappears into the house.

The fragrance of the tea sifts into his consciousness. *Yes,* he thinks. *I could live here.*

He takes a sip, closes his eyes, and listens to the doves cooing in the tree overhead.

*So the girl is a Christian,* he thinks. *I wonder how the high priest feels about the growing number of Christians here. It's time I had another meeting with him. The ordination of his son must be at hand. We must give the boy a gift. The high priest is the key to a contented populace here. I can't afford an uprising—not while the emperor relies on us for grain to feed the army.* The thought pushes him from his tranquil, shady retreat. He finishes his tea.

At the top of the stairs, he is stopped short by a wave of nausea. His head is light; he sits on the top stair. *That's odd,* he thinks. He is there when his aide finds him and helps him to his bedchamber. The young soldier has come to tell him that the temple wall has collapsed and that the high priest is buried beneath the rubble.

"Send Marcus to me," the governor says. "I will want him to organize a rescue party. Hurry!" He leans back on his pillow, all but spent.

---

"We are trying to free him now, Madam," Khenti is telling Alenna, "The governor has sent help."

"Where is my son?" Alenna is gasping for breath, her chest rising and falling. She has run the entire distance from her house, as fast as her legs would carry her down the river road, and is now searching the courtyard, wild-eyed.

"Safe, Madam."

Khenti has to restrain her from going further, imploring her to remain in the courtyard until it can be determined that the other walls are stable. She pulls away from him.

"Bring him to me!"

"Yes, Madam." Her knees give way and she slumps to the ground.

"Mother!"

"Lukhamen, my love!"

He is on his knees and in her arms.

"Have they found father yet?"

"They are working to free him, Lukhamen."

She caresses his face and holds him to her. Khenti turns his face away from this display, this infraction of the rules. The boy is, after all, ordained.

Roman soldiers pour into the temple, directing farmers with donkeys to harness and haul away the great stones, workmen with mallets and chisels to break them into pieces to be carted away. Among them is Simon the stone mason, who sets immediately to work, rolling away a gigantic stone with his bare hands, his muscles straining, great streams of sweat pouring down his back.

Sechmetna the physician arrives running, a bag slung over his shoulder. He must wait, like the rest.

It is dark when the high priest is brought out on a stretcher. Sechmetna directs that he be taken to a room off the courtyard.

---

A single candle lights the darkened cell. Alenna tiptoes up to the stretcher, which has been placed on a small cot. She can barely make out his face; it is dark with dust and blood. His lower body is covered with a blanket. He is very still. She moves to take his hand. Sechmetna steps in between, quickly.

"His hand is broken. Do not touch him, please, Alenna."

She leans over him. "Beloved," she whispers.

"Alenna," says Sechmetna, "Look at me."

She turns to face him. "You must return to your home and instruct your servants to bring me a barrel of boiled water. I need wine, and straight limbs from a sycamore tree. Bring every ointment and bottle of oil that you possess, and clean linens for binding. Send me two manservants and above all, send Semnut."

She looks at him, dazed.

"Now, Alenna!"

"He is alive, then!"

"Yes." *For the moment*, he thinks, *for the moment*.

She turns for one look at her husband, and is gone. Sechmetna turns to the boy.

"Do not worry, Lukhamen. We will do everything we can."

"Yes, sir," replies the boy.

His purple robe is covered with dust, and torn at the shoulder. The bracelets his father placed on his arms catch the candlelight. His eyes are on his father, who is as still as death.

Sechmetna rummages in his bag, his hands shaking, retrieves a pouch of nightshade, and places it on a small table beside the bed.

———◦∞◦———

Marcus the centurion is at the pylons, leaning against the great statue of Ramses. He stands on one foot, the other braced against the base of the statue. His men have worked through the night—removing stones, clearing debris, inspecting the standing walls by torchlight. He is bareheaded; a day's growth of beard shadows his face. He rubs his eyes.

A thin strip of orange is visible above the tips of the mountains across the river. Overhead, the sky is still purple with night, but is giving way to light. Marcus looks toward the sunrise, drains the dregs of beer from a small glass flask. Through the bottom of the glass he sees the woman. She is coming toward the temple. He lowers the glass, the better to see her. The sun is in his eyes; he cannot see her face, only the silhouette of her body. The wind presses against her, and she struggles up the incline from the river road to the pylons. She is leading a small entourage of servants carrying baskets. Four men carry the platform of a sedan chair loaded with water jars and tree limbs.

His curiosity grows as she approaches, and he strains against the sun to see. Even from here he can tell that she is not like any Egyptian woman he has seen. Her gown is silk, and dyed a most delicate color: blue, but also violet, like the sky in the pre-dawn light. Her head is down against the wind; a scarf matching her dress covers her head and blows against her face. As she reaches him, a gust of wind rips it away. He starts to retrieve it, but the old nurse is there and reaches down quickly; he is too late.

She turns her head and looks back at him. The wind lifts her hair; it dances and plays around her face. The scent of orange blossoms drifts toward him. The old nurse replaces the scarf, and she turns and walks away. Marcus stares after her, rooted to the ground. At length he speaks to the Egyptian servant who has come to refill his flask.

"Who is she?"

"The wife of the high priest, Sire."

"The one who was crushed?"

"Yes, Sire."

The servant hands the flask to the centurion, who walks quickly down the long corridor. But Alenna has disappeared.

At midday, he returns to his quarters and falls on his bed without removing his sandals. He sleeps deeply and dreams of a violet-blue scarf floating to the ground.

---

"Your Excellency. Can you open your eyes?"

The mouth moves slightly. It tries to form a word, but there is no sound. Slowly, the eyes open. They are red with old blood. Tears flow from them down the sides of the pale, rigid face. A sound comes from the throat.

"God," it rasps.

The doctor is working quickly, taking the nightshade from the bag, dropping a spoonful into a cup of wine.

"Something for the pain, Your Excellency."

"Ah…Ah!"

Before Sechmetna can give him the red liquid, he faints.

"Oh, God, I cannot bear it!" Alenna is crying, huddled in the corner. Lukhamen stares from the other side of the bed.

"It is all right, Alenna. He has just fainted. This way he cannot feel the pain."

Sechmetna puts his hands on her shoulders, looks directly into her eyes, and speaks slowly, gently.

"Now listen carefully, Alenna. What you have just seen is the sign I have been looking for. He has not lost his capacity to speak, and I believe his sight is unimpaired, although his eyes are still filled with blood. He has had a great blow to the head, but the brain, or at least portions of the brain, are still working. This is important, Alenna, do you understand?"

Her eyes are wide. She stands straight, rigid.

"He is going to recover, Alenna, but it is going to take a very long time. Almost every bone in his body has been broken," *including his spine,* he says to himself.

She clings to the old man, sobbing. Lukhamen stares at his father, who is very still.

*His mind is intact.*

Lukhamen looks at Sechmetna.

"Did you say that his mind is intact, sir?"

"No, I did not, Lukhamen. But that is a very astute observation. I believe that his mind *is* intact. How did you know that?"

"I thought I heard you say it, sir."

Sechmetna feels a slight chill.

---

It is sunset when Alenna leaves for home. Lukhamen walks with her as far as the great pylons, his hand resting protectively on her shoulder. He seems to have grown taller since the accident.

"Try not to worry, Mother. I will be here with him."

He smiles at her, and she tries to return his smile, but her lip quivers. Lukhamen watches until she has rounded the corner and is out of the temple. Then he heads back toward the cell where his father lies in his deep sleep.

The centurion is waiting, but when he sees the anguish on Alenna's face, he neither speaks nor makes any move toward her. He watches her walk unsteadily down the river road, her manservant behind her.

⚬⚬⚬

Dawn. Marcus is looking upriver. He sees a tiny figure coming toward the temple and feels his heart race. It is not until she is almost within arm's reach that he realizes it is the old nurse, Semnut. The sight of her face is like a blow. He raises his arm to stop her.

"And where is your mistress today, old crone?" He is hoarse with disappointment.

"Not well, Sire." Semnut keeps her eyes on the ground.

"Not well? And what is the nature of her illness?"

"She is exhausted, Sire."

He lowers his arm, and Semnut passes by him. He looks down the road again, hoping, aching, to see her. *I don't even know her name*, he whispers.

# CHAPTER 20

*L*

*The Romans put stone upon stone and carved figures into the new wall. Look. You can see the difference between theirs and ours. Look so. We have carved from the inside out and they have carved from the outside in. Look carefully, and you can see the difference.*

# CHAPTER 21

HARAA, HEAVY AND AWKWARD IN her ninth month of pregnancy, sits by Alenna's bed. She shifts in the small, uncomfortable chair. She is restless, clinking with gold bangles and pendant earrings. There is something of the wild in her countenance; the eyes are large and protruding, like those of a gazelle. Her hair, dark as night, is thick and unruly. Even so, she is carefully groomed. Her skin gleams from oils and massage. Her gown is silk, the color of persimmons. Each finger bears a gold ring.

"What you need is wine, my princess." She notes the dark circles around Alenna's eyes. "Wine, wine, wine."

"Dearest Haraa, what would I do without you?"

"What, indeed? Now don't move. I am going to find that decrepit old nurse of yours."

She hefts herself out of the little gilded seat, almost overturning it, and stumbles into Semnut.

"Curses on you, Semnut! You nearly frightened me to death!"

"Pardon me, Mistress."

"Go downstairs. Tell Manut I have said to bring us lotus fruits and wine, the best in the house."

"Yes, Mistress."

"Now!"

"Yes, Mistress."

Haraa turns to Alenna. "There, now. You will drink lots of wine and sleep for two days. Then you will rise from this bed and tend to your baby, your household, and your husband."

*And*, thinks Haraa, smiling to herself, *by then I will have my baby. The seers have foretold it. A girl! A girl, who in time, will be wife to Alenna's son. My daughter will belong to the royal class. She will be wife to a high priest. But dear, poor Alenna—just a few days ago, losing her son to the priests. Now this. How the gods punish us! It seems just a moment ago that I bade him and his father goodbye ...*

The high priest was in the great hall downstairs, about to leave for the temple, young Lukhamen in tow. He allowed her a moment to lean down and kiss the boy.

"Hello, my little pomegranate," she said.

The boy backed away from the kiss. *You'll kiss me soon enough, little pomegranate, when I am your mother-in-law.*

She watched them walk down the river road, the boy a perfect miniature of his father. *The elder Lukhamen is different today... There's something...radiant about him. I wonder...has he taken a mistress? He's beautiful enough, by all the gods! And a high priest! What woman wouldn't...* She blushed.

---

On the far side of the river, a storm is brewing in the desert. The sand, spiraling upward, whirls in dizzy circles throughout the Valley of the Kings. It fills the air and wraps the mountains in a dusty cloak, then soars high above the river, and onto the city of Luxor, darkening the skies. Haraa looks over at Alenna, who is sleeping quietly. She motions for Semnut to close the shutters.

---

Antonious stands before the governor. "The temple was already decrepit, Sire. But they'll likely blame us for the collapse. They blame us for everything else."

*Yes*, thinks the governor, *as they blame you for running down that man in the street with your chariot. You think I don't know about that.*

"No one will *blame* us, Antonious. We are benefactors here, as well as conquerors. Be mindful of that, and of the way a Roman should behave towards a conquered people: Honorably, Antonious, always honorably. I have dispersed my troops to help in the reconstruction of the temple. It is, after all, an ancient symbol of a once-powerful civilization."

"Yes, Sire." *He coddles them like an old woman. I can remember when a Roman governor acted like a Roman governor, not a sheepherder.*

"Incidentally, Antonious, I have asked Rome to send auditors to go over our records and inspect the stores of grain. They will be here within the month. You will need to be ready for them."

Antonious blanches. "Auditors, Sire? But why?"

"To keep us above reproach, Antonious. It is a common practice. It is far more politic to *request* auditors than to have Rome send them unsolicited and unannounced."

Antonious feels a rivulet of sweat trickle down his back.

"And I will want them to validate the distribution of grain to the common people. We do not want our emperor to think that we would impair or starve the people in the province that supplies his armies with bread, now, would we?"

"Certainly not, Sire." Antonious pales, feels the nausea rise in his stomach.

"Well-fed people are good workers. And good workers make more grain for Rome. Well-fed people and good workers do not *revolt*, Antonious."

"Yes, Sire."

"See to it that your books are in perfect order. I take it that you will have no trouble accounting for this year's harvest and last year's stores?"

"No Sire, no trouble at all."

"And the farmers, Antonious—will their physical appearance bear witness to their well-being and a judicious allotment of grain?"

"Yes, Sire." His voice has all but disappeared.

*He is lying, the contemptible bastard. The rumors are true. He is selling the grain to mercenaries. I will give him plenty to squirm about.*

"I want this inspection to go very smoothly, Antonious. I've seen officers crucified for pilfering. That is the one thing the emperor will not tolerate. It is nothing less than treason. I want this province to be a model for good management and good practices. Is that understood?"

Antonious is trembling. "Yes, Sire." The left side of his face has become spasmodic. The governor turns his back on the ugly sight and walks to the window.

"And Antonious."

"Yes, Sire."

"I shall expect you to escort the auditors as they make their rounds, assist them in every way. You will provide them with lodging and meals, and every comfort."

Antonious tries to speak, but manages only a squeak.

"That will be all, Antonious."

"Yes, Sire. Thank you, Sire." It is scarcely a whisper.

Antonious backs out of the room, runs down the back stairs, and once outside, leans against the wall and vomits. A servant girl finds him there.

"May I help you, Sire?"

He raises his head, wipes the soil from his mouth with his sleeve, and rears back. The force of his fist strikes her full in the face. She falls to the ground—stunned, out of breath, blood streaming from her nose. He kicks her in the small of her back. She cries out.

"Shut up, whore!" he shouts. "Shut up, shut up, shut UP!"

He reels off, in search of wine.

———

Red-eyed and exhausted from a nightmarish sleep, Antonious stands unsteadily in his sitting room, staring out the open window. His feet are swollen with serous fluids, the nerve endings on fire. They strain against his sandals. He bends to remove them, is overcome with nausea, and stands upright quickly. There are perspiration stains on the front and back of his robe. His hair is matted.

*Deputy Superintendent of the granaries! What an insult. I tend to granaries for a pittance and am subordinate to an idiot. An* idiot! *As long as he is governor, nothing will ever change for me in this stinking hellhole. I am nothing here, going nowhere. No one in Rome knows my name.*

He paces, slapping the floor with his painful sandals, sweat oozing from every pore.

*That's going to change.*

There is a knock at the door. It is the governor's cook—a big, greasy man with enormous hands. Antonious hands him a small pouch of white powder and a handful of gold coins. They do not speak. Antonious slams the door behind him.

---

"Beloved."

The high priest is unresponsive. Alenna bends down to kiss his forehead. The gash in his head is sutured; legs, arms, hands, and feet are splinted, as is his back, which is tied to a wooden plank.

"Good news, Madam."

"Sechmetna, is there good news?"

The old doctor puts his hand on her arm.

"It is this, Alenna: his breathing is not obstructed. There was some internal bleeding, but I believe that by some miracle, his internal injuries are less than all of our surmising led us to believe. The workers who retrieved him tell me that the altar stone and the statue of Amon fell over him, and in so doing, created a space, a shelter of sorts, that deflected the full impact of the larger stones, an extraordinary act of providence. In other words, Madam, *the Lord Amon saved him.*"

"What?" she says.

"The fact that he can breathe without laboring is very encouraging, very encouraging indeed. I have discontinued the sedative for the time being. I want him to return to consciousness. I want to be sure that the injury to his head has not affected his ability to see, or to speak."

She is not listening.

*He needs to be in his own bed where I can see to him. He'll never get well in this place. He needs to be at home. That's it. I can convert the dining room into a bedroom. It's large, and airy, and has a view of the garden. I will have all of his things brought there, and...*

"Alenna?"

"Yes, yes. Thank you, Sechmetna."

He leaves her, walks out into the courtyard. The sun is good on his aching back. A young acolyte runs after him with him a cup of water.

*I am tired,* he thinks, taking a sip. *Poor Alenna. She has no idea of the severity of his injuries, let alone the consequences. If he is able to see and speak, that will be nothing less than a miracle. But he will never walk again. That I know. The spinal thread is completely severed, and there is nothing I can do about it.*

---

The only sound inside the small chamber is that of workmen outside—stonecutters, chipping and hammering as they have done since the time of the pharaohs. Lukhamen sits beside his father.

"Your Excellency." Khenti puts his hand on the boy's shoulder. "Come with me. One of the other priests will sit with him for a while."

Until now, Lukhamen has only heard the title of *Excellency* bestowed on his father. Then he remembers. It belongs to him as well. He is the next high priest.

"Come, Your Excellency."

"But, Khenti..."

"He will sleep until the sun sets. It is important, the thing that you and I must do."

---

In a little while they are in a small temple boat with white sails, crossing the Nile. Lukhamen takes a deep breath. It has been a long time since he has been out in the open, and he is taken with the idea of space and of deep breaths. He looks to the bright sky, then toward the other shore, to the mountains, then closes his eyes and lifts his face to the wind.

When they reach the bank, Khenti instructs the boatman to wait for them, and they set out toward the mountains.

*I know this place*, the boy thinks. *This is where the divine ones sleep. It is the Valley of the Kings. I have seen it from the other side, with father.*

The walk is long. Lukhamen is beginning to tire, but then they are in a crescent bowl at the foot of the mountains, and he is awestruck. High cliffs surround them. The valley is immense and quiet.

Khenti's voice is deeper here, more resonant. "This is where your ancestors rest with the pharaohs. Your Father's father is here, and his father's father. Look up. There, to your right. There is a place—just there, Lukhamen, above that outcrop. Do you see where I am pointing?"

Lukhamen's eyes follow Khenti's finger until they find a great stone that covers the entrance to a tomb. He can barely make out the single word that is carved into it: *Sa'at*.

"Behold the tomb of the Sa'at high priests, Lukhamen. It is where your father will sleep when it is his time, and it will be your resting place, as well."

Lukhamen inhales sharply.

"Is my father going to die, Khenti?"

"Oh no, Your Excellency. I mean when he is a very old man. A very old man."

The boy exhales. His eyes find the spot again.

Khenti's voice is low, contemplative. "I come here to be close to them. I feel them. They help us, Lukhamen; they guide us. I brought you here so that you could feel them too. You must know that we are not alone in our troubles."

Lukhamen looks around at the bleak landscape, the dusty, dry valley. The feeling of awe is gone. He feels no comfort, no presence, only smaller and more alone than ever.

Khenti walks a little way from him, a bit higher onto a foothill, and is all at once remote, lost in meditation. The boy sits in the shade of a large rock, leans against it, and drifts into a deep sleep.

---

"Lukhamen." Khenti's hand is on his shoulder. "It is time to go."

The sun is beginning its descent, and the air has cooled. He follows the old man down the rocky path toward the river. Khenti walks quickly. Lukhamen, still groggy from sleep, cannot keep up. He hears the wind rise in a wail and echo off the walls of the cliffs. He stops to listen. He looks back at the valley and the mountains, which are beginning to turn pink in the setting sun. The wind blows stronger, and raises the dust at his feet. He resumes his walk toward the river, but a voice stops him in his tracks.

*Lukhamen.*

He turns, but he is alone. Khenti is almost out of sight.

*It is true.*

"What is true? Who are you?"

*It is true, Lukhamen.*

"What is true, what is true?" Lukhamen is shouting now, into the wind. "What is TRUE?"

*You are not alone.*

Lukhamen is rooted to the ground. Like a great weight, the strain and pain of the weeks following the collapse of the wall falls upon him, and he slumps to the ground. The tears flow. Sobs wrack his body, and he is powerless to stop the onslaught of grief.

He is that way when Khenti lifts him into his arms, and carries him like a baby, to the boat.

---

I awake from my trance, and my face is covered with tears. I *felt* it. I felt his aloneness—his deep, abiding, inconsolable sorrow. I am more than an observer now. I am there. I am with him, in him, or he is in me.

# CHAPTER 22

—— ∞ ——

SANDY HAS SEEN ME THROUGH it all. Once, she tried to trick me into going to a recovery meeting with her. That was before I went on my own.

"There's somebody I want you to meet," she said.

"Please, Sandy."

"No, really. He's cute."

"That's what I really need. Somebody cute."

"No. He's *really* cute."

"Sandy…"

"Seriously cute."

"No, Sandy. No."

I was to meet him. In good time.

—— ∞ ——

"This is Bill," she said, pulling me over to him.

"How do you do?" I said, extending my hand, embarrassed beyond words. It was only my second meeting. I wasn't up to socializing.

"I don't shake hands with pretty girls," he said, and gave me a hug.

I wanted to disappear. He and Sandy bantered for a few minutes. He said goodbye, winked at me, and was gone. He had the bluest eyes I had ever seen.

"Didn't I tell you?" she said.

"Don't do this, Sandy."

"Oh, don't worry. He's dating someone."

Thank God.

I couldn't tell her how afraid I was of everything, or explain how safe it felt to be alone.

*I am a living wound, Sandy,* I wanted to say to her. *That's all I am, a joyless automaton. I don't want to meet anyone, and God knows no one wants to meet me. I don't even know why I'm still here.*

---

I've been coming to the meeting for months now, and I see him almost every day. He comes and leaves with the girl he's dating. It doesn't matter to me. I do not want anybody in my life. I have someone.

*He calls me Beloved. Did we live before, together, in another life? Has he come to help me through this?*

I am taken with the idea of reincarnation. I need to explore the ancient concept that we live over and over again, the credo that is embraced by so many in the world, the idea that was first accepted by, then banished from many present-day religions. I wonder why. Didn't young John Bordeaux say that Eddie and I had lived together in another life? I read books on the subject, engrossed, fascinated.

---

Sandy calls. "I hear they're no longer together."

"Who?"

"Ole' Blue Eyes and the girl he was dating."

"Who?"

"Bill. Bill. The cute one, you know, and his girlfriend."

"Sandy, I don't care."

"I know he's for you. I am psychic, you know."

I do notice that he is coming to the meetings alone and leaving alone. Still. It's none of my business.

---

Three months later, he calls. It's May, and a violent thunderstorm has turned D.C. into a maelstrom. It's raining sideways, and lightning flashes over the Washington Monument. I'm staring out of my office window when the phone rings.

"Hi. It's Bill." *Oh no!*

"Hi," I say.

"I was just sitting here in my office watching this incredible storm, and I thought of you. It's gorgeous, isn't it?"

I panic. He continues to talk, easily. *He's going to ask me out*, I think, in pure terror. *Sandy, I am going to kill you.* Did she give him my phone number? Maybe not. I'm easy enough to find. He takes his time, a full fifteen minutes of easy banter before he proposes something very safe: a show at an art gallery on Connecticut Avenue. It's one of his favorite artists. *Think of something!*

"It's an opening. There will be refreshments. It'll be nice."

*I am definitely going to say no.*

"It's Sunday afternoon," he says.

"Okay," I say.

---

I haven't been on a real *date* in twenty-two years. Why did I say yes to this? I'm dreading it. I am a raw human being, a wounded, wary, solitary animal. I need to be by myself.

I am already a pariah to most of my colleagues. They avoid me like the plague—as if they could contract *death* by proximity. That's fine with me. I cling to a small group of friends, mostly Sandy and Martha.

I don't know what to wear. I'm looking at my closet as if I'm seeing it for the first time. My daughter Debbie is visiting from Paris; I ask her to help me. My resident expert on clothes offers her advice:

"You'll look fine in whatever you wear," she says.

This isn't helping, I tell her. She pulls a dress from the closet.

"Here you are. It's red, it's silk, it's afternoon, it's an art gallery," she says. "It's perfect."

She's right. Why am I so shaky? On Sunday morning, he calls.

"Say," he says, "do we have to wait till four o'clock?"

I'm thrown. What kind of a line is that? *What do I say to that?* He gives me no time to answer.

"My son is pitching in a baseball game at one," he continues. "Why don't you come with me to the game, and we can leave from there?"

I don't believe this. *I can't go to a baseball game in a red silk dress and high heels.* My disguise as a normal person going to an art gallery on a Sunday afternoon is shot.

"Okay," I say, but now I'm disoriented. Debbie is not around to help me; I'm on my own. I choose a skirt and sweater, but keep the high heels.

He picks me up at noon, wearing a suit. We are going to a baseball game but he's dressed for our date. *I should have kept the red dress.*

He roots for the pitcher. No doubt who the father of this boy is. I'm surprised. I thought he'd be more...worldly. He is from New York, after all. He's so...sure of himself. Comfortable in his skin. Not jumpy like me.

He proudly introduces me to his youngest son after the game. The boy has his father's startling blue eyes. I take in the baseball field, and the parents and kids laughing and enjoying each other, and I can see, as through a keyhole, life going on outside my world of loss. But I'm an alien. I'm *different.*

Bill is divorced, with four children. *Like me.* This isn't so hard, I think, and he isn't scary after all. He's somebody's *father,* and he clearly adores this boy. At the art gallery, he asks if I have children. I tell him I have three daughters. Just like that I deny Eddie's existence. I'm shocked at how easily it came out, and I wonder if Eddie can hear me. *I'm sorry, Eddie,* I say to him in my heart. *I just can't say the words.* I walk away from Bill, pretending to look at the paintings, because my eyes are beginning to fill.

He knows several people there. I know no one, thank God. He chats easily with them while I force back the tears and tuck my secret deeper into my soul. Still, my lie of omission haunts me, and I am guilty, guilty, guilty.

Later, we stand on the pavement outside the gallery, and it is springtime in Washington. Everything looks new, and I have recovered somewhat. The weather is perfect, and all of a sudden I'm hungry. I haven't eaten all day. *I wonder if there is a place nearby to eat,* I think to myself.

"I'm hungry," he says. "There's a place right up the street on Dupont Circle. They've got sidewalk tables. We could eat outside. Are you hungry?" He is reading my mind. Wait till I tell Sandy.

We find a table; he pulls out my chair, and sits beside me. My chair is too far from the table, so I adjust it. I half-stand, lift the chair, bring it closer to the table, and sit down. On his foot. I nearly fall over, getting up. He makes a joke about it, something about loving pain. God.

The waiter serves us a perfectly awful Salade Niçoise, and he makes another joke.

"Is my *mother* back there in the kitchen?" he says. My brain isn't working; I don't get it. His mother's cooking was so bad, he says, when he got into the army he thought the food was great. I have to laugh a little. My secret is still safe, but my denial is eating a hole in my heart.

He takes me home. He doesn't say he'll call, and he doesn't ask to see me again.

"Ah, well," I sigh in relief. "That's over."

# CHAPTER 23

"A CHILD GRACES OUR HOUSE. What a joy she will be to this old man."

"She will be a joy to us both, my husband," says Haraa, glancing at the babe who is asleep in the arms of a wet nurse.

"We will marry her well." The new mother yawns. "And now, please the gods, I should like to sleep."

The husband kisses her brow and slips from the room.

It is a large chamber, richly appointed with rugs from Arabia and tables with inlays of ivory. A chaise longue, upholstered in dark red silk, sits at an angle in the center of the room. Behind it, on a pedestal, is a large vase filled to overflowing with white Turkish lilies.

Some years ago, the old man, a renowned trader, obtained a hundred of the precious bulbs from the leader of a caravan with goods from the boats at Alexandria. They flourished in the soil of Haraa's garden, and now blooms fill the house with their dizzying aroma year-round. Haraa is overly fond of telling visitors that they are to be found nowhere else in all of Egypt.

She burrows into goose-down pillows and almost immediately begins to snore. Alia, the masseuse who has been folding towels in a corner, quietly takes a bottle of oil from one of the tables, slips it into a small bag, and tiptoes out.

The only air in the tiny hovel is from the open doorway, where a ragged linen cloth is pulled back onto a hook in the wooden frame. On a small, rough-hewn bed, a young woman writhes in the last throes of childbirth. Her cheekbones protrude; the skin is tight around her skeletal face. Her eyes are deep in their sockets; and her gown, drawn up around her waist, is rough and worn.

A midwife, wide and unwieldy in the small space, holds a cup of water to the woman's lips.

'Mahda!" Her voice is strident and grating. "Don't move about so. It only makes the birthing harder, and you'll kill the child."

"I don't care if the child dies," murmurs the young woman. "I don't care if *I* die."

She bears down in a final agonizing contraction and the baby slides onto the little woolen blanket between her legs.

"A girl!" The older woman spits onto the dirt floor. "What a blessing that my son is not here to see this. "It'll be your fault, Mahda, when I starve. I will have no grandson to take care of me in my old age. My husband is gone, my son is gone, and now you have brought this curse on us because you were heedless and *stupid*! I begged you to drink my potions. I begged you!"

She folds the baby carelessly into the blanket and puts it aside into a make-shift cradle. It whimpers weakly.

"Worthless girl." She takes a black powder from a pouch in her pocket, pours it into a wooden goblet, and mixes it with water.

"Kesi! What are you doing?" Alia lowers her head to enter the small doorway.

"I am giving her powered horn. It will stop the bleeding."

"Put it away, Kesi. I have brought something for her," says Alia.

"So *you* think my potions are not good enough, too, don't you? If she had listened to *me*, she would have given me a boy for my old age! But she is *stupid*! Now she has a worthless girl and has started to bleed."

Mahda is trembling violently. Alia pours water from the pitcher into a basin and sponges it onto her spent, overheated body.

"Kesi!" Alia hands her a packet from her bag. "Make tea. There is honey as well in my bag. It's from the rich woman's house. And there is cornmeal, and a jar of goat's milk for porridge. Mahda has not had a good meal in days."

"She needs to fast and drink only palm water!" says the old woman.

"See to it, Kesi, or leave!"

"My husband, if he were alive—may God give rest to his soul—would never let you talk to me this way."

"Do as I say or leave."

Frowning and grumbling, the old woman rummages around in Alia's bag and withdraws a small package wrapped in papyrus.

"What is this?"

"It is soap. Hand it to me."

"What are you going to do with it?"

"I am going to wash them with it."

"You are going to kill them! God! You are going to kill them!"

"Do you want them to be lepers, like Joseph and your husband?"

"Everyone knows leprosy is a curse. If they die, it will be your fault. "I will leave, but..." she smiles slyly, "here is something you don't know, *Mistress Alia of the rich woman's house*: the Romans took the high priest from the temple. I saw them."

"What?"

"They took him from the temple. To his house. I guess he's going to die. Just like *her*, there. You don't know what you're doing, Alia. You think you're as wise as God, but you're not."

Alia sighs with relief as Kesi finally squeezes through the small opening and onto the street.

⸎

She looks at the young woman on the cot who is now sleeping soundly. *Thank God for clover tea and opium.* She smoothes Mahda's hair. *Maybe I should go to the priest's house tomorrow, offer my services. Maybe I can massage his legs. After all, he did give Joseph's father the gold coin.* She looks at Mahda. *She'd like me to do that. Joseph would like me to do that, God give rest to his soul.*

Her friend stirs, and Alia covers her with a clean linen cloth, taken from Haraa's closet.

*She has not had a day of peace since Joseph was arrested. Stealing. As if Joseph would ever steal. Buying dates in the market, and unlucky enough to be spied by Antonious, that was his sin.* She looks over at the child, who is also asleep. *Lucenkep. We will have her baptized, and call her Lucenkep.*

---

Six priests carry his litter. They walk slowly, carefully, lest they jostle their precious load. At the governor's request, Marcus leads the Roman guard escort.

The wall gate to the front courtyard is open; they are expected. The soldiers enter first and station themselves along the walk. Marcus the centurion walks to the door and knocks.

The great door opens, and *she* is standing there. He stares dumbly.

She speaks. "Centurion."

His throat is dry. "Madam." He is barely audible.

"Thank you for escorting my husband. And now," she looks over his shoulder, "shall we get him out of the sun?"

He moves aside quickly, and the litter is brought through the door, across the great hall, and into the dining room, transformed now into a bed chamber. He follows as if in a dream, but stops short of the inner room. He stands alone in the great hall, and waits.

He removes his helmet, the better to see the high ceiling, the immaculate floor of polished stone, whitewashed walls, and columns carved in the same papyrus design as those in the temple. It is simple, elegant, and quiet. Servants come and go without making a sound, floating through the house. They do not seem to be aware of him. He notices the stairway leading up to the bedchambers. *I suppose there is where she sleeps.*

In his mind he sees her mount the stairs, a lamp in her hand to light the way, her hair falling down her back in dark waves, her pale, transparent gown floating in slow motion around her body. She turns to look at him, and smiles.

"Centurion?"

She is standing before him. He looks down into green eyes and thinks he might lose his balance. She turns to the manservant beside her.

"Something cool to drink, if you please, Manut." She turns to him again. "You must be thirsty from the walk, Centurion."

"You are too kind, Madam." His voice is hoarse.

"Please, sit down while the priests see to my husband."

She beckons to a low bench. He sits carefully, adjusting his sword so that it hangs to one side, and places his helmet on the floor. She sits beside him, turns toward him. He breathes in her soap and bath oil. Orange blossoms. Cardamom. He can hear her small, shallow breaths. He imagines her heart beating beneath her breasts.

"Here we are. Thank you, Manut. Ah. Pomegranate, my son's favorite."

She hands him a silver goblet, and his fingers accidentally touch hers as he reaches for it. A small shock sets him aback, and he almost spills the contents. She appears not to notice and takes a sip of her drink.

"It was kind of the governor to provide an escort. I have had to visit my husband in the temple ever since the accident."

"Yes, Madam," he blurts out. "I was assigned to the reconstruction of the temple wall. I waited every day at the pylons for you."

*Stupid!* He immediately regrets his remark. She takes another sip from her drink, stands, and places her goblet on Manut's tray.

"I hope you will forgive me, Centurion, but I must see to my husband. We must do everything we can to make him comfortable."

He stands, stricken. *I'm being dismissed. What a boorish, stupid thing to say!*

"Forgive me, Madam, what I meant to say was…"

"It's quite all right." She gives him a cool little smile. "Manut will see you out."

"If there is anything I can do…"

"We shall certainly call on the governor. Please give him my regards, and thank you again."

"Good day, Madam."

She turns her back to him and walks toward the inner room, and then she is out of his sight. He stares at the place he has last seen her. After some time, he is aware of Manut standing next to him, still holding the tray. He places his goblet carefully, next to hers, and heads for the door. Manut opens it quietly, and he is out in the courtyard. His men, who are lounging in the shade of the wall, snap to attention. When he is onto the street, the heat of the sun reminds him that he has forgotten his helmet. He walks the few paces back to the courtyard. Manut is standing in the doorway, the helmet in his hand.

# CHAPTER 24

⚭

☥

Young Lukhamen is sitting at a small desk under a tree, propped on his elbows, daydreaming of battles, soldiers, and chariots. A hoopoe bird hops into his view, pecking for grubs with a long, curved beak, his red-tufted head bobbing up and down like a *shaduf,* the draw-well farmers dip into the river to fill their irrigation buckets. The boy's eyelids grow heavy.

Khenti's voice from within the house breaks his reverie. He sits up abruptly and picks up a brush. The bird skitters off. Khenti stands over him, inspecting the papyrus sheet. "Your characters are quite good, Your Excellency," says Khenti.

"Yes, Sire."

"Soon you will be able to read; and read you will of the great Pharaoh Ramses II and his defeat of the Hittites. You will know the names of all the ancients and the gods. You will know whatever you desire to know—history, mathematics, engineering, astrology, medicine." The boy stares into Khenti's eyes, unable to comprehend this great promise.

"Sire?"

"Yes, Your Excellency?"

"Will you call me Lukhamen, as my father does?"

"If you wish. In the presence of others, however, you must always be addressed as Your Excellency."

"I do wish it, Sire."

"Then you may address me as Khenti. Agreed?"

"Agreed."

"When we are alone."

"Agreed." Lukhamen smiles at the old man.

*Don't grow too fond of the boy, Khenti, you will have to give him up. And soon.*

A servant interrupts them.

"The high priest is calling for you, Sire."

"I must go now, Lukhamen. We will have a lesson another time, tomorrow perhaps."

"May I come with you, Khenti?"

"Not now, Lukhamen. Your father wishes to speak with me."

---

A morning breeze parts the sheer white curtains as Khenti passes through the archway. The high priest lies still in the high bed.

"Greetings, Sire," says Khenti. His voice is low and tender.

The high priest looks up at him through bloodshot eyes. "You are changed, my friend." His voice is raspy and weak.

"I am the same, Sire."

"Too thin. Tired." A pause. "I am glad to see you."

"As am I you, Sire."

A pain seizes him. He closes his eyes tightly and lets it wash over him, take him, run its course. When it is over, he opens his eyes.

"Are they saying that I am going to die?"

"If you mean the ignorant, unwashed multitude, they are always ill-informed, Your Excellency."

The high priest smiles. "How long have I been here?"

"You were brought from the temple ten days ago, Sire."

"The boy?"

"He is well, learning to read."

"He is much on my mind."

"Yes, Sire." A long silence follows.

"You have something to say, Khenti. What is it?"

"I can delay it no longer, Sire, now that you are conscious."

"What is it?"

Alenna is suddenly upon them, like an angry storm. Wearing an apricot silk robe, her hair tousled, her feet bare, she hurls herself into the room and in her haste, trips. She regains her balance quickly, but her cheeks are aflame with anger and embarrassment.

"He tires easily, Khenti. I trust you are not burdening us with unnecessary worries."

"No, Madam. I am sorry if I have awakened you."

"You have not awakened me. No one *awakens* me. I have a young baby to attend to, you know."

She leans over her husband.

"Beloved," he rasps, "Do I smell coffee?"

"Yes."

"I should like to have a little."

"I shall see to it." She frowns at Khenti before leaving, stepping carefully over the raised stone in the doorway. They hear her voice down the hall, calling for the servants.

"Quickly, Khenti!" says the high priest.

"The council is here, Your Excellency."

A pain strikes and the high priest pales, but he breathes slowly, steadily through it. He lets his body float on the waves of nausea and lightheadedness.

Alenna is back, walking quickly, a servant girl behind her carrying a tray.

"Khenti will assist me, Alenna," says the high priest.

"No."

"If you please, Alenna."

"Then let me give you the medicine Sechmetna has *instructed* me to administer. Do you think I cannot see your pain?"

"It clouds my mind," he says. She stands rooted, glaring at Khenti.

"I shall most certainly report this to his physician," she says to the older priest. She whirls around and heads toward the doorway, hair swinging wildly, bare feet pounding the stone floor. "I shall most certainly report it!" she says at the threshold before disappearing. The servant girl runs behind, taking the coffee with her.

From his bed, the high priest can see the garden through the arches. His eyes move toward a flamboyant tree and settle on its blazing, scarlet flowers.

"I had forgotten it was summer," he says to Khenti. "Are the white birds on the river?"

"Yes, Your Excellency."

"And the temple at Philae is under flood and the priests of the council are here at Karnak for the annual convocation."

"Yes, Sire."

"And what occupies them, Khenti?"

"The boy, Sire."

"What are they saying?"

"That they must see to his education, since you..."

"Will be dead soon?"

"Oh no, Your Excellency. It's just that he is already nine years of age..."

"They are right. I have injuries that even Sechmetna cannot see. I know they are there. I can feel my life force ebbing."

"Your Excellency..."

"They wish to take him to Philae?"

"Please, Sire."

"Answer me. They wish to take him to Philae?"

"Yes, Sire."

"When?"

"When the waters recede. They want to begin immediately as they ..."

"...do not want the Temple of Amon to be without a high priest for long."

Khenti does not reply.

The next pain flashes through his spine like lightning. He tenses, but breathes again—slowly, steadily. He is learning to surrender to it, to conserve and redirect his energy. When it passes, he speaks again.

"My father has come to me in dreams, Khenti."

A pain takes him again and this time he grimaces.

"Ah…"

Khenti's eyes grow bright with tears.

"Tomorrow I shall cross over into the spirit world. He beckons me."

"Sire…"

"Tonight," he takes a deep breath, "go in secret to the repository. Retrieve the white crown and leopard skin. Keep them with you throughout the night. In the morning, at sunrise, bring them to me."

"Your Excellency!"

"Take great care, Khenti. If you are discovered by the Romans, it will mean death."

"Sire…the crown is forbidden…the Romans do not know it exists."

"Ah, but it does, Khenti! And as long as it exists, Egypt exists! They are afraid of it. It repudiates their emperor and reminds the people of who they are! But I tell you that the day will come when the people will again see the white crown and leopard skin. They will see with their own eyes the Egypt they thought was lost."

It is a while before he can speak again.

"My father wore the crown on the day of his death, as did his father, and his father's father. Shall I not, too, be properly dressed for my rite of passage?"

Khenti relents, and with bowed head says, "Yes, my Lord High Priest."

"Will you assist me, then?"

"Yes, Your Excellency."

"Alenna…"

"Yes, Sire?"

"Alenna is not to see me die." His voice breaks, finally.

"Yes, Your Excellency."

"Go to the woman Haraa. Tell her she is to take Alenna away. You need not explain why. She will do what I ask of her. She has ambitions upon my son and my family name. She thinks I do not know."

A pain comes and passes. He smiles at the old man.

"It is all ordained, my friend."

"Yes, Sire."

"Bring two of your most trusted priests with you, but do not tell them why."

"Yes, Sire."

"Until tomorrow, then."

The old priest turns to go. Tears blind his eyes, and he does not see the doctor in the doorway.

———— ⊸∞∞⊶ ————

"Good morning, Sire."

"Ah, Sechmetna. My wife has sent you to scold me."

"Indeed she has, Sire. I hope you have not exerted yourself too greatly this morning." He looks closely at the man in the bed. "I think Alenna need not have worried. It seems to me that your color has improved. There is a new energy about you."

"Then remove these splints immediately, all except the one which binds my back."

"Your Excellency..."

"Remove them, and all traces of opium from this room."

"Your Excellency!"

"Do it now, Sechmetna! Now!"

# CHAPTER 25

—⁕—

"Would you like to go to a baseball game?" It's Bill.

"I'm in a league—real estate guys, you know, and we have a game on Saturday. Would you like to come?"

I don't believe it.

—⁕—

He seats me on a bleacher with wives and girlfriends. I have this funny feeling that I *belong* somewhere, belong to someone. I never felt that in twenty-two years of marriage. *Don't be stupid*, I warn myself. *You don't belong to him.*

He looks so easy, so natural on the field. I like watching him. Halfway through, reaching for a fly ball, he grabs his side. He's out of the game. He comes to sit next to me.

"Well, that's it for me. I'm through."

"Forever?"

"Maybe. I keep pulling the same muscles in my side. I probably shouldn't push it, quit while I'm ahead."

"But you're such a good baseball player."

"I know," he says, and smiles at me.

"Do you think you should go home?"

"No. I'll stay."

I'm glad he's out of the game. He sits by my side, rooting for his team, hunched over, his baseball cap in his hand. He's so handsome. And he's here.

With me. My husband was never with me. He was always with somebody else when he was with me.

The game is over, and he turns to me. "Would you like to go out to dinner?"

"Okay." I really don't want the day to end, this feeling of *being* with someone.

"I'll have to go home first and change my clothes, okay?"

This is awkward. I don't want to go to his apartment. Is this how it's going to end? I feel so disappointed. *I guess they're all alike, after all.*

*Wait a minute. Don't jump to conclusions*, a little voice inside me says. *You know how to say no. Give it a chance.*

Maybe he isn't trying to get me into bed and then dump me. Maybe he really does want to go out to dinner. I gamble.

---

His apartment is awful; the furniture is right out of Goodwill. Newspapers are piled in the corner.

"Grim, isn't it?" he says.

I laugh, and relax. This is no seduction scene.

"It's so bad, when burglars come, they leave things. They left me all this."

He makes me laugh. I can't remember the last time I really laughed.

He comes out of his bedroom, dressed in a suit. "Let's go," he says.

---

Dinner is over and we are sitting outside my apartment building in his car. *Now* it's awkward. I don't know what to do. I'm forty-three years old, and I don't know what to do. I think people have sex now, automatically. I'm from another world. I can't do this. I hardly know him. I thank him for dinner, say goodnight, get out, slam the door, and run to my door. *I slammed the door!* He must think I'm an absolute idiot. That's okay. I'll never hear from him again anyway.

---

"What are you doing next Sunday?" It's Bill again. I don't believe it.

"Some friends of mine are giving a party. Would you like to go?"

I hate parties. It was always at parties that my husband would disappear with the first girl who fell for his charming lies, while I sat alone through the night, humiliated, too ashamed to look for him, too afraid to find him, drinking myself into a stupor.

"Okay."

At the party, Bill knows everybody, and disappears right away into the crowd. *I knew it.* In a few minutes, he's back, with two plates.

"Food looks good, doesn't it?" he says.

He never leaves my side, even when he is talking to someone else. I don't know his friends. I don't have much to say, so I watch him talking, listening, laughing, enjoying them. Sometimes he reaches for my hand, as if to make sure I'm still there. I feel tears coming. This is something new.

# CHAPTER 26

♀

THE GOVERNOR LOOKS UP WEAKLY from the basin into which he has vomited. A servant girl wipes his face and takes the basin out to empty it. He sits in his dressing room, trying to garner strength. "Send for Marcus," he says to the aide who has come to dress him.

A short while later, the centurion stands before him.

"Marcus. Welcome."

"Sire."

"Close the door, Marcus. I must speak to you in privacy."

Marcus closes the door quietly. "Are you well, Sire?"

"It shows that plainly, does it?"

"You look...tired, Sire."

"My condition is much graver than that, Marcus. I am dying. I do not have much time."

"Sire!"

"I am being poisoned from within my own kitchen, but I cannot prove it. I believe Antonious is behind it."

"I will execute him with my own sword! Give me leave, I beg you, Sire."

"I cannot prove it, Marcus. I have changed every cook, every maid, more than once. Still, I believe Antonious' gold goes from hand to hand."

"Gold? He is but a minor officer, Sire, in charge of..."

"Wheat, Marcus, wheat—the precious commodity that makes this province of inestimable value to the Roman Empire. We are the province that feeds the armies, and Antonious is the keeper of our treasure. It was a mistake to give him such a post. He is a petty little man with unrealistic ambitions, and a thief. I have reason to believe he has pilfered wheat and sold it to Arabs and to Egyptian insurgents. He has used the money to have me poisoned and is probably preparing to launch a campaign within the Roman Senate for my seat."

"He is a traitor, Sire! I shall crucify him with my own hands!"

"I have summoned Roman auditors to conduct an inventory of our granaries. They will arrive within a few days and will undoubtedly discover a deficit, a loss for which he, as Deputy Supervisor of the Granaries, is responsible. Rome will take care of Antonious, Marcus. Starting immediately, I want you to place sentries on every road, inspect every caravan, every wagon, every conveyance traveling in and out of the city. Find every grain of wheat that might still be in transport, and confiscate it. We may be able to trap Antonious' coconspirators and *persuade* them to give him to us."

"I shall find the grain, Sire, and the insurgents. I promise you."

"Use only your most trusted men, Marcus. I do not want Antonious to know that we are onto him."

"Trust me, Sire."

"I do, Marcus. Your father was a great friend of mine."

"He still is, Sire."

"Good. Go, then."

"But Sire, you…"

"I have seen a brilliant Egyptian doctor, the one known as Sechmetna. He has confirmed that I am poisoned. There is no antidote."

"Sire…permit me to bring you provisions from my own mess."

No need now, Marcus. The harm was done a long time ago, before I realized what was happening. I eat very little these days, in any case. Now that the poison has done its work, they have probably stopped giving it to me. Go quickly, Marcus. I shall write a letter to Rome, recommending that you be appointed acting governor until the Emperor can appoint one."

"But I am only a soldier."

"You are a centurion. Your father is a senator. Upon my death, this office shall pass to you. I shall also recommend that the emperor make it a permanent appointment."

"But Sire..."

"That is all, Marcus."

"Yes, Sire."

He watches the tall, stalwart soldier walk away. *You will do well, Marcus. You are your father's son.*

---

Haraa holds a lock of Alenna's hair between two fingers.

"By all the gods, Alenna, you look like a peasant's wife."

She drops the lock of hair as if it were ridden with vermin. "You will come with me to my hairdresser. Now! No arguments, no arguments. Take my broach, wear it. Here, I want you to have it." Haraa takes the broach that is pinned between her breasts and hands it to Alenna. "This was made for your blue robe. It's lapis lazuli. And just look at the gold work! It's perfect."

"Haraa...I can't leave him. You know that."

"Oh, but that is just foolish. What can you do in a few hours that Sechmetna and all the servants are not doing already? You are the wife of the high priest! It will raise his spirits to see you looking well-groomed and beautiful."

"Haraa..."

"Come, come, Alenna. Do it for *him*."

"Haraa..."

"My sedan chair is waiting outside."

"He does have Khenti with him, and he has brought two other priests as well. I cannot keep them from him."

"So there. What can happen in a few hours?"

---

A breeze lifts the curtains of the sedan chair, allowing Alenna a glimpse of the mountains in the distance. Along the river, the air is fresh and clean. Flocks of white birds float on the swollen Nile. They pass the marketplace, brimming with stands and merchants selling spiced lamb sausages, almond rice, and teas from the Orient.

Alenna takes a deep breath. She sighs. "Oh, it's good to be alive! You were right. I needed a breath of fresh air!"

Harra smiles to herself. The high priest will be pleased with her.

The sedan chair comes to an abrupt halt.

"And what goes here?" says Haraa, poking her head out of the curtain.

"Excuse me, Madam, but I must ask you to alight from your chair."

Marcus holds the curtain up with one hand and extends the other to Haraa.

She is stunned for a moment, but recovers quickly. Her eyes take in the tall centurion, and she gives him her most devastating smile.

"Gladly, Sire," Haraa purrs. She puts her hands on his shoulders, forcing him to lift her to the ground.

"Must I alight as well, Centurion?"

He had not seen Alenna.

"Must I alight as *well*, Centurion?" she repeats.

He cannot speak.

"*Centurion?*" Haraa says loudly.

He clears his throat. "A thousand pardons, Madam," he says to Alenna.

"Is this a new practice? Is there a regulation of which I am unaware which forbids the passage of Egyptian ladies through the city?"

"No, Madam, certainly not. We are conducting a routine inspection of moving conveyances, is all. I am truly sorry."

"A routine inspection would not seem to merit the attention of a *centurion,*" Haraa purrs.

He extends a hand to her, eyes still on Alenna. "Allow me, if you please."

"Of course, Centurion, of course." Haraa gives him a new, winning smile. Once again, she puts her hands on his shoulders, and he lifts her into the chair.

He looks past her, to Alenna. "I hope your husband is improved, Madam."

"He is gaining ground daily, Centurion."

He cannot take his eyes from her face. He is faintly aware of a blue gown, a touch of gold sparkling between her breasts, and of his heart, which is beating wildly against his chest.

"Alenna…" says Haraa.

"And shall we pass now?" Alenna's voice is cold.

"Yes, most certainly." He stands aside. *Alenna. Her name is Alenna.*

The sedan chair moves on, leaving him standing in the middle of the road. He watches the bearers as they move away, achingly aware of the growing distance between them. He stays thus until they turn a corner.

———— ✺ ————

Haraa's eyes are wide.

"You *know* him?"

"He brought my husband from the temple."

"By all the gods, he is beautiful."

"Haraa!"

"Well, he is. By all the *gods*!" Haraa runs her fingers through her hair.

"He is a Roman, Haraa."

"Roman or no, he is still beautiful. Such eyes. Brown…with little flecks of gold in them. You can tell a lot about a man from his eyes."

"I will not listen to this."

But Haraa's thoughts have turned to the strong arms that lifted her from the chair.

"And the way you let him touch you. You should be ashamed, Haraa."

"I think I will have a red henna rinse this time…What do you think?"

"I think you need to consider your delicate status as an Egyptian woman, Haraa, a *married* Egyptian woman."

Haraa shifts in her seat, thinking of her empty bed and her old merchant husband who travels to all parts of the world and sleeps with countless foreign women.

# CHAPTER 27

THE BOY IS HIDING BEHIND a pillar, watching closely as Khenti, chanting softly, swings a censer at the foot of the bed. The room is fragrant with frankincense. The high priest is still, eyes closed.

"Lukhamen!"

"Yes, Father?" the boy calls from behind the pillar.

Khenti is shaken from his trance; the chanting stops. "Lukhamen! What do you there?" he says.

"Let him stay, Khenti."

"Sire…"

"The boy's education will begin here, now."

"Yes, Sire."

"Come, Lukhamen," says the high priest.

The boy walks slowly to the bed.

"My son."

"Yes, Father."

"I will permit you to stay, because you are a high priest. But you must play your part."

"Yes, Father."

"You are to watch. Nothing more. Can you do this? Can you be still and silent?"

"Yes, Father."

"It is important that you obey this rule, absolutely."

"I understand, Father."

"I am about to journey, of my own free will, into the spirit world."

"Yes, Father." His voice is barely a whisper.

"Khenti's prayers and chants will guide my soul on its journey. You must not interrupt him."

The boy's eyes are locked onto his father's. He stands rigid, still, afraid to move.

"You must not be frightened. Can you do this?"

"Yes, Father."

"Remember that you are the High Priest of Amon."

"Father?"

"Yes, Lukhamen?"

"Why are you going to enter the spirit world?"

"My father has asked me to come, Lukhamen."

"But why, Father?"

"He will tell me when I come to him."

"Is it because you are very sick?"

"Yes. I believe so."

"Will you die, Father?"

"I do not know, Lukhamen."

"I do not want you to go, Father."

"Would you have me disobey my father, Lukhamen?"

"No, Father." The boy's eyes grow bright. His lip quivers slightly.

"And now, I want you to do exactly as I have told you. Are you ready?"

"Yes, Father."

"Very well, then."

The high priest closes his eyes, and the boy backs away from him, into a corner of the room.

Khenti pours water into a basin, assembles sponges and soap, and towels. His hands tremble a bit as he removes the sheet. For the first time, he sees the bruised, fractured body, the legs that are beginning to atrophy. He unties the lacings that hold the splint to the high priest's back, soaks a sponge with water, and squeezes it over his body. He lifts his head slightly and pours water down the back of the neck he has so often tenderly massaged. Khenti's eyes brim with tears at the sight of the sores that score his back.

The high priest is breathing deeply. The movement has caused great shocks of pain to shoot up and down the crushed vertebrae. For a moment he loses consciousness. When he opens his eyes again, Khenti gently soaps his body, rinses it, and towels it dry, but does not lift his head again.

Exhausted, the high priest falls into a light sleep. Khenti lays a purple robe over him while the two priests who have accompanied him remove the water, sponges, and soap, and clean the floor around the bed.

In a moment, the high priest awakens. "Khenti."

"Yes, Sire."

"Water."

The old priest holds a cup of water to his lips.

"I would speak with Lukhamen once again." Khenti motions to the boy to return to his father's side.

"Lukhamen," he says, "this journey that I am about to take..."

"Yes, Father?"

"My spirit will journey across a sacred lake, in a sacred boat, to the place where my father waits for me. My spirit will be safe, Lukhamen, always, for Amon the Merciful will protect me."

"Yes, Father."

"I may appear as dead, but you must not fear. I sense your fear, Lukhamen. You must put it away."

"Yes, Father."

"You are the High Priest of Amon. As his priest, you must trust that Our Lord the Merciful will keep me—keep us all—safe."

"Yes, Father."

"Khenti! Let us begin."

Khenti returns the boy to a bench that sits against the far wall and asks the priests to wait in the great hall. He closes the door behind them and lowers a crossbar, locking it in place. He retrieves a bag from beneath the bed, and from it he removes a leopard skin and a white crown, the *hedjet*. In a low voice, he begins the ancient prayer:

*Oh Lord of all, protect your servant Lukhamen as he gives himself wholly into your care...*

With trembling hands, Khenti places the leopard skin over the high priest, gently places the crown upon his head, then kneels before the last remnants of Egypt's greatness, the royal raiment of the great pharaoh, Ramses II.

A cloud passes over the sun. The high priest convulses, and then is still. His breathing becomes slower, more measured, then imperceptible. The boy watches as the blood drains from his father's face, as it becomes an ashen mask.

The birds are still. The only sound is of Khenti's droning chant. From the censer on the floor, whiffs of frankincense float above them in milky waves and dance in and out of the shadows.

---

He is in a boat, crossing a great, dark void. The vessel is colored as a rainbow, and the eye of Osiris is drawn upon the bow. A boatman guides it along with a long pole. They move easily, swiftly, without sound. Square sails of purple silk billow above him. The boatman turns to him and smiles, then looks forward again. They are moving toward a pinpoint of light. The boat begins to speed toward it, faster and faster; but when he looks to the boatman, he is gone.

He tries to cry out, but collides with the light instead, and amidst a great shimmering, silent explosion, is flung from the boat. He is in air, twisting and turning as if in a great vortex. He is drowning in a whirring cacophony of voices surrounding him, wailing in words he cannot understand.

The voices merge into one; he is brought to stillness and alights, on his feet. The voice speaks his name, like a thousand echoes: *Lukhamen.*

He can see a temple shimmering in the sun. He is propelled toward it, his feet not touching the ground. He passes through great pylons, and enters a corridor that leads to a courtyard where a circle of high priests await him. They beckon and smile, encouraging him. One of the priests steps forward, his arms outstretched. He is young and handsome.

*Why have you come?* he says.

Lukhamen cannot remember. He struggles to recall, and then it comes to him. "My father has beckoned me," he says.

*We are all your fathers, Lukhamen, and we all have beckoned you, for there is something you must know, something you must see.*

"What must I know?" he asks.

*First, you must behold.*

The young priest smiles, embraces him, then holds him at arm's length, and Lukhamen shields his eyes from the light that radiates from his body. It illumines him from within—a shimmering, translucent, silvery light. Its beauty brings him to tears, fills him with love.

*Now behold your spirit, Lukhamen.*

Lukhamen looks down at his own hands, his feet. They are radiating the same light, the endless, eternal sun-moon light that comes from he knows not where.

*Behold your spirit, Lukhamen. Remember its beauty, and know this: it is not your son, but you... who shall be a light unto your people.*

At this, there is a humming in his ears. It grows louder; the light begins to fade, and the temple and the priests with it. He reaches out for the young priest, but he is not there. He feels himself being pulled backwards. *No, no*, he mouths silently into the darkness. *No! Let me stay!* He falls backward, and down, into a dark abyss. A voice whispers in his ear: *You will be a light unto your people.*

He hears praying as if from a great distance. "Amon, Lord of Light, protect your servant. Lord of All Creation, who art the source of all strength and holy reason, hold him in your arms..."

*No, No!* he shouts. He falls and falls, closer to the praying.

"Amon, Lord of Light, be our everlasting source of strength. All-seeing, all-knowing God of Light and Life, stay with us."

He breathes.

The moon through the archways lights the room. The boy is asleep on the floor, his head on a pillow propped against a pillar. Khenti is sleeping in a chair beside him, his head resting on the edge of the bed. The hand of the high priest reaches out and touches the silvery hair, ever so gently.

# CHAPTER 28

———∞———

I HAVE A DREAM. IN the dream I am walking down a flight of stairs. I turn. A young man is following me. He looks familiar, but I cannot place him. His hair is in great, brown curls that fall over his shoulders. He is wearing a white robe. *I know him.* Love washes over me. Something from long ago is saying *I remember you.* I awake, but the dream and the deep love stay with me. Who is he?

———∞———

I have not seen Reverend Brown for two years, but the dream is so real. I decide to see him again.

He is pleasant, as always. I place my folded card in his hand. On it I have written only one thing, a question: *Is it true?* I don't elaborate, but in my mind I want to know if I am channeling, or if what I am recording is fantasy. When I am in Egypt, grief is suspended. But in real life, it is still a deep hole in the center of my being. Part of me is missing. Still, I can't live in the spirit realm. I need to know how to live in the world, if I can live in the world.

He prays. "Mother/Father God, we ask you to open the door to the two worlds and that the guides and teachers will come through and give our sister all that is for her higher good. We pray that she shall be uplifted and that her teachers will guide and direct her."

"There are great energies coming in," he says. "I can feel them. There is an ancient Egyptian standing behind you." I lose my breath.

"He is wearing robes, jewelry on his arms, a breastplate, and so on," says Reverend Brown, "and he is saying, *It's true, it's true*." I don't know whether to laugh or cry. "There is a big 'L,'" Reverend Brown says, "and he *becomes you*." I am stunned.

It goes on, flowing from this man like a fountain. "Wonderful, wonderful," he is saying to someone I cannot see. "You will be using your hands," he says to me. "You are channeling, and there is healing in your hands. There is a pencil in your hand...something about a book. Spirit is working through you. You need to stop worrying. Eddie? Eddie? He is here, helping you. Oh, yes, they are working through you astrally and in dreams." *In dreams.*

"I see you traveling to Egypt." The words are spilling out of him. "They want to encourage you," he is saying. "Do not worry. Spirit is channeling through you. Let it flow, make sure you record it." He repeats this a few times, and in a minute it is all over. I thank him and stumble out of his office as I did that first day, shaken, awed, elated. Out on the street, I laugh out loud. *Lukhamen came to Reverend Brown,* I say to myself over and over. *Lukhamen came to Reverend Brown!* A loop has closed, a great, cosmic loop.

———— ∞ ————

A door opens for me, a new way of understanding the experience called death. Now, it is more than a parting, more than separation. I see it as a passageway through which we return to another form of energy.

Books find their way to me in which I read that in spirit, we assess our human experience and can choose to return to a physical state to learn, for as many times as it takes, the lessons that teach us to be kinder and do less harm, to understand that the Universe is a mirror, and as we do unto others, we do unto ourselves.

In the physical life, we are born with amnesia, unable to recall the beauty of our spirits, who we really are, and from whence we have come. I think of the high priest, beckoned to the other world to behold his own spirit, who with this knowledge can *be a light unto his people* in spite of his broken body, in spite of Roman rule and subjugation.

It is no wonder that life can be beautiful and awful, sweet and horribly bitter, but always purposeful. And always too short. One thing I know from what I have learned thus far: one lifetime is not enough.

———— ⚬⚬⚬ ————

Lukhamen is teaching me, like so many great teachers and masters before him, with a story, his story. It is not merely a distraction from grief. It has a purpose.

# CHAPTER 29

⚤

☥

I AM SORRY TO INFORM *you, sir, that your old friend the governor has died, and that I am now Acting Governor of the provinces of Luxor and Thebes. I did not seek this post, Father. Upon his deathbed the governor bade me accept it, and I did not know how to refuse him.*

*Oh, but his death is a travesty of all that is just. He was the best of all Roman governors, and a gentle, wise man. Before he died, he confessed to me that he had been poisoned by a Roman upstart and traitor known as Antonious, a man he suspected of pilfering wheat and selling it to insurgents. I have decided that we shall handle this scandalous affair here in the province. I see no need to bring the matter to Rome; but be assured I shall do all that is in my power to bring the culprit to justice, even though he has, so far, escaped what is due him.*

*Auditors found our stores of wheat short, but not so short as to affect the armies' yearly allotment. The traitor, who was Deputy Chief of the Granaries, reclaimed wheat from the Egyptian farmers' personal stores to cover the losses; he was clever enough to refill the granaries before the inspection. The farmers shall go hungry if I do not return an allotment of wheat to them. We shall, therefore, start out the year with a deficit of grain.*

*After blaming what shortage there was on "thieving insurgents," Antonious made a half-hearted attempt at suicide, which the auditors regarded as a noble act of contrition. But I know him for what he is, and I shall catch him yet, Father. I have relieved him of all responsibilities. He is a virtual prisoner in his house, guarded by my own troops.*

*I have taken up residence in the governor's villa, and a public announcement has gone out to all the residents of Thebes that the authority of governing the province now rests with me. Lest you worry for my safety, I eat nothing that is not prepared in my old soldier's mess by my own cook, a soldier long under my command, a man loyal to me and to the emperor.*

*Governing a province is infinitely more complicated than I would have thought, Father. It is a job I am not qualified for, one I have never wanted. I know that I am a simple soldier, nothing more. Please pray that I shall be up to the task until a real governor can be dispatched to our outpost.*

*Please convey my fondest regards to my wife and son.*

*Your obedient servant,*

*Marcus*

---

"Marcus Aurelius. Marcus Aurelius. How presumptuous...to bear the name of one's own emperor..."

Haraa is seated beside her latest souvenir, a rose-colored marble fountain, brought from the Far East at great expense by her husband. It had, he lied, originally belonged to an emperor of the Han Dynasty. It is his custom to bring her prizes from foreign lands, mementos of his guilt that she collects like trinkets on a bracelet.

The fountain's trickle has distracted the little man who kneels at her feet. He stares at it, transfixed.

"Well, go on," she says. Her tone is sharp, commanding.

He turns to look at her, nervously picking at his ragged robe.

"He is the son of a senator and the grandson of a general, yes, yes, and that same general, his grandfather you see, had served under the great emperor, Marcus Aurelius, yes, yes. Marcus Aurelius himself." He spits out the words, then stops and waits to see the surprise in Haraa's eyes. Delighted and emboldened, he offers more:

"I hear from very good sources that he is married and that his wife is still alive in Rome."

"What else, you little weasel?"

"By all the gods, great lady, be merciful. I have not eaten in three days." Haraa drops another coin into the outstretched hand.

"Oh, thank you, thank you, great lady. My children thank you, my children thank you." He bows nervously and continues.

"His wife's father is also a senator, he has a son, and it is said that..."

"Yes?"

"It is said that, as a soldier, he had an appetite for strong wine and cheap women."

*How Roman.*

"Well done, little weasel. Now get out."

Haraa beckons a manservant who lifts the little man by the back of his robe and carries him to the garden gate, his feet scrambling, searching for ground.

"Keep your eyes and ears open," she calls after him, "and I may have something for you another time. And bathe before you come into my garden again!"

*Slimy little bastard.*

Haraa is in the aftermath of her husband's latest visit. Within a fortnight of his return, when he had rested, eaten well, sold his contraband to local merchants, and grunted his way through several disappointing *encounters* with her, he left. Soon after, Haraa began to suffer from a painful, pustular infection.

"It is not as serious this time as it is painful, Haraa," said Sechmetna. "I want you to sit in a bath of warm beer several times a day and apply this unguent of eucalyptus." He gave her a small jar. "And upon his return, I shall prepare a cotton swab moistened with acacia, carob, and honey that you are to insert before intercourse with him. It will guard against infection and prevent pregnancy. In the old days," he chuckles, "they used a plug of dried crocodile dung. Can you imagine?" But his face grew serious again. "If he continues to live as he does, Haraa, he will die from one venereal disease or another. I see no reason why you should die with him, or why you should bear a malformed child. You have enjoyed exceptional good fortune until now, but further infection is inevitable and, Haraa, listen to me carefully…potentially fatal."

---

Fully recovered, Haraa sits by her fountain, staring vacantly out into the garden. It is extravagant, even by her standards. A cohort of gardeners is about—pruning, watering, and coaxing her courtyard into a breathtaking oasis. But she is partial to the white Turkish lilies from her errant, infected husband. Great bronze bowls filled with the prized lilies perfume her rooms.

*I shall host a dinner party. He needs to see how Egyptian aristocracy lives, how we have always lived and how we shall always live. He needs to know that we were here before Rome and that we shall be here when Rome's banners have disappeared beneath our desert dust. He needs to know who we are, and I shall teach him. I, Haraa, shall personally teach him.*

She thinks for the thousandth time of the strong arms that lifted her from her sedan chair and the gold-flecked brown eyes that could not tear themselves away from Alenna.

*I saw how he looked at her. A hopeless cause, handsome centurion, now Governor of Thebes. It is I to whom you shall turn, not Alenna. One night with me, Marcus Aurelius, and you shall cease pining for the pious wife of the high priest.*

She stands, smoothes the lemon-yellow silk gown around her hips, then picks a lily, tucks it between her breasts, and orders hibiscus tea to be taken in the garden. Afterwards, she will go to the nursery to play with her little girl, who is growing prettily.

---

Marcus, a man unaccustomed to great amounts of correspondence, sifts through a pile of letters. He selects two. The first is from Antonious.

*Excellency,*

*It is with a humble heart that I implore you to hear my case. I am an innocent man, Sire, and a loyal citizen of Rome. I cannot believe that you would allow me to languish imprisoned in my quarters without a hearing and the opportunity to speak in my defense. I have spent my life in the service of the empire, Sire.*

*I am in great sorrow at the loss of our beloved governor, whom I admired and esteemed greatly. I am sure Your Excellency will understand the duress and strain of the last days of this great man and understand, as do I, that charges made under such terrible circumstances must reflect the pain and delusions of sickness.*

*I hold no ill will. On the contrary, I am filled with sympathy for the very sorrowful circumstances that surrounded him at the end. Nevertheless, Sire, I must insist that the charges brought against me are unjust and unsubstantiated. I am sure that once you have heard my answer to this unsupportable indictment, you will be assured of my innocence and allow me to return to my duties. My only desire is to serve you and my emperor.*

*Your obedient servant,*

*Antonious*

Marcus turns to his secretary.

"I have no choice but to grant this man, however despicable, a hearing. He is a citizen of Rome, after all, and is entitled to a hearing and to counsel. Arrange it, will you please, and set a date when he is to appear before a judiciary council."

"Yes, Sire."

Marcus opens the second, a small, delicate roll of scented papyrus. A white Turkish lily is carefully folded inside. In classical Latin and written in Haraa's bold hand, it is an invitation to a dinner party. He sighs and addresses his secretary:

"Please take another letter."

"Yes, Sire."

*Dear Madam:*

*I am honored by your kind invitation to dinner, and it is with deep regret that I must decline. Unhappy circumstance prevents me from enjoying the pleasure of your company. We are in a period of official mourning and protocol forbids me to attend any social function for at least thirty days following the funeral of our governor.*

*Your invitation is nonetheless greatly appreciated. As acting governor, I am looking forward to a happier time when this office is able to become a better part of Egyptian life and culture. Thank you again for your kind thoughtfulness.*

Marcus Aurelius

Acting Governor of the Province of Luxor and Thebes


"I will sign it myself."

"Yes, Sire."

"That is all."

"Yes, Sire."

Marcus walks to the window. White puffs of cloud hang suspended in the clear blue sky. Small fishing boats sway gently on the river, their sails billowing in and out, as if they are taking deep breaths. A flock of white birds rises from the river and turns gracefully downstream.

*I'm beginning to understand why the governor loved this place.*

A breeze touches his brow. He closes his eyes.

*If I could hold her in my arms just once, I would never be lonely again.*

His secretary comes back through the door.

"It is time, Sire."

"Thank you."

He walks upstairs to his private quarters where a valet awaits him with the dress uniform that is mandatory for funerals.

# CHAPTER 30

☥

IT IS MIDDAY. THE SQUARE is abandoned, except for an emaciated goat, foraging around the well for that which is not there. The well is the nexus of the Christian Quarter, the center of a labyrinth of squalid, dusty hovels. Two women enter the square; one carries a small tub, the other a baby. One tree grows in the square, an old sycamore. A dry leaf floats to the ground, and the goat runs quickly to it, snaps it into his mouth and chews hungrily.

"Thank God for this bit of shade," says Alia. "And for this bit of solitude. The city is so crowded today. I don't think I've ever seen so many soldiers."

Mahda shoos the goat. "Get away, get away!" He trots off, leaving the well to the women.

There are dark circles around Mahda's eyes. Her dress hangs on her like a drape over a scarecrow, and it is stained with perspiration. She jiggles the baby on her bony hip.

"They're planning something," she says.

Alia lowers the tub into the dark shaft.

"They're always planning something." Mahda scratches at her arm.

"It's the governor's funeral," says Alia, drawing the tub to the top. "They've come from all over the province. I overheard my rich woman say that even the high priest may attend."

She unties the rope and places the tub on the stone platform, then takes the baby from Mahda and lowers her into it. The child is surprised by the cool wetness on her skin, but soon begins to play, her little hands splashing the water onto her face, into her eyes. Alia dries them with the blanket. She smiles and splashes again, with more vigor.

Mahda scratches at her arm. It is raw and bloody where she has torn the skin away.

"He wouldn't go to a Roman governor's funeral, even if he could walk!"

"I only know what I heard, Mahda."

"The governor should have died in that cell instead of my Joseph. That would be justice! *That* would be justice!"

"Dear God!" Alia whispers. "You know very well it was Antonious who arrested Joseph, not the governor. And keep your voice down!"

"What difference does it make?" Her voice is rising. "They're all the same. They won't stop till we're all *dead*." She screeches it: *Dead*. It echoes around the circle: *dead, dead, dead.*

"Stop it, Mahda! You're putting yourself and your baby in danger, and me."

She takes Mahda by the arms, pins them to her sides, and looks directly into her eyes. They are wide—wild with fear. Alia speaks slowly, deliberately.

"Your baby is to be baptized today, Mahda. You must be quiet while I bathe her."

Mahda is flushed, feverish, her body damp with sweat. She pulls away from Alia, and walks briskly round and round the well, arms crossed, hands locked under her armpits.

Alia pours water over the baby and lathers her with the fine soap she has purloined from Haraa's luxurious bath. Lucenkep waves her little arms and splashes merrily. She smiles at Alia, dimpling her cheeks.

Mahda peers around the corner of a house. "No soldiers here. They don't like it here. Too much sickness, too much *leprosy*."

"Thank God they *don't* like it here," Alia whispers to herself, giving the baby a final rinse.

She wraps Lucenkep in the blanket and holding her in one arm, empties the water onto the dusty ground. Alia places the precious soap in her pocket and looks around for Mahda, who is suddenly in front of her, pointing back at something over her shoulder.

"Look, there. Is that a snake?" she whispers, "Is that a snake?" She is trembling.

Alia turns, and seeing only an old rag that has blown into the road, says quietly, "Come, Mahda. There is no snake. It's just an old rag. Here, carry the tub. I have a salve for your arm at home, and a lovely tea for you to drink. Come, my love."

She puts her free arm around Mahda's shoulder and leads her gently into the labyrinth.

---

A tiny dress of fine, white linen is on the small wooden bed. Mahda smoothes it with a trembling hand; calloused fingers caressing the fine cloth. She takes a sip of the tea Alia has made with hibiscus and a pinch of white powder.

"It took my whole allotment of grain to buy this linen," Mahda says slowly. "The merchant cheated me, as he does every Christian. But by the time Antonious came to steal our grain, mine was already gone." She smiles at the memory, pulls the dress over the baby's head, and smoothes it down awkwardly.

"Joseph would be proud to see her like this." Tears drop slowly from her eyes onto the little dress. In the gloom, Alia can see the hollowed-out cheeks, made deeper by the shadows. She puts her arm around the frail shoulder, feels Mahda's trembling ease a bit. *Thank God for Haraa and her powder*, she thinks.

"Let me put this salve on your arm, Mahda," she says quietly, taking a jar from her bag.

"She'll never have another dress like this, Alia. Not in her entire life."

Alia spreads salve onto the ravaged arm and bandages it with a piece of clean linen she has brought from Haraa's vast supply.

"We don't want to keep Abba Michael waiting," she says, and helps Mahda to her feet.

---

THEY MAKE THEIR WAY THROUGH the crowded, dirty alleyways, toward the river. An old woman calls from the doorway of a wattle mud hut.

"God be with you, Mahda!"

Mahda smiles weakly at the old woman, who throws a bucket of foul-looking liquid onto the street. They step forward quickly to avoid its contents.

"Thank you," whispers Mahda.

Alia steers her on, out of the airless alleyways onto the river road. A cool breeze lifts the veils on their heads and, without thought or notice, they breathe in great doses of the clean air.

"The waters are receding every day. It is a good sign, Mahda. The earth will be rich again and ready for planting."

Mahda's eyes are dilated; she frowns in the bright sunlight. "Maybe we will even eat next year if the Romans don't take every bit of grain from us."

"I'm telling you again, Mahda. It was Antonious. He sold the grain to Egyptian insurgents, who are trading it for arms. Everybody knows that."

"If it weren't for *them,* we wouldn't have to buy our own grain, and we wouldn't need arms." Her voice is rising.

"In the name of God, Mahda, lower your voice!"

They step aside as a troup of soldiers marches by, their helmets gleaming in the sun.

"Where is your head, Mahda? People are *executed* for less."

Mahda's lip trembles. She stares after the soldiers, reeling slightly. Mahda takes the baby from her.

"Oh, my poor love. I don't mean to scold you, but my God, you need to think of your baby. Where will she be if you end up on a Roman cross?"

"You're right, Alia. I am just so tired. I can't think any more." Mahda stops.

"Keep walking, Mahda. We're almost there."

"I have nightmares. I can't sleep." She is sobbing softly.

"Oh, Mahda…"

"It's always the same—men in the wheat fields, a hundred men, hanging from a hundred crosses…blood everywhere…flowing from their hands and feet, from their eyes! Oh, God!"

"Mahda…"

"I can't stop it. I don't know how to stop it."

"I had nightmares, too, Mahda, after my husband died." The image of him under Antonious's chariot chokes her. She clears her throat. "It will stop. Eventually." The lie comes easily.

The little chapel stands before them, like a small beacon of hope. Alia takes a deep breath.

"We will think only of Lucenkep today, Mahda. This is a holy day for her, a day of peace and blessings. Perhaps her life will be different." The second lie.

Mahda forces a smile. "I'll try."

"Come, then. God waits for our baby."

The small chapel is dark, lit only by a few candles on the altar and at the baptismal font. Their eyes slowly become accustomed to the dark. The kneeling figure of Abba Michael emerges from the gloom; he is at the foot of the altar, deep in meditation. The baby whimpers, and the sound brings him back from where he has been.

He rises slowly. He is short and round. His robe is torn at the hem, and a strap on one of his sandals is broken. It flaps on the dirt floor as he limps toward them, smiling, his eyes crinkling at the corners.

"Welcome, welcome! Are you alone, then?"

"We are widows, Abba," says Alia.

"My husband's name was Joseph," says Mahda.

"Ah yes, now I remember. Be comforted, daughter. You are not alone." His eyes are kind. "I will get Abba Paul and Abba James to stand with us—for Joseph. I won't be long."

He shuffles off, and in a while he is back with two young priests.

At the baptismal font, Mahda's trembling ceases, at last. She is safe in the cool darkness, quieted by the merciful white powder, the soothing voice of Abba Michael, and the presence of God. Her heart no longer races, but her eyes are yet bright with tears as the other priests speak for Joseph, their voices young and gentle, their faces sweet in the candlelight.

Abba Michael trickles water over Lucenkep's forehead and whispers, "I baptize you, Maria Lucenkep, as John baptized our Lord. May the spirit of Jesus the Christ, who is risen from the dead, enter you now and remain with you all the days of your life and after."

Lucenkep whimpers as the water spills over her face. Abba Paul wipes it away with a small cloth. She looks up and smiles at him. His eyes fill with sweet tenderness. And in that quiet, loving moment, Mahda is free. She closes her eyes and lets everything go. She feels a presence beside her. Something like a feather brushes her face. *Joseph.*

"Mahda." The young priest is holding the baby out to her.

"Maria Lucenkep is now a member of this church and of the family of Christ."

The feather floats away. "Thank you, Abba," she says in a voice barely above a whisper. The old priest touches her shoulder.

"Go in peace, Mahda. God is with you."

Mahda's only thought is to lie down, rest, and sleep.

———⟨≈⟩———

Alenna is standing in the arched doorway to the garden, her back to her husband. The day is bright; bougainvillea cascades over the far walls in splashes of fuchsia.

"Can you not send one of your priests, Lukhamen?"

"There is no better representation of myself than you."

She turns to face him. She is wearing a simple white linen robe and a single golden bracelet.

"He was a Roman, but the best of them, Alenna. I believe it is because of him that our people will have what little they will eat this season."

"But..."

"And I want you to take young Lukhamen with you."

"To a Roman funeral?"

"Yes. He is the next High Priest of Amon."

It is useless to argue with him. He is another person now, changed since *that night*, the night he locked her out of his room, and out of his life. He is distant, a stranger, closer to the coarse, redheaded stonemason called Simon who has fashioned a strange chair for him, a chair with wheels in which he sits day and night—an awkward, ugly contraption he uses to propel himself around his room.

He sleeps little, infused with restless energy. He opens and closes his scrolls constantly, searching, searching for something he never finds. He confers with Khenti by the hour, but his conversations with her have become no more than requests for meals and baths. He has not touched her since his *journey*. And now, he has commanded that she attend the funeral, and she will go. And she will take the boy.

———— ❦ ————

She curtsies. "Your Excellency."

Marcus cannot speak.

Her eyes are fixed on the ground. "I bring the sorrowful condolences of my husband, Your Excellency. He wishes me to convey to you his great regard for the governor who saw to the needs of our people and whose generosity caused our temple to be repaired. We shall not forget him."

*Alenna.*

When he does not answer, she forces herself to look at him, to see the reason for his silence, and she is caught, trapped in his eyes, in his pain, stark and pure, in his inconsolable love.

A gust of wind lifts the veil from her hair and onto the ground. He bends, retrieves it, holds it for a moment, feeling the silk in his hands, wondering how it would feel to lay it on the crown of her head, wrap it softly around her shoulders. An old man coughs and breaks his dream, giving him the presence of mind to put it in her hand.

Now it is her turn not to be able to speak.

"Sire." It is the boy. "Sire."

Marcus tears his eyes from her and looks at the boy. He is handsome, tall, and confident, with a grave countenance far older than his years.

"Sire. My father wishes me to convey his deep sympathy."

*By all the gods. He has sent the boy.* This time Marcus finds his voice.

"Thank you, Your Excellency."

He is glad that he has thought to call the boy by his exalted title. They stand there in the awkward silence, until Lukhamen tugs at his mother's gown.

"Mother," he whispers.

She comes to life and curtsies, then quickly turns and walks away.

"Mother, what is it? Are you all right?"

Alenna's face is flushed. "I am fine, Lukhamen. I am uncomfortable with Romans, is all."

"But he seemed to be a nice man, Mother."

"Yes, Lukhamen. Perhaps he is."


They walk toward their sedan chair, and a flock of white birds rises from the river and circles in a graceful arc, then comes to rest again on its surface.

"Mother..."

"Yes, Lukhamen."

The birds rise again, and her heart seems to lift and soar with them, into the bright blue sky. They swirl again and form a perfect formation, fly downriver, and disappear. She looks after them and feels a sudden, deep sense of loneliness. She turns. He is speaking to another, but she had seen it. It was unmistakable, unspeakable, but he had been unable to withhold it from her. And now she knew.

"Mother?"

"Yes, Lukhamen. It is time to go."

Later, in her bath, she watches the setting sun reflected in the water. She closes her eyes, and his come to haunt her, deep and dark, with their golden flecks of pain and misery. She opens her eyes quickly.

"Semnut!" She startles the old nurse. "Semnut! A towel! I can't stay in this bath forever. I must see to dinner!"

"Yes, Mistress."

The old nurse holds out a large towel and Alenna steps into it.

# CHAPTER 31

♀

ANTONIOUS GRUNTS AND RELEASES HIS semen into the belly of the servant girl who lies crushed beneath his heavy body. He lies where he finishes, unconscious, mindless of his dead weight. His breath, stale from old wine, sours the room. The girl struggles to free herself, fumbles under the bed until she finds the purse that Antonious has hidden there. She removes a silver coin, puts the purse back in its place, and dresses quickly. She opens the door, stops, walks back to where Antonious lies stiff-legged and swine-like, and spits in his face.

The next day, Antonious appears before the judiciary council, badly shaven and sweaty, but brazen and ready with his defense. He cites his long career, his spotless record, and his abiding loyalty to the emperor. He points to the lack of evidence linking him to the governor's death, the frailties of mind and body of the unfortunate man. He ends with a sad salute to an aging, delusional governor who has unwittingly accused him of the preposterous charge of murder.

He prepared for his hearing by allotting himself just enough wine to quiet his morning tremors, but hours later—when the council's decision to acquit him is announced—he is shaking uncontrollably, and overcome with nausea.

He runs from the judicial chambers to the back of the building, where he vomits against a tree.

That night, he celebrates alone in a tavern at the edge of the city, a seedy haunt of insurgents and mercenaries. By midnight, he is unconscious in a dark corner, his head on a table. The tavern owner carries him to his chariot, drops him unceremoniously onto its floorboard.

"Take him away," the grizzled proprietor growls at the driver, "and when he wakes up, tell him to find another drinking hole. My wife is tired of mopping up his piss."

Shortly thereafter, Antonious is recalled to duty and assigned to the Department of Lands, where he is to keep records of farms in the district—their abeyances and crops. The office, on the ground floor of a small, windowless building, is occasionally visited by farmers registering purchases of land. The door, therefore, must always be kept open—a situation taken advantage of now and then by a stray chicken. Antonious's new apartment, above the lands office, consists of two small, stifling rooms.

⸙

Downriver, on the second floor of the governor's residence, Marcus holds a small piece of papyrus in his hand, Haraa's second invitation to dinner. It notes, in Haraa's bold handwriting, that the event is to be in honor of the high priest and his marvelous recovery. The high priest and his wife, Alenna, will be the only guests—besides the governor, of course.

Marcus closes his eyes, remembering the scarf falling from Alenna's hair onto the ground, feeling the silk in his hands. The moon rises over the river. He calls for his valet to prepare a bath.

⸙

Haraa's steward ushers Marcus into an entranceway lit by small, latticed lanterns. Bronze statuary line the wide steps to the great hall, where black granite floors shine like glass and reflect the candlelight that flickers from wall sconces. He feels lightheaded.

The steward leads him into the dining hall, where Haraa awaits, her back to the garden. After a full morning under the buffing stones of her masseuse and an hour slathered in rich oils as she lay in full sun, Haraa is luminous—her skin appears lit from within. Her hair, newly hennaed dark-red, is caught in a gold clasp. She wears a white décolleté linen sheath with a sheer, pleated shawl. Gold earrings and bracelets catch the light as she moves toward Marcus, smiling. She is the sun, burnished copper, candlelight, and gold. A white Turkish lily is tucked between her breasts.

"Good Evening, Your Excellency. Welcome."

He is shocked by the beauty that surrounds him. He has seen only one Egyptian home: Alenna's. Where it was quiet, elegant, and understated, Haraa's villa is exotic, and unapologetically opulent. The room opens onto the garden, where Haraa's pink fountain trickles water into a pond. Small, silvery fish flash in and out of the dark water. A harpist sits nearby, playing softly. Haraa watches Marcus take in the furnishings, the tapestries, and the sculpture.

"These are treasures brought to me from foreign lands by my husband, Your Excellency. They are all I have of him."

"I am sorry."

"Oh, no," she laughs, "There is no need to be sorry. He is very much alive. He is a merchant, you see. He travels."

*Such wealth.* "Apparently a very successful merchant."

"Very successful indeed. But these...*things* do not keep me company at night, Marcus."

She has used his given name, and the room is suddenly, shockingly...intimate. A servant enters with wine, pours it into silver goblets. Unlike the sweet Egyptian wine he has known, it is harsh and bold.

"I hope you like it, Marcus. It is from Tuscany."

He does not respond. She looks at him, a question forming on her brow.

"Forgive me, Madam. I am not accustomed to hearing my name spoken anymore."

"Forgive me, Your Excellency. It is just that..."

"Please do not apologize. When Rome sends a permanent governor, which will be soon, I hope, I will be simply Marcus again. I look forward to it. And yes, the wine is splendid."

She leads him to cushions set before a low table, fills his goblet anew. In a moment, they are surrounded by servants with enticing tidbits, hotly spiced lamb on skewers and vine leaves stuffed with perfumed rice. *Where is she?*

"Please excuse me for a moment. I must see to dinner."

"Are we not to wait for——" he almost says, *"Alenna?"* then catches himself. "——the others, then?"

"I'm afraid they will not be joining us tonight, Your Excellency."

Across the room, a candle flickers and goes out. Haraa rises, lights it with a taper from the table. "Is the high priest taken ill again, then?" Marcus asks in a hoarse voice.

"On the contrary. He is better every day. He performed a ceremony this morning for the young high priest, who will be leaving soon for Philae, where he will receive his training. The exertion seems to have taken something from him. Alenna has sent a note saying he needs to rest."

Haraa takes a deep breath. "Now if you will excuse me, Your Excellency, I won't be long."

She leaves quickly, not wishing to see the disappointment in his eyes, the pain that flickers across his face. He motions for the servant to fill his goblet. He drinks it down and holds it out again.

# CHAPTER 32

ALL WEEK ALENNA PACKED AND repacked the boy's belongings—his clothes, the toy soldiers that lay idle ever since he learned to read. The overstuffed bag now stands in a corner. Alenna has been informed that nothing from home shall go with him.

"Lukhamen."

He does not move.

"Lukhamen. You must wake now."

He turns over and pulls the sheet over his head.

"Lukhamen, dearest love."

She sits on the bed, pulls the sheet away. He opens his eyes and looks up at her, drowsy and tousled. Alenna feels her heart ache.

"Good morning, Mother."

"Good morning, Lukhamen."

He sits up, at once awake. "Is it time, Mother?"

"Yes, Lukhamen. It is time."

"This is the last time I shall wake in my own bed."

His words cut her to the quick. "Oh no, my love. Your room will always be here, waiting for you. Father says you will come home to visit every year when the river rises. You will come with the priests from Philae."

"But it won't be the same, will it, Mother?"

"No, Lukhamen. It will not be the same. But nothing stays the same, does it?"

He throws himself into her arms. She cradles his head and holds him close. No one is there to forbid it.

"What I mean is that I shall continue to love you with all my heart, even when you are not here. I shall love you no matter where you are. You will grow and change, and live in another place, and I shall love you every day. I will be here, waiting for you. Do not be sad, my love. The time will pass, and you shall return to me."

The room disappears behind her tears. He holds on to her tightly and does not let go. Finally, she takes his arms from around her waist, removes the medallion she is wearing, and puts it into his hand.

"Here, now. Here is a part of me to take with you. Your father had it struck the night you were born. See how it is engraved with images of Isis and Horus, mother and son? Every night when you go to bed, put this medallion under your pillow. It will be as if I am there with you. It will keep us together."

He looks at her, his eyes brimming. Tears spill over and run down his cheeks. Alenna feels her heart break.

"This is the last time we shall be allowed to cry, Lukhamen, before we have to be brave. All eyes will be upon you today. Our people will watch you as you walk in the procession. It is a very old custom, a custom some wait a lifetime to see. Some never see it. You are their hope. Like your father, you are all of Egypt that is left to them. When they see you, they will see Egypt as it was, and as it will be again. When they see you, they will remember who they are."

He looks at her and wipes his eyes.

"I shall be strong, Mother. You will see." She holds out her arms again, but he slides off the bed, out of reach.

---

The high priest is dressed, in his wheeled chair. Lukhamen enters the room still in his night robe. His feet are bare, his hair tousled. At the sight of him so young, so childlike still, his eyelashes damp from tears, the high priest feels a great lump in his throat. He swallows hard.

"Good morning, Lukhamen."

"Good morning, Father."

"This is your day, my son. Are you ready?"

"Yes, Father."

"You will go with Khenti, take the bath, and be dressed at the temple. Your mother and I will follow."

"Yes, Father."

Alenna enters the chamber.

"He will have breakfast first, *My Lord*."

"Khenti is already here. He can breakfast at the temple."

"He will breakfast *here*. With *me*."

He has never heard her speak thus. He does not challenge her.

"Come, my love. We shall have breakfast together." She puts her hands on the boy's shoulders and steers him toward the corridor. "We will eat in the kitchen. With Semnut."

The high priest keeps his silence.

Later, Alenna stands at the door, adjusting the boy's robe, smoothing his hair. "I will be there shortly, my love."

"Yes, Mother."

She bends down to whisper in his ear. "Do you have the medallion?"

He opens his hand. The medallion's gold catches the sunlight. They smile a secret smile together.

"Remember, if they see it, they will take it from you. You are forbidden to take anything from home."

"I will remember, Mother."

Khenti helps the boy into the sedan chair and draws the curtains.

—⊶∞⊷—

At midday, the procession appears in the corridor of the Temple of Luxor. Moving through the great pylons, it spills out onto the Avenue of the Sphinxes, the broad byway connecting the temples of Luxor and Karnak. At Karnak's quay, a boat awaits that will take the young priest on his long journey, past the island where crocodiles bask in the sun, and over the white cascades, to the great temple of Isis that sits in the middle of the Nile, on the Island of Philae.

The crowd, gathered since dawn, presses forward, but is held back by Roman soldiers. The temple percussionists come upon them, striking large frame drums and cymbals. The slow, steady beats resonate in the midday stillness. The crowd is suddenly quiet.

The high priest appears in an open sedan chair, borne by six priests of the Temple of Luxor. He is dressed in the purple robe of his office and the simple ornaments he is permitted to wear in public: a pair of gold bracelets and a pectoral of gold, silver, and semi-precious stones. In the center of the pectoral is a scarab with a falcon's tail and wings, carved out of translucent chalcedony. Exclamations of wonder ripple through the crowd. All reports were that the high priest had been too gravely injured to appear in public; but he is of good color and handsome, the gray at his temples the only outward sign of his ordeal. His eyes are riveted on his destination: Karnak.

Khenti walks beside him in a simple white robe, his halo of silky white fluff floating in the breeze.

Behind them is the young high priest, walking alone. He, too, is wearing a purple robe with a small collarette embroidered with gold thread, and gold bracelets that match his father's. The rich brown curls are gone. His head is shaven.

The crowd strains for a look at him. The boy walks slowly, bravely, head held high, eyes ahead. "Take your time, Lukhamen. Listen to the drums. Do not move too quickly," his father had said. "The people need to see you."

Mahda's eyes fill with tears. "Look, look!" she says, a little too loudly. "His head is shaven!"

"Quiet, Mahda!" says Alia. "Be quiet."

Simon is with them. "Yes, lower your voice, Mahda," he says.

"But look!" she insists. "He is *shaven*, like the old ones, like the ancient ones!"

The crowd strains for a better view of the young priest whose straight back and slow, measured steps bring tears to the eyes of the old men, bowed and broken from years in the wheat fields.

They press forward to get a closer look, but are pushed back by Roman soldiers.

"*They* don't belong here!" hisses Mahda. "*They* don't *belong* here," she says, a little louder. Several people in the crowd look toward her, alarmed.

"Mahda!" Alia whispers, "For God's sake!"

Simon touches her shoulder. "Be careful, Mahda."

He takes the baby Lucenkep from her and lifts her onto his shoulder.

"Look, little girl," he says, turning her toward Lukhamen, who is now drumbeats away. "One day that boy may be all that is left of Egypt."

Their eyes turn toward Alenna, who is in a long, violet tunic, pleated and tied beneath the breasts. Her eyes are lined in kohl. A gold band around the crown of her head holds her scarf in place.

Mahda points at her. "Look, look!" she says gleefully, clapping her hands, jumping up and down.

"Quiet!" someone in the crowd hisses.

"And that is my rich lady," whispers Alia, nodding toward Haraa, who glides by in a surprisingly simple linen robe, a costume befitting a future mother-in-law. Still, her rich red hair is fiery in the midday sun, and she wears an excessively ornate necklace of square cut emeralds. A nurse walks in back of her, carrying Lukhamen's hoped-for betrothed. The crowd draws in a collective breath as they pass, but Haraa is unaware of them; she is somewhere else. She smiles, ever so slightly.

Temple singers and musicians end the pageantry, and the crowd disperses as their chants and tinkling finger cymbals fade away down the long corridor of sphinxes, who remain alone and impassive in the stillness.

---

Lukhamen and Alenna are permitted a moment together at the top of the stairs that lead to the dock.

"Was I was brave, Mother?"

"All of Luxor is proud of you today, my son. I am the proudest of all."

"Goodbye, Mother."

"Goodbye, Lukhamen."

On the dock, Lukhamen kneels before his father's chair. The high priest places his hands on the boy's head.

"Amon's blessings upon you, Lukhamen. Go now, in the name of the Lord of Heaven and Earth. Be diligent and faithful, and return to us as a full priest of Amon."

The priests of Philae lead him into the boat, and as it gently rocks away, he turns to look back. Oars dip in and out of the water; the dock slips backward and away. He can see Alenna standing next to his father's wheeled chair, her violet scarf waving in the breeze. As the boat moves upriver, his father's pectoral catches the sun with a blinding flash. The boat rounds a curve, and when Lukhamen can see again, they are gone.

Children wave to him along the banks. As the boat reaches the Temple of Luxor, the wind lifts the sails, and the boat moves away from it, swiftly. When he can no longer see the hills of Thebes, he turns his face toward Philae.

"What is in your hand, Lukhamen?" a priest asks him.

Lukhamen opens his hand to reveal a small gold medallion. And then, it, too, is gone.

# PART TWO

———⊰∞∞∞⊱———

*Blessed are they that mourn, for they shall be comforted.*
*~ Matthew 5:4*

# CHAPTER 33

―――⊗⊗⊗―――

"WE HAVE TO WATCH THE sun rise," says Bill. We sit on the sand in front of the rented beach house and wait as darkness lifts and the last stars twinkle out of sight. We are quiet in the sky's rose light. I do not have to do anything, be anything. We are just there, together. The sun rises out of the ocean and bathes us in gold. Seagulls squawk, fly out over the water, then turn back again, settle down on the sand, and bring the beach to life.

"Thank you," I say to him.

―――⊗⊗⊗―――

We are warriors of battles fought and lost, Bill and I. We have known the agonies of divorce, and are therefore, not afraid to wait, and watch, to see where this...*togetherness*...will lead us. We do not conjure the future; we live one day at a time. Our conversations are not filled with breathless, blithe declarations of love.

We talk about our children. He knows his children well and thinks about them deeply. He inspires me to observe my daughters more closely, to see them in detail and depth. He cannot imagine what losing Eddie has been like, he tells me, but I see in his eyes when he speaks of it the fear only a parent can know: that of losing a child.

Sunday mornings belong to us. We linger over coffee; we explore and chart where we stand on everything from politics to philosophy. We probe and provoke, but never proselytize; we've had enough of strife. Still, we have to know who we are.

Marriage has made me suspicious of love, and death has taught me that nothing lasts. I can't be easy to know. He is more comfortable in his skin than I am in mine, but we are not open books. Not yet.

I have kept a secret from him: Reverend Brown. I do not discuss mediums, channeling, or the Egypt story, with anyone except my precious little circle—Sandy, Martha, and my children. I am not ready to be ridiculed.

But one Sunday morning, I gamble. If it's now or never, it's now. It's time. Life after death, communication with the dead, reincarnation…I'm nervous, but I put it all on the table.

He listens quietly and does not interrupt as I describe my journey into the mystical world of metaphysics: Reverend Brown, Egypt, Lukhamen, all of it. I finish and wait. *Maybe I've made a mistake.* For the first time in a long time, I feel safe with someone. And now I have pushed everything to the far corners of believability and sanity. I can hardly breathe.

In a calm, steady voice, he says, "I haven't had experiences like yours, but I have studied Transcendental Meditation. I've never told you this, but I met the Dalai Lama once, through my meditation group. We were in a large crowd, but I managed to get close enough to touch him, and something happened. I felt a force of some kind. It was real. And I can't explain it."

I think of the Buddhist admonition to ask oneself three questions before speaking: *Is it true? Is it necessary? Is it kind?* Bill has spoken well.

He wants to hear more, and I tell him the story of the people in Egypt as it is unfolding, and how I am receiving it in a way I cannot explain. We begin to talk about Lukhamen as if he is someone we both know, a friend.

The long, dark night that began on a Sunday morning years ago fades slowly into the sunlight that streams into Bill's living room. The world around me seems to relax, and I am aware of an open window, a breeze, and the sound of a bird somewhere.

A minute ago, we were lovers, even friends. Now we are something more, something closer, something infinitely more precious. We have embarked on a journey of trust and love, on this earth, in this time.

# CHAPTER 34

———⊗⊗⊗———

I AM IN BED READING, when I hear the door open and slam shut. Bill, who has been at a recovery meeting, appears in the doorway of the bedroom, looking rattled.

"We don't have a *relationship*, do we?" he asks, his voice a bit strained and high-pitched.

I look up from my book. "No, of course not," I answer.

"Whew. That's a relief!"

"Why do you ask?" I reply with a straight face.

"The meeting tonight turned into one about *relationships*. I *hate* it when that happens!" Apparently, the term *relationship* is frightening.

"Me, too," I say.

I look down and smile behind my book.

I'm in his apartment because there is a rat in my condominium.

Harold's second wife, a beautiful Hopi woman, had persuaded him to give me a share of the proceeds from the sale of the house we once owned together. It is meager compared to his, but it is enough for a down payment on a home of my own. I call her my wife-in-law.

The condominium is near Dupont Circle, a section of Washington, D.C. favored by young urbanites. I have hired an ineffectual exterminator, who tells me that the neighborhood is zoned for large sewers, which will accommodate restaurants and...rats. Further lectures about the gelatinous skeletal systems of Norway rats and their ability to squeeze through holes as narrow as a pencil are not helpful. The "expert" looks around my apartment, finds no "evidence," suggests that I have imagined the rat, and leaves a sticky trap in my living room.

The next day, I find the trap empty, but with paw prints on the sticky surface. Finally, Bill baits an old-fashioned spring trap with peanut butter and dispatches the rodent.

Feeling relatively secure, I go back to my apartment, but now I hear movement in the walls at night. The other condo owners (there are nine of us—all women) tell me that there is a "rat run" throughout the hundred-year-old converted mansion that nobody seems to be able to find and seal. I hire a specialist. He's a builder and a rat run finder. He finds no entry ways, no runs, no rats. Maybe there is no "rat run." Maybe I just got the odd one. Maybe the sounds in the wall are my imagination. It doesn't matter. My precious purchase is now a nightmare and I can't sleep at night. Bill invites me back to stay with him.

Going back to my apartment only to confer with workmen, I install new carpeting, have every room painted, and put my condo up for sale. It's a beautiful apartment, after all, in a very good location, and it sells right away.

The new owner has to move in immediately; the sale is not contingent on my ability to relocate. When I sign the papers I will be homeless.

"Move in with me," Bill says. Bill's offer is like he is—easy, casual. No labels. We are not "living together." I'm just there.

My furniture, the contents of my home office, and my piano, quickly convert Bill's apartment into a maze of furniture. He doesn't complain, but all too soon, he grows quiet. Very quiet.

I have the sinking feeling that we have—that I have— made a big mistake. He finally loses his temper when, in the middle of the night, on the way to the kitchen, he stumbles into my piano seat and bruises his shin.

"I can't live like this," he says.

"Fine!" I reply.

I'm shaken. I have to move quickly. I can't afford to get hurt again. I toss and turn on the couch, and at first light, pack an overnight bag and before Bill can say or do anything, I flee to my daughter Michaela's apartment nearby. I'm hurt. I'm angry with myself for being so *stupid*. I'm full of false pride and discouraged at how fragile I still am.

My office is in Bill's apartment, and I go back every day to work, but I'm careful not to leave signs that I was there, and I'm gone before he comes home in the evening. He doesn't leave me a note and I don't leave him one.

I search the newspapers frantically for a place to live, but my mind is jangled, and I can't get organized. *I thought I was okay*, I say to myself over and over. The truth is I love him and I'm afraid it *is* over.

In a few days, Bill calls and tells me that he has pulled some strings with the management and that a studio apartment is available for me in the same building. He is being chivalrous, but I don't want to live there. Why would I want to be there every day to see him coming and going with somebody else? *I knew this wouldn't last.*

Misery returns, my natural state. I didn't really expect anything else. *Did I?*

I move into the studio because I want to get out of his apartment as quickly as possible. I can figure out what to do later. Besides, it's the dead of winter.

---

Bill doesn't call. I'm glad; it's easier this way.

Bob, a friend of ours, calls and invites us to his New Year's Eve party. I tell him I can't come because Bill and I aren't together any more.

"That can't be," he says. "Bill and Helen are like one name."

Choking back a sob, I thank him and tell him that he should invite Bill alone.

Later that day, Bill calls. The sound of his voice makes me cry.

"Let's go to Bob's party," he says.

"I thought it was all over," I sob into the phone.

"I never said it was over," he tells me. "I said I couldn't live like that. How could you think it was over?"

And then he tells me that he has been busy. Looking for a house. For us.

---

The New Year's Eve party is joyous. The lights seem brighter, and everyone is prettier and handsomer than usual. Bob is glad to see us.

Bill is his usual jovial self, greeting and talking to everyone, but at midnight, he walks across the room to kiss me.

Everything he has ever said to me, everything he has ever done, has led to this moment: the point in time when I am able, finally, to let past betrayals and distrust dissolve into dust, the miraculous moment when I am able to see love in a pair of impossibly blue eyes and return it without reservation.

# CHAPTER 35

———∞———

I HAVE A DREAM IN which I see a wooden arbor on the side of a house. Inside the house is a sunken room. Two stairs lead up to the rest of the house. It's hardly a dream—just an image that appears for a second, then is gone.

Not long after the dream, Bill calls. He's been searching for a house for weeks. I don't have his patience; after the first six or seven unsuccessful tries, I give up. Commercial real estate is Bill's business. Combing neighborhoods and walking through properties is not a chore for him—it's a project.

I am in my studio working when the phone rings.

"Stop what you're doing," he says. "I have found our house."

I turn off my computer and race for the Metro. When I arrive at the Bethesda stop, he's waiting at the top of the escalators, beaming.

"I've found our house," he says again.

We walk a half mile from the metro stop to a quiet street that seems a world away from Wisconsin Avenue, the street that takes traffic through downtown Bethesda.

The houses sit primly behind hundred-year-old trees that line the street. We walk down and then up a gently sloping hill. As we near the top, Bill points to a house on the corner of a side street.

The house is perched on an ivy-covered knoll, and from my vantage point below, I can see an arbor that has been built onto the railing of a side deck. The house is empty, and while we wait for the real estate agent to show us through, we walk around back, then onto the side deck, and peer through the window of a sunroom. The sunroom has apparently been added to the original house and is sunken to accommodate the downward slope of the hill. Two steps lead up to the rest of the house.

"This is our house," I say to Bill.

I don't question dreams and visions any more. That would just be ungrateful.

———⚬⚭⚬———

Spring is one beautiful surprise after another. Our street is a horseshoe curve, a pink, flowering crescent of dogwood trees. Azalea bushes bloom in shades of pink and fuchsia and peek over the windowsills in the sunroom. The ancient trees on the side street sprout tiny leaves. Black tulips appear at the bottom of my ivy hill. I fill the sun room with ferns and a potted orange tree and plant a wisteria to climb over the arbor.

Bill's children come to visit—Billy, Sean, Patrick, and Laura. I sense in them a bit of reservation, a determination to wait and see if this…home… is real before they invest their feelings in it. Our children have had more than their share of disappointment, and they must find the faith, as I have, that sometimes something extraordinarily good happens in the universe.

As for me, there are times when the sun is on my back and my hands are deep in fragrant soil, that I feel a sense of balance; I am able to view life as it is in winter—cold and dark— and as it is now in springtime— verdant, vibrant, and new. I am able to see it always changing and always continuing, as seasons come and go, and come and go again.

# CHAPTER 36

———— ⦿⦿⦿ ————

REVEREND BROWN ONCE ASKED ME to imagine myself in a boat, floating down a river. "Think of people who have passed into spirit as if they are standing on a cliff above the river," he said. "You can only see what is ahead of you. They can see around the bend. They aren't God, and this isn't magic. It's just a matter of perspective."

———— ⦿⦿⦿ ————

I am sitting before him once again. "I don't usually say this to people," he says, "but Spirit wants me to tell you this. I see a circle of American Indians. They are dancing, rejoicing, getting ready to welcome your father into spirit."

I am not surprised. After surviving cancer and three heart attacks, my father, who is almost ninety, has had a massive stroke.

I dread the visit to the hospital. What will I say to him? He can no longer talk. My father makes it easy. He looks at me and smiles. I know that smile.

———— ⦿⦿⦿ ————

It is Christmastime. He comes in from the cold and sits down at the kitchen table, still in his policeman's uniform. My mother gives him a steaming cup of coffee. I push my chair as close to him as I can get, waiting for the story. He always has a story, and while my mother is cooking dinner, I've got him all to myself.

"Guess who *I* saw today?" he says.

"Who?"

"Santa Claus."

"Oooh..." I say. I know that Santa Claus is in the department store on Market Street, where Daddy works.

"He told me something."

"What?" I am breathless.

And then he smiles that *I-know-a-secret* smile.

"What did he *say?*"

"He said he knows who you are."

"He knows who I *am?*" I am practically screeching.

"Shhh," he says. "Don't tell anybody."

"Okay," I whisper, so excited I can't sit still.

"He told me he was going to bring you that thing you really want for Christmas."

I can still feel the world light up, as it did that moment, when Daddy and I shared the best secret in the world: I was going to get the doll with the real hair.

—⊗⊗⊗—

He is almost ninety years old, and cannot move or speak. He looks up at the ceiling. His eyes are following something. He looks at it, then looks over at me, looks at it again, and looks at me. I look up.

"I can't see it, Daddy," I say.

His eyes are merry and shining. And then, he smiles the smile at me. It's our last wonderful secret: Someone, or something from spirit is here.

"I know, Daddy," I say to him. "I just can't see it."

The next day when I visit, the nurses have just finished bathing him and are adjusting his pillow, trying to make him comfortable. I talk to him, try to get his attention, but for the first time in my life, my father is not interested in me. He has gone away somewhere.

He dies the next day while I am at work.

It's an old-fashioned funeral, my mother's generation's funeral. Daddy is in an open casket. He is beautifully dressed; the funeral home is elegant. Family has gathered from all over, my friends and colleagues have come in numbers to pay their respects. My brothers and their wives are teary. My mother, who is sinking deeper into Alzheimer's disease, is withdrawn, preferring to sit in an anteroom. She is like a stone.

My father's pastor gives an affectionate, funny eulogy, and later, the family gathers at my house. It's been a long day. I see to the guests, thank everybody for coming, and later, when my mother is resting and Bill and I are washing the dishes, I remember my last visit to Reverend Brown. "I see a circle of American Indians," he had said. "They are dancing, rejoicing, getting ready to welcome your father into spirit." In the hectic, exhausting months of dealing with my mother's Alzheimer's and my father's stroke, I hadn't thought much about Reverend Brown's words. But now, it comes to me: My father's father was Native American.

That night, I go to sleep thinking of my father in his hospital bed, smiling, looking at a circle of dancers, led by his father. There is no need to cry. Death is not what it used to be.

# CHAPTER 37

⚬

☥

Rising from cascades in the river, the small island of Philae is crowned by the great Temple of Isis. The river laps gently at its shores, where fuchsia bougainvillea grows in profusion on the rise leading to the temple. An old priest cuts armfuls of the blossoming branches and places them in a basket. He pauses to watch as a Roman customs officer signals for a small barge to dock.

*Even here they will not let us be. What sacrilege! Tax collecting! Here!*

He turns away and walks up the embankment with difficulty, his legs stiff and arthritic, and makes his way across the great open courtyard that leads to the temple. High above his head, carved into a pylon, is the colossal figure of Isis, wearing a headdress of cow horns with a solar disk between them. Her profile is slender, her expression stoic. Isis, the enchantress-goddess who reassembled the dismembered corpse of her husband, Osiris, then gave birth to Horus, one of the great gods of Egypt.

Seated majestically on its own island, its perfectly fitted ochre stones a testament to master carvers, the Temple of Isis at Philae is the center of learning for Egyptian clergy. It is newer than the Temple of Luxor, and well preserved; its carvings and columns are colored in hues of red, blue, and gold.

A bronze statue of Horus in the form of a falcon sits on a base at the entrance. The old priest touches the falcon's claw with a trembling hand before passing through the cool, dark corridor. He stops at the inner courtyard, sits on a bench that is tucked between the giant columns, and waits for his breath to return to normal. After some time, he stands and looks out at the green waters of the Nile in time to see the small barge as it passes, the oarsmen pulling mightily against the current.

*I suppose they are going to Edfu,* he thinks, *no doubt a bit poorer than when they docked.*

He walks on, passing the small cells on the left—the sleeping quarters of the student priests. They are dark and empty. He turns to the right, and enters a spacious dining hall. Seated on both sides of a long table are his charges, the young men who will go forth from this island temple steeped in the secrets and magic of Egyptian antiquity. They are the last vestiges of a royal class, princes of the ancient religion, who will preserve Egypt's past until her Roman occupiers grow weak from internecine conflicts, or simply tire of pillaging, and retreat. They will hold Egypt's secrets close, and pass them on to others of their class, until Rome's adventure is over. Time is irrelevant; their view is a long one. They are, therefore, content.

The old man arranges the bougainvillea in earthenware pots that sit on the floor, speaking first to one and then another of the young priests as he passes them. Each rises as he is spoken to, bows his head, and folds his hands in front of him. Lukhamen is not among them.

The old priest fills the last pot with his blooms, and walks out into the second courtyard, shielding his eyes from the sun that is now rising in the bright blue sky. Between the columns, he can see sunlight sparkling on the water. He smiles. He has been here since he was a boy and can remember no other home.

He enters the darkened corridor that leads to the sanctuary. Inside, he waits until his eyes are accustomed to the dark. At the foot of the altar he sees him sitting on his heels. His back is straight, and his hands rest palms-upward on his thighs.

Lukhamen is his favorite. Like his father before him, the boy had accepted the life of rigorous study and discipline without question or complaint. Even when the medallion, a parting gift from his mother, was taken from him, he did not protest.

In the lonely darkness before dawn, he is the first to step into the river's cold water, and at night, at study in his small cell, he is the last to extinguish his lamp.

When, at each rising of the river, he was told that he would not return to Luxor with the others, he went to the city of Edfu to study at the Temple of Horus without a word, and excelled there in Greek and Latin. He was a brilliant student, and took to the life of unending work as if it were the thing he desired most in the world.

---

The old priest waits patiently, and after a long while Lukhamen stirs, stands, bows before the image of Isis that is carved into the back wall, and turns.

"Good morning, my son."

"Good morning, Sire."

"Will you come with me?"

"Yes, Sire."

Lukhamen follows him into the small corridor, and through a side opening to the outside, ducking his head as he passes through.

He is tall and strong. He has come to know the weight of the wooden yoke, as he must climb uphill from the river with buckets of water for the parched plots of vegetables and grain that feed the priests. His body is hard from the labor, his skin dark from years in the sun. He follows the old priest to the rise above the river. They sit beneath a small sycamore tree.

"The waters will rise soon, Lukhamen."

"Yes, Sire."

"And you will go with us to Luxor."

Lukhamen is speechless. He stares at the river without seeing it.

"You will have your final ordination in the Temple of Amon at Luxor. Your father will officiate."

The old priest stands, touches him on the shoulder, and leaves him alone. At length, the river comes back into view, and Lukhamen watches a small barge as it struggles to navigate the rough current.

*The river is much calmer at Luxor.*

It is the first time in twelve years that he has allowed himself to think of home.

———— ∞ ————

Aahmes, Alenna's youngest son, hides behind a palm tree, waiting. He is a stocky, healthy boy, calm in his demeanor; his movements are deliberate and unhurried. He spies the girl as she comes from behind the oleander shrub, skirting the plots of her mother's Turkish lilies. She is stealthy, on tiptoe. She comes closer, closer, and he covers his mouth with his hand, so as not to laugh and give himself away.

Femi, Haraa's daughter, is tall, like her mother. Even at the age of thirteen, it is clear that she will inherit her mother's voluptuous figure. She is a striking girl—strong, and confident. Closer and closer she comes, until he can almost touch her.

"Arrrh!

He jumps from behind the tree and she screams in terrified delight. She attacks him with both fists, but he holds her wrists, laughing as she wriggles to free herself.

"You are my prisoner, Femi," he says in a little singsong voice, "I have you and there is nothing you can do about it."

"You will pay for this, you dung-eating ass!"

"What language!"

He lets go and runs, and she runs after him, and tackles him to the ground. They wrestle, he laughing, she screaming, until she pulls free from him, feigning anger.

"Now see what you have done! My mother will be angry!"

Femi's sleeve is torn. It hangs from her dress, exposing one shoulder.

"What do you care? You have lots of dresses."

"I know, but my mother does not allow me to tear them, you idiot!"

He mocks her: "My mother does not allow me to *tear* them, you *idiot!*"

"Oh!" she screams, and takes off after him as he races toward the house.

"Children, children! What is this unseemly behavior?"

Haraa sits on her terrace, in the shade of a flowering vine. She is pouring tea. Seated across from her is the governor, reading. He looks up and smiles at them.

"Sorry, Mother," says Femi coquettishly, looking at the handsome man with the deep brown eyes. There is a touch of gray in his hair.

"Sorry, Auntie Haraa," says Aahmes.

"Femi, change your dress at once, and you, young man, go into the dining room and sit. Lunch is ready for you both. And see if you cannot comport yourselves with a little more dignity, will you?"

"Yes, Mother," says Femi, twisting from side to side, looking at Marcus, flirting shamelessly. Aahmes gives her a little punch on the arm.

"You heard your Mother. Change your dress."

"Goodbye, Governor," she says sweetly.

"Goodbye, Femi." He smiles at her.

Haraa sighs as Femi disappears into the house. "She's incorrigible."

"I agree," says Aahmes. "Incorrigible."

Haraa looks at him sideways and narrows her eyes.

"Go, young man. Now."

"Yes, Auntie Haraa." He gives her a kiss on the cheek.

"And don't try to charm me, you imp."

He smiles at her, bows to the governor, and disappears into the house.

"Lukhamen will be home soon, you know," says Haraa. "I wonder what he will think of his little brother. I'm sure he hardly remembers him. He was an infant when he left."

She hands Marcus a cup of mint tea.

Marcus remembers Lukhamen as he was on the day of the old governor's funeral, when he was still a boy, the day Alenna stood so near to him, the day her scarf fell to the ground and he retrieved it, put it into her hands—the day *she knew*, because his eyes had betrayed him.

"I remember him as a poised young man, very much in command of himself."

*His eyes were like Alenna's.*

"Yes, indeed," says Haraa. "We hear that he is everything a high priest should be."

Haraa remembers that time as well, with relief. They are past that now.

Aahmes pokes Femi's arm. A lunch of lamb and rice with almonds sits untouched before them.

"You're incorrigible."

"What?"

"You're incorrigible."

"What's *incorrigible?*"

"You're not well-behaved."

"Ha! You should talk! You're the one who ripped my dress."

He makes a face at her, and she throws a spoonful of rice at him.

"Femi!"

"Sorry, Mother."

She has been seen, and caught. He brushes the rice from his robe, smiles wickedly, then delicately and deliberately picks up a piece of lamb and puts it in his mouth.

"You're a big baby. You may try and act grown up, but you're still a baby."

"That's what you think, Femi the Incorrigible. I'm almost a physician."

"A *physician?*"

"Yes, a physician."

"You are not."

"I am. Or, I will be soon. Mother says I may study with Sechmetna. Even though he is practically blind and cannot hear well, he is still the most brilliant physician in all of Egypt."

"Oh, but that's perfect— a teacher who is blind and deaf for a student with no brains!"

He reaches out to swat her with his napkin, and knocks over his glass of tea. The contents spill into his lap, and he jumps up from the table. "Ah...ah...!"

It starts as a giggle but soon escalates into helpless, rollicking laughter. She tries to catch her breath, banging her feet on the floor and rocking from side to side. In a minute, they are both wailing like braying goats, holding their stomachs, tears rolling down their cheeks.

On the terrace, Haraa smiles. "He will miss her when she marries Lukhamen."

"Yes," says the governor, "I am sure he will."

# CHAPTER 38

⚑

✠

IT IS LIGHT IN THE garden now. The high priest can see it, pale and violet, through the sheer curtains. He closes his eyes and imagines the sun rising above the river—red-orange and blazing like fire over the water.

He sits in the wheeled chair designed for him by Simon. It is painted purple and bears the family name *Sa'at* inscribed in gold on its side.

He hears Alenna down the hall, giving orders to the servants as she nears his room. She enters, all hustle and bustle. A servant girl runs behind her, bearing a tray. Alenna walks directly to the alcove that opens onto the garden and pulls back the curtains. The sky is streaked with pink. Bougainvillea vines on the far wall move slightly in a soft breeze.

Alenna's hair is tousled; a robe of saffron-colored silk flows in her wake. She turns to her husband.

"Breakfast, my love," she says, beckoning the servant girl to come forth with the tray.

"Good morning, Alenna."

She leans down to kiss him on the forehead. There is a knock at the front door.

"That will be Simon," he says.

"Then I will be upstairs. I must get dressed. I have a busy day ahead … Manut!" she calls to the head steward. "The door, if you please!"

She turns from her husband and runs up the stairs, calling down from above:

"Do not forget, Lukhamen …we will be dining with Haraa and Femi this evening!"

He glances at the cheese and warm bread the servant girl has left on the table next to his chair. Pushing it aside, he looks up into the smiling face of Simon.

"Ah. Good morning, Simon. Let us be off, shall we? We have much work to do."

*We?* thinks Simon.

"Yes," he says, as if he has heard Simon's thought, "We have much to do."

"Yes, Sire."

And not knowing what else to say, Simon wheels him toward the door.

---

Semnut, the old nurse, is sponging warm, sudsy water over Alenna's back.

"Quickly, Semnut, a towel. I will have no massage today. Just oil, please. I have a thousand things to do before dinner."

The old woman fumbles among the oils on a small table, flustered by Alenna's impatience. In her haste, she drops a bottle and its spilled contents fill the room with a memory. A memory Alenna would prefer to forget.

---

She had made the best of her life, such as it was. She dined alone with her husband much of the time, their younger son preferring to take his meals at Haraa's house, which was always lively and of course, home to Femi.

Except at meals, Alenna saw her husband only in passing. He still slept in the airy, spacious room on the first floor. Once a dining room, it was now a library, its walls lined with shelves and scrolls. He visited the temple every day. She heard that he kept the priests from their duties, perplexing them with strange, esoteric theories. By night, he consulted the scrolls, sleeping little, unfurling one and then another, making great piles of them on the floor, discarding them as, one by one, they failed to reveal whatever it was he sought. Each morning, after he had left for the temple, Alenna would have Manut roll them neatly and return them to the shelves.

Her husband made little use of the remainder of the house and the garden, and spoke to her in small, direct ways. He was always polite, and when she engaged him, they spoke about the weather, or the state of the garden—subjects which held little interest for either of them. She slept on the second floor, where once they slept together, before an aging temple wall changed everything.

---

Semnut covered the spilled oil with towels, but the scent would remain in the room—lingering, hurting her. Because of Marcus. He had told her that he would never again be able to bear the scent of orange blossoms.

It was the night she had stepped into Haraa's garden, into the moonlight, when Marcus followed her. He had spoken to her intimately, touched her hand, and it had moved her. She had wanted to put her hand in his, feel it close around her own. She had resented the way he drew her to him and she had pulled away. Then he had wounded her with his words: *It is never her, Alenna. It is always you.*

She had been outraged. She was angry with Haraa for her scandalous liaison, angry that Haraa's evenings now boldly included *him*, angry that she was forced to be in his company, angry that she was moved by him, by the pain that never left his eyes, angry at the awful twist of fate that had left her alone in the sweet summer of her life.

*How dare you*, she had hissed at Marcus, the tears burning her eyes. *Do you think we are all your whores?* That had hurt him, as she intended. He stood pinned to the moment, unable to move, as she walked back into the house.

---

"Never mind, Semnut. The maid will take care of it. I should have another scent anyway. I am growing tired of this one. I shall get another."

But she knew that she would not. She would wear it whenever she saw him. She would haunt him, hurt him for his weakness and ... *Haraa*.

---

"Hold on tightly, Sire," says Simon as they approach the downward slope to the temple's entrance.

"Simon?"

"Yes, Sire?"

"Will you take breakfast with me this morning?"

Simon stumbles. He has never been asked to have a meal in the temple. Or with a priest.

"If you wish, Sire."

"It is done then. Join me in the dining room after the bath."

"Yes, Sire."

---

Later they are seated at a long table, alone, the other priests having long ago eaten and gone about their duties. A boy brings tea, a warm loaf of bread, some cheese, and bowls of yoghurt with honey. They eat silently for a few minutes. Then the priest speaks.

"I knew your Abba Michael, you know."

Simon stops eating. His eyes grow wide.

"You knew Abba Michael?"

"Yes. Before he died, we got to know one another. I liked him. He was a good man."

"Yes, Sire. He was."

"It was in the days when Antonious was stealing the grain. I gave Abba Michael a portion from the temple's stores."

Simon's face darkens at the mention of Antonious' name.

"Once I vowed to kill him, Sire."

"I will wager you are not the only one, Simon."

"He killed a friend of mine with his chariot. My friend and I, we built the church together. Antonious would ride through our quarter at top speed, to frighten us. My friend was not the only one to die under his horses. He killed a child once."

"Many people suffered from Antonious' cruelty, Simon. But it is what brought us together, Abba Michael and me. More tea?"

"Thank you, Sire."

"Simon?"

"Yes, Sire?"

"I would like you to attend Lukhamen's final ordination."

"Me, Sire?"

"Lukhamen would be pleased, I know."

"He probably doesn't remember me."

"He saw you move the stones. He watched as you lifted me out of the rubble of the temple wall. He will not soon forget you, Simon."

"I will be honored, Sire. And I am grateful for the work you have given me all these years."

The high priest pours himself another cup of tea. "And now I have something to ask of you."

"Anything."

"I want you to teach me."

"*Teach* you, Sire?"

"Yes, teach me."

"What could I possibly teach you, Sire?"

"You can teach me what you believe, Simon, what the Christians believe." Simon looks into his eyes. They are bright and penetrating. "I want to know everything. I want to know if there is one thing that makes us Egyptians, one common thing that makes us one people, despite our differences."

"Differences, Sire?"

"Differences in how and whom we worship. We must not allow these differences to alienate us."

Simon is thinking hard, trying to understand the word *alienate*.

The high priest continues. "The Romans believe they have suppressed us, Simon, but they are wrong. We were here before Rome marched on us, and we shall be here when their banners lie buried in our dust. Egypt shall never belong to them, not while we have our memory. Do you see that?"

Simon frowns. "No, Sire."

"When they have gone," the high priest's voice is quieter now, conspiratorial, "we will have our memory to teach us who we are. Amon is as old as anyone can remember. Amon *is* Egypt, just as Osiris, and Isis, and Horus are Egypt, just as the Pharaohs who sleep across the river are Egypt. If *they* are not here when the Romans leave, who will we be, Simon? We will be the shadows of those who have conquered us. We will be like sand in the desert wind, blowing this way and that, scattered and separate! There is nothing greater they can take from us than the memory of who we *are*, Simon!" His eyes are like burning coals.

"My people do say that you are the only ones who remember, Sire."

"Then you must teach me, Simon. Abba Michael and I did not discuss such matters. We were more concerned with food, with sustenance to keep the people alive. But now, I would like you to help me understand who your god is, and whether or not he is Egyptian."

Simon thinks a bit. "Well, Sire, his son Jesus was here in Egypt when he was but a babe in his mother's arms."

"Your god was here? In Egypt?"

"Yes, Sire."

"Come, Simon. Take me to my anteroom, just off the bath chamber. I must hear more."

"Yes, Sire."

Simon wheels him out into the sun. They cross the courtyard, and Simon is growing increasingly uneasy. He does not know where this is going, but it is sure to be troublesome.

───※───

The river is wild at Philae, where white foam dances high into the air and over the cascades. The small, delicate feluccas that dot the river at Luxor do not sail here. Here, only barges dare venture. This is where the Nile bursts open. Boatmen who do not know where the great stones lie beneath the rushing water dash their barges into splinters and often perish.

It is midnight, and the Dog Star has appeared faithfully beside the full moon. Its appearance heralds the rise of the Nile waters, and Lukhamen's return to Luxor. The island is lit as day. Lukhamen sits at the river's edge, a papyrus scroll in his lap, the letter that arrived two days ago. It is from Alenna.

*My Dearest Love,*

*They have told me that now I may write to you, after twelve years. Twelve years, Lukhamen! I am afraid you will not know me, although it will be you who has changed more.*

*I cannot sleep some nights, so I go into your room and sit there. I have changed it only a little. Aahmes now sleeps in your old bed and I have had a larger one placed in your room, one fit for a man. It is strange to say it, Lukhamen: fit for a man. Oh, I pray that you will remember me! I have thought of you every day, my son. Every day you have lived in my heart.*

*Your father is well, considering his condition. Simon— the stone mason— has fashioned a rolling chair for him, and although I hate to admit it (I am not at all fond of Simon), it is quite cleverly put together. Your father goes to the temple every day, just as he used to, with Simon rolling the chair. (Oh, how the people talk at this strange sight!) Your father says there is no pain, and that not being able to walk is just an inconvenience. His eyes light up at the mention of your name, and although he is more circumspect than I am, I know he is just as excited that you are finally coming home.*

*Your brother has grown into a fine, intelligent boy. You will be proud of him. He has begun to study with Sechmetna. Yes, Lukhamen, he wants to be a physician. He is four years older than you were when you left. So hard to believe!*

*I have saved the best news for last. Yesterday Auntie Haraa and I completed all the legal proceedings, and your betrothal to her daughter, Femi, is now official. Oh, Lukhamen, she will be a wonderful wife. She is very bright, and she is beautiful, and comes from a very old (and may I say very rich) family. I cannot imagine someone more perfect for you. Her father died some years ago, but he left Auntie Haraa a great deal of money, and she has provided Femi with a bountiful dowry. You will want for nothing. Of course, you will have to wait until she comes of age (she is thirteen, like Aahmes) before you marry.*

*A wonderful life awaits you, Lukhamen. Come home.*

*All my love,*

*Mother*

He tries to remember how she looked, tries to recall his mother's scent. What was it? Her face eludes him. He used to dream of her when he first came to Philae, dream that she would put her hand on his face, and call him her dearest love. But in time, the dreams stopped. And her face left him. He never cried, not even in the darkest night.

He looks out at the river, all leaping crystals and foam, sparkling in the moonlight. Its beauty has never moved him. When he arrived on the island of Philae, his only thought had been to survive. He had turned inward, found the refuge of silent uncaring, and it had saved him.

He had given himself totally to his masters, and they had taught him Latin and Greek, history, mathematics, and theology. At some point, he was no longer aware of longings, or of loneliness. But now he sits here with his mother's letter in his lap, and feels its power pull him toward home.

*A wife!* He has not thought of a wife, or of any life other than the one he knows: the solitary, scholarly life of a man who is to be the servant of Amon. Still, he will accept her. He knows he can make no choice as perfect as the one his mother has made for him. He watches the river as it plays and dances in the moonlight.

From somewhere on the hill above him, a sleepless young man places a flute to his lips and sends a sweet melody into the night air. It washes over him and drowns him in a new feeling: loneliness. He puts his hand over his heart as if to ease its hold on him. From that day on the river, from the moment he turned his head away from Luxor and from all who loved him, he had, without knowing it, emptied himself of everything that could cause him pain. The emptiness had served him well. It was why he excelled, unlike those who constantly longed for home. Unlike them, he was not distracted by love.

The scent of night jasmine floats around him, sweetening the warm night air. It reminds him of something from long ago, but he cannot remember what it is. He lifts his other hand to his heart, and holds the pain close.

———— ✺ ————

From his bed, the high priest cannot see the moon, but it floods his room with blue-white light. He cannot see the Dog Star, but he knows it is there. The waters will rise soon.

*Lukhamen, Lukhamen. The next moon will find you in my house again. Oh my son, I have such plans! There is so much to teach you!*

He thinks back to the morning, and his talk with Simon. It had surprised him how closely the Christian father god, the son Jesus, and the mother they call Mary, resembled the Egyptian gods Osiris, Horus, and Isis. Were not both Osiris and Jesus resurrected from the dead? And Jesus, like Horus, was the son of a god, and a god in his own right. Isis, although much more heroic, is Mary.

Resurrection, father, son, mother of God. The new religion, with a few minor exceptions, is built on the concepts of the old. It is as he hoped it would be: essentially, undoubtedly, indisputably *Egyptian*. He closes his eyes.

*Yes, my son, there is so much to teach you.*

He smiles and is asleep instantly, the scrolls forgotten, neatly rolled and put away.

# CHAPTER 39

"EAT YOUR MIDDAY MEAL, LUCENKEP. Don't give it to the birds. I've made the bread you like— the one with coriander seeds and honey. It's still warm. And there are olives and cheese. I want you to eat all of it."

"Yes, Mother, I shall."

Mahda kisses her daughter on the forehead.

"I shan't be long."

"Mother, may I go with you, *please?*"

"No, no, and no again. For reasons known only to God, the lepers do me no harm, but I do not know what would happen if you came among them."

"Mother…"

"But that is all, Lucenkep. Now be careful of the scroll Abba John has let you borrow. It is delicate and precious. And it belongs to the church."

"Yes, Mother."

Lucenkep watches her mother disappear down the river road, toward the leper compound, then settles in under a tree. She unrolls the scroll. It is the Gospel of the Apostle Marcus, the "lion of the desert," the friend of Jesus, the first one to bring news of Him to Egypt. She breaks off a piece of the bread, puts it in her mouth, and searches through the scroll with her finger until she finds the passage she is seeking:

*A leper approached him with a request, kneeling down as he addressed him: "If you will to do so, you can cure me." Moved with pity, Jesus stretched out his hand, touched him, and said: "I do will it. Be cured." The leprosy left him then and there, and he was cured.*

A breeze blows gently against her face. She leans back against the trunk of the tree and closes her eyes. *Jesus,* she prays, *be moved with pity now for our poor lepers.* And with the sweet, earnest faith of her youth, she whispers another request: *And give my mother the power to heal them.*

The day is warm, and the river is still. A cloud of tiny dragonflies hovers above the surface. Locusts drone in the distance. She tries to read more, but her eyelids grow heavy, and in a few minutes, Lucenkep is asleep.

———— ∞ ————

At first the chanting is low and far away, and she is not sure if it is a dream. But it grows closer, and Lucenkep sits up to see a barge coming toward her, filled to capacity with temple priests. Even from here she can see their robes of crimson and purple and the glint of gold around their necks.

She rushes to the river's edge as the barge approaches, and she sees a young priest—deeply bronzed, dark hair blowing in the breeze, eyes straight ahead, still as a statue. His robe is not colored richly like the others. It is white, and he wears no ornaments. As he passes, she sees him in full profile—half-lidded eyes shadowed by heavy lashes, straight nose, a mouth that is gentle and solemn. Her heart leaps from her body and is borne on the air's warm current toward him, like the white river bird that follows the boat. She stares at his back until the barge rounds a bend and disappears behind the tall rushes.

She puts a hand to her chest, over the spot where her heart had been.

———— ∞ ————

Lukhamen has not seen her. His eyes are fixed on the temple ahead, and the dock, where his father and mother await him.

—∞∞∞—

Mahda walks quickly, trying to outdistance her dread; but it will not be left behind, no matter how blue the sky, or how sweet the song of the bird above. It overshadows her as she approaches the compound and folds her tightly in its murky hold.

There are no sweet oleander shrubs to enclose it, no bougainvillea to give color to its borders. Only a field of tall dry rushes separates the lepers' small village from the lonely road. No one travels here except the Christian priests, the Abbas.

"Mahda! Mahda!"

The cry goes out, and the lepers come from everywhere—rushing forward, overjoyed at seeing her. For an instant, Mahda thinks she will be overrun by them, and she pales; but then, seeing her distress, they stop. They will not come too close; they will give her time. Mahda takes a deep breath, and smiles.

"Good morning!"

"Good morning, Mahda!" they cry in chorus.

"What did you bring us, Mahda?" cries a little girl. Her face is aged and misshapen. She hops toward Mahda on one leg, balancing herself with a crutch made from a tree limb.

"Shush...That's not very polite, now!" says the older woman with her, whose face is shadowed by the rags that cover her head.

*Jesus give me strength*, whispers Mahda. "Well, what do you think?" she says to the little one.

"The special bread, the special bread!"

"Yes. I have brought the special bread. And olives."

The little girl jumps up and down, loses her crutch, and falls. She begins to cry. The older woman helps her up, sets her crutch aright.

"Pay no attention, Mahda. She gets too excited. Come, come. Sit down."

Mahda follows them to a courtyard that is shaded by a majestic old sycamore tree. A few battered chairs sit beneath it, leaning precariously. The best one is brought forward for her; and they arrange themselves in a semicircle at her feet. Mahda gives the older woman the basket of bread. With trembling hands the old woman removes the cloth, puts her face close to the mounds of loaves nestled inside, and breathes in.

"Ah…it smells like heaven. God bless you, Mahda."

Precious morsels of the fragrant bread are passed from one to another. No one speaks. No one takes a bite until everyone has been given a piece. Then they begin, chewing carefully, savoring, never taking their eyes from her. A bag of olives is passed around; and they take one apiece, delicately, carefully. The rest are put away for later.

Then Mahda produces a small bottle of oil. "Ahh…" comes a sigh from the group. "This is from the house of a rich woman. My friend Alia is her masseuse."

"Did she steal it, Mahda?" the little girl blurts out, the olive pit still in her mouth.

"Shh…!" the old woman scolds her.

Mahda laughs. "Her maid forgot to put it away, is all. No one in that house will miss it." They stare at Haraa's gold colored liquid, sparkling in the sun. Mahda stands. It is time.

"Come, Mahda. I will go with you," the old woman says.

Mahda follows her into one of the little hovels. It is dark, and she stops just inside the doorway, allowing her eyes to become accustomed to the gloom. There is a mattress of sorts on the floor, a mat covered in rough cloth, filled with dried reeds. A small figure lies very still, wrapped in linen, curled up like an old rag doll. A mouse scampers from beneath the mat.

"Shoo! Shoo!" says the old woman, stamping her feet. "We must watch constantly, Mahda. The mice eat at our legs if we do not." Mahda is suddenly lightheaded. She steadies herself against the wall. The old woman continues, as if she has said nothing out of the ordinary. "Look, Kesi, Mahda is here."

The small figure stirs. The old woman kneels by the mat, and lifts her head. *This is the woman who used to terrify me*, Mahda thinks. *She used to be so fat.*

Two small, unseeing eyes stare out at her from beneath a turban of rags. "Mahda…?" a small, raspy voice comes from the mummy-like figure.

"Hello, Kesi. I have brought you something." The small figure does not respond. "I have brought you a lovely oil, Kesi. We are going to bathe you and change your linens."

"No…" the raspy voice protests, "No…"

"Now, Kesi," says the old woman, "There is no need to protest. Mahda has seen all of this before."

"No..."

Mahda turns to the old woman. "Bring me water, and soap, and the linens I left under the tree." The old woman leaves, and Mahda turns to the little figure. "Kesi, you remember Joseph, don't you?"

"Joseph...?"

"He was your son."

"Joseph was my son?"

"Yes, Kesi, your son and my husband."

"Where is he?"

"He is with God."

"Oh."

The tiny figure seems to drift off into sleep. The old woman enters with a basin.

"I'll remove the linens, Mahda. It is better if you do not touch them."

Mahda backs into a corner of the room while the old woman begins to remove the linens, lifting the tiny figure now and then to unwind them. A sickeningly sweet odor fills the small, airless room. Mahda slides down the wall and sits on the floor. *Jesus, help me now.* She watches as the old woman takes the pile of bloodied rags outside to burn. *This is for Joseph*, she mouths to herself.

Kesi's body is skin and bones, the face unrecognizable, leonine. All fingers and toes are gone, and what is left of the limbs is ulcerated from top to bottom. The eyes are closed tight in shame. Mahda stands, comes closer.

"Don't worry, Kesi," she whispers, "We are all the same to God."

Tears fall from the tightly closed eyes, flow down the tiny face whose features are all but gone. Tears blind Mahda's eyes as well, and she brushes them away as the old woman enters with a basin. The revulsion is gone now, and she is mindless of the odor as she wraps her hands in linen and squeezes soapy water over the poor skeleton that lies motionless before her. Gently, gently, she pats dry the little body that is like the dried reeds it lies upon, and pours streams of oil down the arms, over the chest, and down the legs. Then Kesi is turned on her side so that Mahda can bathe her back. The sores there are the worst, having come together into one large wound. Kesi whimpers pitifully as the water touches it.

"It's all right, now, Kesi. We are finished."

They pour oil onto the back wound and cover it with clean linen. When Kesi is fully bound, Mahda places a clean sheet on the soiled mattress.

"These linens also come from the rich woman's house," she whispers to the old woman. "They will not be missed either." She turns to the mummy figure. "I shall come again soon, Kesi," she says. But Kesi has slipped into unconsciousness.

Out again in the sunshine, Mahda stands upright, takes a deep breath, and hands the bottle of oil to the old woman. "Use it where it is most needed," she tells her.

"I think you must come again soon, Mahda. Kesi can no longer swallow. She can neither eat nor drink."

"I must work tomorrow. Tomorrow is the day I bake bread for my rich lady. I will come the day after."

The old woman walks her to the edge of the compound. The lepers follow at a distance, to wave goodbye. When they are almost at the road, the old woman stops.

"Mahda?"

"Yes?"

"When Kesi dies, will you come no more?"

A long moment passes. "I will come." The old woman smiles, and Mahda turns onto the road.

In the dark hovel, the unseeing eyes open wide. "Joseph?" the raspy voice whispers, "Joseph, is it you?"

———— ❦ ————

As Mahda reaches the river road, a barge floats slowly downriver, toward Luxor. Her knees give way; she sits down and leans against a tree, watches it pass. It is filled with priests of the old religion.

The water laps at the sandy bank, then drifts out again. A small white bird comes from nowhere and settles at her feet. It looks at her for a long moment with small, bright eyes, then flies off downriver.

---

An old man enters the small, dark room that houses the Department of Lands. At the far end, Antonious sits slumped over his desk. The room reeks of urine and stale wine. The old man goes to a small desk, opens a drawer, pulls out sticks of incense, sets them in a bowl filled with sand, and lights them. Wisps of smoky perfume begin to weave a curtain between him and the rancid odor that emanates from the back of the room.

Sitting down at the desk, he takes a quill, dips it in ink, and writes on a piece of blank papyrus.

*Dear Sir:*

*It is with great regret that I tender my resignation. On this day, I intend to present myself at the governor's office with an application to become a pensioner. I have worked in this office for thirty years.*

He can think of nothing more to say, and so he signs his name, *Masru.* He walks to Antonious's desk, places the papyrus on it, anchors it with a smooth stone, and walks out.

He blinks in the sunlight, and almost falls against the wall as someone jostles him. The streets are filled with people, all headed toward the pier at Karnak. He stops a small boy.

"Where is everyone going, boy? What is the excitement?"

The boy turns to him, breathless. "The barge! The barge from Philae is here!" He runs on.

"What barge?" Masru cries out after him.

"The barge carrying the priests!" shouts the boy, over his shoulder.

*What do I care of barges carrying priests?* the old man murmurs to himself. *I have more pressing things to do.*

In the dim Office of the Department of Lands, Antonious raises his head. The commotion from the street has called him back to consciousness. There is a loud ringing in his ears, and a blinding pain in his throbbing temples. He dares not move. He sits there, as if deaf and dumb, and watches through the open door as people filled with the merriment of a holiday run past. The smell of incense incites rising nausea, and try as he may, he cannot contain it. He vomits into a basin that he keeps near his desk.

It is some time before he notices the letter. He reads the few lines without comprehending. Somewhere, however, in a far recess of his mind, he becomes aware of being completely alone. He has no friends, no political connections, and now no one to run the office that he has held onto by the thinnest thread for the past twelve years. The end of something has come. In his miserable fog, he cannot explore the concept, but he knows that he is at the nexus of his troubles, that he has plumbed the depths of a sea of darkness. Even though he does not know it at that moment, Antonious makes an important decision. He decides to live.

He climbs the stairs to the living quarters above the office, where he falls onto his bed and sleeps a fitful sleep presided over by nightmares. He hovers in and out of consciousness for three days, awakened finally by a rap on the door. He opens it to find a young Roman soldier, cleanly shaven and smelling of soap, standing tall and straight before him. Without a word, the young man hands him a scroll, turns sharply, and walks down the stairs. Antonious stands in the doorway, the scroll shaking violently in his hand.

He closes the door, and collapses again on his bed, the scroll still trembling as if it had a life of its own. At sunset, he summons the courage to break the governor's seal and read the official notice. He has been relieved of all duty to the Roman Empire and is to vacate his apartment within four days. He is entitled to a small pension, which he may collect as soon as he presents himself. He is not to enter the Office of the Department of Lands or any other Roman office in Egypt, except of course, the Office of Pensioners.

It is what he has been waiting for, the final humiliation that gives him the strength to survive. His upper lip curls into an ugly sneer. He looks around at the filthy, sparsely furnished room and finds the one robe that is not stained with urine. He dresses himself with great difficulty, dropping the robe several times before he is able to slip it over his head. His sandals are the most challenging, for he must lower his head to tie the straps. And he cannot do that without stabs of pain rendering him blind.

It takes a long time, but finally it is done. He descends the stairs carefully, grasping at the wall with each step. It is dark, and he is grateful that no one sees him walk a few paces down the narrow street, then fall to his knees. He stands and begins again, heading toward the public baths. After a bath, he plans to go to the nearest inn. There he will try to eat a little soup, perhaps a bit of bread.

As he makes his way through the dark streets, something begins to grow inside. He can feel it swell, and wane, and swell again. It shimmers and grows powerful and violent. By the time he reaches the baths, Antonious is transformed. The dark thing now owns him. He feels wonderful for the first time in years. A lifetime of resentment, jealously, and disappointment has formed into an entity, a living thing inside of him. He feels it organize, assemble, and fashion itself into something palpable. Solid. As he sits in the steaming water, it enters his soul. Like an exhilarating fire, it breathes life into him. It becomes his alter ego, his obsession, his devoted companion. Revenge is upon him; it wraps him in its tentacles, and folds him in a tight embrace.

---

Lukhamen helps Manut lift his father onto the bed. The high priest has finally shown signs of fatigue after the spectacular banquet that was held to welcome his son home. Hosted in the great hall, the banquet was an elegant, glittering affair, and included all the priests from Karnak and Luxor, their wives, the governor and Haraa, and the intended bride, Femi. Lukhamen was overwhelmed. He was not accustomed to noise, or to women. The chatter of the guests, the colors of their costumes, and the complexity of their jewelry confused him. He was grateful when his father asked him to roll his chair into the garden.

"It is a little hard to bear at first, Lukhamen, but you will adjust. You have been sequestered for a long time."

"Yes, Father."

"Tomorrow we will go to the temple. Khenti is anxious to see you again."

"As am I to see him. Is he well?"

"Yes, but a little older…as am I."

"You are the same, Father."

"No, Lukhamen. Your mother is the same. I am older."

"How are you, Father?"

"My physical life, Lukhamen, is all but lived from this chair. Ah, but real life is lived in my mind."

"Aahmes must give you great joy."

"Yes. He is a gift for the heart. But he is his mother's child. You were always mine."

Lukhamen touches his father's shoulder. "I shall try to make you proud of me, Father."

The high priest looks at him closely. Lukhamen is taller than he'd expected, and strikingly handsome, but something lonely follows him like a shadow.

Alenna breezes in with Aahmes to say goodnight. The boy goes immediately to Lukhamen and puts his arms around his waist. Lukhamen is surprised by this artless expression of affection. He has had no physical contact with another human being since he left home. He puts his arms around the boy and smiles down at him.

"Ah, a room filled with Sa'at men. What could be more wonderful?" says Alenna, as she runs her hand playfully through Lukhamen's hair. She bends over the high priest and kisses him.

He smiles at her. He has never seen her looking so young, so radiant. She is dressed in a gown specked with gold that caught the light of every lamp in the great hall. A gold medallion hangs from a gold chain around her neck. Her hair is piled high on her head. Carefully arranged tendrils are at the nape of her neck.

*She is still so beautiful. The way Marcus looks at her…He is consumed with her, and she is aware of it. I wonder if she…*

"Well now, my sons. It has been an exciting evening, and your father must rest."

"Good night, Father," says Aahmes.

—⊗⊗⊗—

Upstairs, the boy follows Lukhamen into his room and sits on his bed. He is quiet for a moment. "Sechmetna doesn't know how to cure Father, you know."

"What does he say of Father?"

"He says the things that caused pain in Father's back died, and that is why he has no pain, but that he will never walk again."

"Aahmes..." Alenna pokes her head into the room.

"Yes, Mother, I am going."

"Lukhamen is tired. You can talk to him tomorrow."

"Goodnight, Lukhamen."

"Goodnight, brother." Lukhamen ruffles the boy's hair. Aahmes winks at him, and is gone.

"Welcome home, my love," says Alenna, as she leaves, closing the door.

"Thank you, Mother."

Lukhamen removes his robe and lies on the new bed. It is soft, and the pillow smells of jasmine. For twelve years he has slept on a hard cot with coarse sheets, and he wonders if he can bear this luxury, but a wave of fatigue overtakes him and he turns out the lamp.

—⊗⊗⊗—

Through a space in the roof, Lucenkep can see the stars. Sleep will not come to her this night. Over and over Lukhamen's face comes to her: the wind in his hair, the boat as it takes him away from her, the rushes that hid him from view. Her mind retraces it all, the lashes that hid his eyes, the silence that seemed to surround him. Lucenkep's heart beats against her chest. It has returned from its flight, but it is no longer hers.

*Sweet Jesus,* she whispers into the night, *let me see him again.*

# CHAPTER 40

———— ✾ ————

IN A WHITE MARBLE CLINIC in Paris, my daughter Debbie and her doctor are singing a little French lullaby. Debbie's husband, Francis, is standing next to me in the delivery room, pressed against the wall. At 10:37 a.m., a baby enters the world, my first grandchild. A girl. Debbie is crying happily. Francis is gray, but still standing. A nurse wraps the baby in a blanket and the doctor brings her to me. He puts her in my arms and in a beautiful French accent says, "Are you going to cry, too?"

"Oh, yes," I say.

I look down at her through my tears and think, *If I had died when I wanted to, I would have missed this.*

She yawns. Her name is Céline. I put her into Francis's arms. His grayness dissolves into delight, awe, and love.

Céline's French grandparents are waiting outside. I leave so they can have their moment with her. And I need to get back to Bill, who has come to Paris with me, and is in bed with stomach pains.

I walk back to Debbie's apartment with the good news. She and the baby are fine, I tell him, whereupon his pains promptly subside.

———— ✾ ————

Bill fell in love with Paris the first time he saw it, two years ago. I've been coming here for over twenty years, but he knows it now better than I do.

"Let's go out," he says.

We spend the afternoon walking, stopping at Notre Dame on the lovely Île de la Cité. Sitting in the great cathedral, I think about Eddie.

Reverend Brown asked me once, "Was there ever a time when Eddie almost died?"

"Yes," I say. "He was about twelve. We were at my boss's house. Everybody had gathered around the pool. My boss had given Eddie an impromptu swimming lesson, and as soon as we turned our backs, Eddie, invincible as only the young can be, jumped into the pool's deep end. He was sinking when I screamed and my boss pulled him out. I'd forgotten about that."

"He was ready to go then," said Reverend Brown, "but he loved you all so much, he decided to stay a while longer. This was a soul decision, you understand."

I have come to understand that God does not punish us with death; He created it for us—the bridge between the corporeal and the spiritual life, the doorway through which we pass again and again.

I look up at the great rose windows. *I understand,* I whisper to Eddie. *The timing was up to you, not to me, not to any of us.*

---

Debbie has gone to the clinic for a post-partum checkup. Bill is out seeking the perfect baguette, and Francis is at work. I am alone with Céline for a precious moment. I hold her in my arms and search the dreamy little eyes that look up and around, up and around, seeing what I cannot— another world, remembering what I cannot— another time, another place. Love floods my heart.

*Where have you been, little girl?* I say to her. *Did you see Eddie there?*

# CHAPTER 41

———— ✸ ————

BILL HAS A FRIEND WHOSE daughter has died. A suicide. "Come with me to see her," he says. "You're a mother who has gone through this. Maybe you can help her. She's devastated." The last thing I want to do is to see another mother going through this. But I don't know how to refuse.

I walk into her living room. It is crowded with friends and family, but she is sitting in a chair, alone, her head bowed, her hands clasped in her lap. I walk toward her, filled with trepidation. *God help me to say the right thing.* I kneel before her, take her hands, and whisper, "This is the worst thing that can happen to you. I know. It happened to me." She raises her head and looks into my eyes. "If you can survive this," I say to her, "you can survive anything." We put our arms around each other and weep.

I am not alone. There are so many of us whose children have died. I believe there is a way for us all— if we want to live.

———— ✸ ————

I have a friend whose son woke from his coma and said, "Oh, Mother, I have been to the most beautiful place, and I am not sick any more." He smiled at her, went to sleep again, and passed on the next day. "If he had not told me that," she told me later, "I would not have been able to live." He was her only child.

I have another friend whose only child, a daughter, died in her arms. Bill and I flew to Europe to be with her at the funeral. I wanted her to see me. Alive.

From the beginning, she spoke of her daughter as if she were *just there*, a little way from us, in spirit. It's been years since her daughter passed over, and always, when we speak of her, we cry. My friend has survived, with her daughter's twin sons to love, and the vision of her beautiful child, no longer ridden with cancer. At the funeral she said to me, "Am I still a mother?" And I answered, "Of course you are still a mother. Your child is *just there*, in spirit."

These mothers are far braver than I, for I have three daughters who are still with me, in whom I rejoice, and for whom I am eternally grateful.

There are those in this world who will rationalize that one can endure the death of a child only by denying that the child has died. This is perfectly logical. I have nothing against logic, reasoning, or the power of the mind to intellectualize or shield itself from pain too great to bear.

And yet, the unalterable, timeless belief that we are more than our bodies is held not only by mystics and men and women of faith, but by philosophers, theoretical physicists in the field of quantum mechanics, psychiatrists, nurses, and physicians. The endurance of this belief by people everywhere is a mystical phenomenon, as is mankind's ceaseless quest to understand the part of the self that has consciousness, that intuits, that thinks and observes its own thoughts. There are many names for it. The one I like is Spirit.

---

My memories of Eddie are precious. At first, when they came unbidden, I pushed them away. I was afraid to recall his smile, the little huskiness in his voice, the vision of him dancing around my piano as I practiced a Bach Invention, a caper that always reduced me to laughter. I was afraid to remember how full of joy he was, how smart, and funny. I thought memories of him would break my heart again, and kill me. I did not know then how to remember with love.

---

On the day Debbie is to leave for college, my husband Harold and I and our four children are living in the same house, but my marriage, in truth, is over. On that day, however, we drive to Princeton, New Jersey, as a family.

As we near the university, I am on the verge of tears, but like all of us, I am pretending that all is well, that after today we will still be a whole family. *We are just having a ride.* But Debbie is leaving us, and her leaving is like a thread pulled from a woven garment. The next year Niki will leave, her thread will pull, then Eddie's, and Michaela's, and the garment will unravel until it is gone. We are falsely cheerful and full of hollow jokes.

As the campus comes into sight, something makes me turn around. In the back seat, Eddie is looking out of the side window, and he is crying. Our family is unraveling, and he is the first to acknowledge it. He gives us all the courage to cry, to be true to the day, and the passages of life. It will be less than five years from that day that Eddie, too, will leave us. But that dear memory of his face, wet with tears and love, is mine forever.

---

Two years later, another little girl has come to join us. Bill and I travel to New York to meet her. She is so small that she fits into Bill's hands. She is vibrantly present—screaming, screeching, twisting, and rebelling with all her might against her infantile helplessness. When she sleeps, finally, I ask to hold her. Bill passes her to me. She is Michaela's little girl and her name is Elenni.

When she wakes, I gaze once again, as I did with Céline, into dreamy little eyes that are not yet ready to focus on the world. Michaela says that when she was born, the room was filled with tiny white lights. *Thank you for coming to us, Elenni,* I think, *but stay in your world of lights just a little longer. There is plenty of time.*

# CHAPTER 42

———⊗∞⊗———

JANUARY 17, 1991 WAS THE day the war in Iraq was codenamed "Operation Desert Storm." I was seated at my computer when a thought came to me: *How many mothers will lose their children before the day is over?*

The day that began with tears for the mothers of sons and daughters in that war was the day that love walked through the door and changed me and my family once again.

"Say," said Bill, taking his coat off, "If we live together in this house through the summer without killing each other, what do you say we get married?" Like Eddie, Bill could always lift my spirits and make me laugh.

"Be still my heart," I answer him.

———⊗∞⊗———

In the county courthouse in Rockville, Maryland, Bill and I wait for the clerk who will preside over our civil wedding ceremony. It is January 6, 1992, a crisp, cold morning, a little less than a year after his romantic proposal. We have lived together in harmony throughout the summer, throughout the fall, and into the winter. We have met our own criteria and passed our own test.

The clerk arrives. She is petite with white hair, wearing a dark suit and a frilly white blouse. She is calm, smiling, and quite beautiful. She takes her time, and greets us as if we are the only people to get married that day, even though there is a waiting room full of couples. She begins solemnly.

Bill and I have been together for ten years. As we stand before her and repeat the vows, I feel as if we have been married for a long time, and this rite is a reflection of our marriage, like the moon reflected on the surface of a lake. Over the years, we built our marriage one step at a time, in increments of love, laughter, tears, and trust. Always trust.

When the clerk asks if there is anyone present who knows why we should not be lawfully married, Bill and I, as if on cue, turn and feign warning glances at our children, seated behind us. Everybody laughs. In a few short minutes, the clerk pronounces us man and wife. Sandy, who is my witness, signs the court's official document, and Billy, Bill's oldest son, signs for him.

We take our family to lunch at the Phoenix Park Hotel in Washington, D.C., an establishment known for its Irish charm. The Dubliner, a pub on the hotel's first floor, is a favorite on Capitol Hill and is owned by one of Bill's friends. But for our wedding luncheon, we choose the elegant restaurant on the top floor.

Bill and I are seated in the middle of a long table. Our children sit all around us, forming a new circle with its own symmetry. I had one son. Bill has brought me three sons. He has one daughter. I have brought him three daughters.

Bill's sons have brought more daughters into the circle—Sue, Billy's wife, Shari, Patrick's wife, and Sharon, Sean's sweetheart. My daughters are all single. Debbie and Francis have parted, Michaela is not with Ezra, Elenni's father, and Niki is without a partner at the moment, as is Laura, Bill's daughter. There is symmetry here, too—Bill has two sons who are married, and I have two daughters who have children. All the boys have partners and all the girls are without partners. Interesting balances.

Billy, Bill's oldest son, toasts us, and my mother, the eldest member of my family, rises to do her part. My mother is remarkable. She has been diagnosed with Alzheimer's disease. She is still mourning my father, and yet here she stands, brave and lovely, and tells Bill, in elegant, lucid language, that she is sure he will make me happy. She is dressed beautifully, and she is out in the world with us, which I know is frightening for her. I seat her next to me. Niki also stays close by, talking to her often.

Michaela is at one end of the table, struggling with six-month-old Elenni, who is twisting and vocal. Céline, who is two years old, very French and very proper, takes a side look at Elenni, then goes around the table from person to person, tugging at their sleeves, whispering loudly, *Elle a rempli ses couches! Elle a rempli ses couches!* She wants the world to know that very un-French-like, un-lady-like Elenni has *filled her diaper.* But no one, except her mother and I, understand her. She is visibly frustrated. And a little smug.

But for the most part, we are a calm, happy assemblage. Bill's children are joking good naturedly with him. Their love means so much to him. My daughters, who have not been close to Harold over the years, have loved Bill from the beginning. They now have a father. Bill's children and my children like each other. I look at them around the table, laughing, smiling together. We were wise to give them time.

After lunch, we take pictures in front of the Christmas tree that is still in the hotel lobby. Bill's children return to their homes in Maryland. My children, who have traveled from Paris and New York, retire to our house in Bethesda, and Bill and I drive to the grand old Willard Hotel in Washington, D.C. for our "honeymoon."

That night, there is a power outage throughout the city. The only lights we can see on Pennsylvania Avenue are those in the White House and those that have been generated by the Willard Hotel and the ice skating rink in its plaza. We decide to join a merry few who have come to the rink, and we skate, holding hands. The city is dark —except for the lights that shine on us.

# CHAPTER 43

*Home again at the rise of the river. I was Father's vessel, fired, gilded, and painted with lilies, handled with care, beloved, and empty.*

☥

The voice of the High Priest of the Temple of Luxor resonates throughout the courtyard.

"Our survival depends on alliances. It is our only hope."

"Alliances?" says the High Priest of Karnak. He is young and ambitious, anxious to make his mark. "We are a divided people, Your Excellency."

Lukhamen, in the back of the group of priests, tries to concentrate.

His father continues. "If we form an alliance with the Christian clergy, we may be able to bring the insurgents into the fold. We must convince them that armed resistance is impossible, a hopeless cause, one that will have unthinkable consequences. Our aim must be to band together, act together, think together, as one Egypt."

"To what end, *exactly*," the young priest pauses over the word, "is this unity directed, Your Excellency? Together or apart, we cannot overthrow the Romans. Surely this is not what you are suggesting."

"No," the high priest answers. "The Romans must be made to leave Egypt of their own accord."

"I'm afraid I do not understand."

"The *glory* of Rome…" he cannot keep the irony from his voice, "…its greatest moments, its ambitions, have been no nobler than conquest and pillage."

"That is obvious, Sire. I still do not see where you are leading us."

"*We* are the more civilized of the two. We must teach them." There are sneers in the crowd.

"Teach the Romans to be civilized?"

"Yes."

Some are laughing outright. The high priest presses on. "But we must begin with ourselves. We must understand that it is not physical force that defeats us. Defeat begins and ends in the mind. No civilization can be fully conquered until the mind of that civilization has been captured, until its sense of self, its identity, its *authenticity,* has been lost. *That* is the real danger we face, my brother!" His voice reverberates off the columns and echoes throughout the courtyard.

"Please go on, Your Excellency," says an old priest from Philae.

"The Romans think little beyond the unholy conviction that they have the right to take what belongs to others."

"Yes, yes," some of them murmur. With this he has their attention.

"The Roman mind may be blind and arrogant, my brothers, but it is crafty and manipulative. They take what is ours, and lead us to believe they have the right because they are militarily superior. The idea is as old as slavery. We, too, have been guilty of it in our past, have we not?"

Murmurs go up from the council. The young High Priest of Karnak stands and holds up his hand to silence them.

"Excuse me, Your Excellency, but the reality is that our wheat feeds the Roman army and half the Roman population. The *wheat* is what they want, not our minds. You said they must leave voluntarily. Are you suggesting that they will just…let us have the land back because we acquire an…*identity,* or a bit of knowledge of the inner workings of the Roman mind?" He sneers a little and looks around for approval. He is enjoying this joust with the older priest.

"That is *exactly* what I am suggesting." The gathering becomes noisy.

"Silence, please!" Khenti intervenes. "Let us hear His Excellency out! If you please!"

"Thank you, Khenti," says the high priest, continuing. "You see, the Romans have missed something. Their plan is flawed. We will give them a better one."

"I have never been impressed by their intelligence, Your Excellency, but what, may I ask, have they...missed?"

"They have missed the fact that a nation of self-sufficient people, free to invent its own society and spawn its own innovations, can produce more wheat than a nation under siege, that *trade* is a greater motivator than force."

This surprises them. He lets it settle a moment before continuing. "I am not suggesting that we act as anarchists, but as *strategists* to disabuse the Romans of the illusion that our slavery is in their best interests. We must convince them that buying wheat from a supplier is cheaper than supporting an army to keep Egypt subjugated. Let us approach them with one strong voice, one strong idea, that freedom is more profitable than servitude."

Some of the priests begin to talk among themselves, nodding. Others are deep in thought. Lukhamen looks at his father. He is alive with passion and fervor.

The High Priest of Karnak speaks. "With all due respect, Your Excellency, and assuming this goal is achievable, what is the basis of your proposed outreach to the Christian Egyptians? What makes you think they will respond favorably?"

"I have begun to study their movement, and if what I think is true, we have more in common with our Christian brothers than one would suspect."

"Elaborate, Your Excellency," says the old priest from Philae.

"Simply put, the religion has its basis in ours. It is an alternate version, but basically the same. God the Father is their vision of the God of Creation, Osiris. God the Son, or the one they call Jesus, is a reflection of Horus, the son of Osiris. The Virgin, the Mother of Jesus the Son, is none other than Isis, the mother of Horus. The legend of their resurrection of the Son is based on the resurrection of Osiris. There are too many similarities not to be noticed: prophets, visions, miracles of healing, the immortality of the soul, the afterlife. There are variants, of course, but in general it is all borrowed from our theology, which predates theirs by centuries. The religion, my brothers, is basically *Egyptian*."

Again, he lets this idea settle while the priests murmur among themselves.

Lukhamen is lightheaded. His head aches. He leans over to Khenti, who has joined him in the back row, and asks if he might be excused.

"Just a while longer, Your Excellency," Khenti whispers. "It would not do to walk out just as your father has captured their imagination."

Lukhamen wants to stand, stretch, and escape to the river bank where he can be alone, away from this talk of unity and the Roman mind, this political dialogue that makes his head ache. He looks at his father again, who is lit in the glow of sunset, full of energy, alive with discovery and insight.

He thinks of the days following the accident, the days when *he* was filled with fervor, when he talked with his father of faith and dreamed of faith—faith strong enough to cure the incurable, faith that would restore life to his father's legs. Somehow, during the years of discipline and study, the hours spent in prayer, the fasting and meditation, and despite all his striving, faith had slipped away from him. *It was a boyish faith.* He huddles in his chair. The light is almost gone. The novitiate priests light lamps in the courtyard, and he feels the chill of evening. He folds his arms and rocks back and forth to stay warm.

"Your Excellency," whispers Khenti.

He is instantly still, as still as the statues of the great Ramses that line the courtyard, now in shadows. He will never again succumb to fatigue, or cold, or any form of weakness. He is to be ordained tomorrow.

---

"Give me a beer."

Simon sits at a side table, his back against the wall. The tavern is small, windowless, and dark. The air is rank. It is a place of intrigue, a den where men look over their shoulders, a precarious, slippery place. It is where the bitter and desperate gather to whisper of rebellion and revolt.

"Well, Simon," says the tavern owner, "To what do we owe this honor? It's been years."

Simon looks up at him, unsmiling. "Just the beer, Tamut. Spare me the sarcasm."

"Of course, Simon, of course." Tamut calls over his shoulder to a small, pockmarked boy who is sweeping the floor. "Bring Simon here a beer, boy!"

He sits down, across from Simon. "What brings you here, Simon?"

"Can I not have a beer after a hard day's work when I want one, Tamut?" The boy sets a beer before Simon, who drinks it down in one gulp.

"Another, boy. Bring Simon another, a good one this time."

Tamut lights the small lantern on the table, casting shadows along the wall of the small room, and light onto Simon's face.

"You are welcome here any time, Simon."

"Move the lantern, tavern keeper."

Tamut moves the lantern to the next table.

"I don't usually favor places that cater to the likes of Antonious." Simon takes a sip from the beer that was placed before him.

"You needn't be concerned about him. He has been dismissed from his post. The Romans have humiliated him. He's nothing now, just a drunk who doesn't have a job."

"Is that true?"

"Of course it's true. Would I tell you otherwise?"

"I hear he comes here still. I hear he talks with men in the back room. I hear he has abandoned his bad habits and that he fancies himself a rebel."

Tamut smiles, showing stained teeth. Several are missing. "You've heard quite a lot, my friend."

"I am not your friend, Tamut, and there are no secrets among the down-trodden. This is Egypt, and whatever transpires in *secret* is carried on the wind into every corner of the desert night." Simon takes another swig of beer, never taking his eyes from Tamut's face. "You keep questionable company, tavern keeper. If I were you, I'd be careful."

Tamut shifts in his chair and looks over his shoulder at the front door. He answers in a low voice.

"I appreciate the warning, Simon, and I return the favor. Everyone knows of your vow to kill Antonious. He did kill your friend with his chariot, after all.

Some think you have forgotten, but I see you have not. If I were you, I would not underestimate him, my *friend*."

"Beware of traitors, Tamut. They are not trustworthy."

"Lower your voice, Simon."

"…especially Roman ones. Antonious does not belong in our movement. He is a venomous snake who is in this for himself. He is not interested in our freedom."

Tamut leans in and whispers, "…and who knows better than this venomous snake where we might find cracks in the Roman armor?"

Simon finishes his beer and stands. He grabs Tamut by his robe, lifts him from his chair, and hisses close to his face: "When we are ready, my *friend*, Antonious the traitor will be the first to die. You would do well not to be near him when he does."

Simon lets go, and Tamut falls against the table. By the time he has regained his balance, Simon is gone. Tamut sits down, shaking, and calls for the boy to bring him a beer. It is early yet, and the tavern's denizens have not begun to arrive. Only the boy and an old drunk in the corner have witnessed his humiliation. He bends and retrieves the coin that Simon has tossed onto the floor.

---

Simon veers through the darkened alleyways, more affected by the beer than he'd expected. It was his first drink in years. He comes to a small, well-kept house and knocks on the door.

"Alia! Are you there?"

"Simon?"

He stoops to enter the small room. It is lit by a single lantern. She looks closely at him.

"What is it, Simon? What has happened?"

"Nothing. I just need to be here for a while, is all."

"Come. Sit down." She pulls out a chair for him and he sits at the small table.

"You wouldn't have any beer, would you?"

"No, but I have a little wine."

She fetches two goblets and a jar from a shelf and pours a small amount into both cups. Simon downs his immediately.

"What is happening, Simon?"

"Nothing. Everything." He bows his head. She touches his hand. He looks up at her.

"I've always loved you, Alia, even when you married my friend."

"I know, Simon."

She looks at his rough hands, smoothes the mass of copper hair that has never learned how to lie peacefully on his head.

"You know that I have long vowed to kill Antonious for what he did. It is only because of you that I haven't."

"You know, Simon, that I have never condoned that vow. It is not what we do."

"He killed him, Alia, plain and simple. He killed your husband. My friend."

"I was there, Simon."

"Do you think I can just forget that? Why should Antonious be free to murder again, to steal grain from hungry children, to break the ones we love under his chariot?" He suppresses a little sob.

"That was a long time ago, Simon, and you're a little drunk."

"Alia?"

"Yes, Simon?"

"May I stay here?"

"Here?"

"I will sleep on the floor."

She looks at the red-rimmed eyes, sees the exhaustion on his face. "You may stay. But you may have no more wine."

"Yes. No more wine."

He gets up from the table and lies on the floor, by the door. She takes a blanket and covers him, puts a pillow under his head.

"I am not a bad man, Alia."

"I know, Simon, I know." She soothes his brow. "But it is never right to kill."

"I have no choice."

"We always have a choice."

But he is asleep and does not hear her.

# CHAPTER 44

"COME IN, MY LOVE, COME in!" says Harra. She is in a caftan, fresh from her bath. The scent of jasmine floats around her like a cloud. Her damp hair hangs loose about her shoulders.

"And how is our young priest?" she asks.

"Serious and quiet," says Alenna, "too quiet."

"He has just spent twelve years in seclusion, Alenna. He needs time to adjust, is all."

"I'm sure you're right."

"Come."

Haraa leads the way to a stone terrace and a small table beneath a bower of bougainvillea. A servant girl brushes stray pink blossoms from the table and sets down a tray with a silver pot of tea and glass cups that are set into silver filigreed holders. She fills the cups with steaming red tea and withdraws.

"And how are you, Alenna?"

"I am well."

"You look tired."

"I'm fine. Sechmetna says I am just growing older. He has given me a tonic."

"That's not it."

"What do you mean?"

"Sad, Alenna. You look sad."

"Why should I be sad, Haraa? By all the gods!"

"Because you are still a young woman who is living with a man who spends nearly every waking hour in his temple, a man who is paralyzed. Your marriage is not a marriage."

Alenna's eyes flash with anger. "You will not speak that way to me, Haraa, even if you are my friend. You know nothing of my marriage!"

"You have no marriage."

Alenna looks away. Tears sting her eyes. "And what do you know of marriage? *You* never had one."

Haraa thinks of her husband, old and diseased, who traveled to many lands and slept with foreign women, who died in the arms of a Turkish whore. "That is how I know."

Alenna stands and turns her back to Haraa.

"Alenna." Haraa stands and put her hands on Alenna's shoulders. "Forgive me, Alenna. I am not myself today."

Alenna turns and faces her. "I am sorry, too, Haraa. I talk too much."

"At least your husband loves you, Alenna. No one loves me. No one has ever loved me."

The pain in her voice is so real, the sorrow so unlike her. She begins to cry, and Alenna is alarmed.

"Haraa, what is it?"

"Unbelievable, isn't it? Not one day in my entire life has someone loved me."

Alenna puts her arm around her. "That's not true. I love you. I've always loved you. Your daughter loves you."

"You know what I mean." Haraa pulls away, takes in a sharp breath. "Marcus is leaving me."

"What?"

"He's leaving me. His wife has announced that she is coming to Egypt to live, and she is bringing their son. She says it is time he was introduced to his father."

Alenna is struck dumb.

"He was never in love with me, anyway. I am not losing much." Tears stream down Haraa's cheeks.

Alenna takes a moment to answer, then feigns disbelief. "That's utter nonsense. He has lived with you for twelve years."

"And why wouldn't he? I am rich, I have made his life luxurious and comfortable, and I am desperately in love with him. Why wouldn't he stay with me?" Haraa wipes her eyes. "But I have never been the one he wanted."

Alenna freezes.

"He could never hide it. Not from me, not from Lukhamen, and certainly not from you. It was always there...in his eyes."

"Haraa..."

"Oh, I know nothing has happened, but still, there it is. You have always been between us."

"Haraa..."

"It's all right. It's not your fault."

"Haraa, I would *never*..."

"There are times... with me... when he calls out your name."

Alenna catches her breath.

"At least I won't have to hear *that* again."

Alenna has not seen Haraa cry since they were children. "Haraa, I'd give anything if..."

Haraa wipes her eyes. "No matter. It's over now."

"He is a *Roman* after all, Haraa."

"What did that mean to me?" says Haraa with a bitter little laugh. "To me, he was simply Marcus—beautiful, wondrous Marcus..." Haraa's voice breaks. "How amusing...the only man I ever loved was a Roman—and he did not love me. I believe he tried, Alenna, he tried to love me." The tears fall again, and Alenna puts her arms around Haraa, and lets the pain envelop them both.

---

Alenna pulls back the curtains of her sedan chair. She needs to breathe. *He calls out my name.* In spite of herself, she feels a rush of pure, unmitigated joy. The thought stays with her throughout dinner, and her bath, and long after she lay in bed watching the stars through her window.

———⊱∞⊰———

The sun is almost directly overhead. The crowd is restless. Most of them have been there since dawn. Lucenkep sits on the ground near her mother, Mahda, and Alia, a scroll under her arm. They are among the lucky ones, with a place under a sycamore tree.

"Mother…" she says, her breath coming in short bursts, "will we see him, truly see him?"

"Yes, we will truly see him," says Mahda.

Simon appears out of nowhere and kisses Alia on both cheeks.

"Ah, my little treasure!" He lifts Lucenkep and holds her over his head.

"Simon! Put me down!" Her face is flushed with embarrassment. He puts her down and chases her round and round her mother, allowing her to elude him. She giggles uncontrollably.

"Stop it now, both of you!" Mahda smiles at Simon and hits him playfully. He is the only one who can make her daughter laugh. She is serious, Mahda contends, because she is fragile and reads too much. Lucenkep is out of breath. Her chest heaves and she begins to cough.

"Very well," says Simon. "Time to stop. Your mother is right." He puts an arm around the girl, and she leans against him. He strokes her hair. "I have to leave you now," he says.

Alia turns to look at him. "Where are you going?"

"To the temple," he answers. "There is a place for me in the courtyard. I must hurry. The ordination is taking place, even as we speak. It will be over soon, and I must be in the courtyard to greet the young high priest when he leaves the sanctuary."

"Simon!"

"It is true. The high priest himself has invited me and…"

"You jest."

"I do not."

Alia notices the new robe.

"Where did you get this robe?"

"The high priest gave it to me."

"Well! You look…very handsome."

Simon blushes. "I must be off."

"Goodbye, Simon," Mahda and Alia say in amazement.

"Goodbye, Simon," says Lucenkep.

Alia turns to Mahda. "I can't believe it," she says.

---

The road leading into Luxor is empty. Everyone who can walk is by the river, waiting for the procession. The river is still high and covers the fields; there are no farmers about.

A small but elite honor guard escorts the caravan from Rome, which carries supplies and weapons, the wife of the governor, and his nineteen-year-old son, Marcus the Younger.

Antonious, the self-appointed new leader of a band of ragtag outlaws, crouches in an irrigation ditch with his charges. They are criminals, wanted men, men on the run, desperate, dangerous men from the outlying desert, mercenaries who lust for spoils and violence.

"The rear guards first!" whispers Antonious.

As the caravan passes the ditch, the band attacks them from behind. By the time the guards at the head realize what is happening and turn to fight, the rear guards have been dragged from their horses and their throats slit.

The boy, who is riding at the head of the honor guard, surveys the carnage at the rear, bravely draws his sword, and turns his horse back toward his mother's sedan chair, the front guards in his wake.

"No! Sire!" a guard shouts after him.

The governor's wife opens the curtains in time to see a turbaned, masked raider ride past on a Roman horse, waving a sword into the swirl of dust that surrounds him. She screams.

"Mother! Mother!" The boy has reached her. "Stay inside!"

Antonious watches from a distance as the outnumbered guards fall one by one. He smiles crookedly at the men he now commands, feral and frenzied with adrenaline.

"There, that one." He points to a magnificent white horse. "Bring me that one."

One of the men leads the animal to him and helps Antonious to mount. Covering his face with the ends of his turban, he trots into the fray.

"Quickly, now! Supplies! Weapons! Quickly!" One of the men drags the hysterical woman from the sedan chair. Antonious looks at her and smiles under his mask.

"Leave her," he says calmly. "There are more important things to attend to."

In a matter of minutes, the band has swept clean everything of value. Laden with swords, wine, and rations, they gallop off on Roman steeds. At the edge of the desert, they head west for a camp near the border of Libya.

Antonious rides in another direction, galloping at top speed to a small village a few miles north of Luxor, where he hides the Roman horse in a ramshackle stable behind the small farmhouse he has rented from an old man who had gone blind years before.

---

The governor's wife wanders in and out among the dead, whimpering and mumbling incoherently. She sees the boy, who is lying beneath a Roman guard. He is covered in blood.

"Marcus!" She rolls the large man away with superhuman strength, trying not to look at the great, gaping wound in his back. The boy beneath him is unconscious, but alive.

"Marcus!" She cradles the boy's head in her arms, and rocks back and forth, wailing loudly. "Marcus, wake up!"

---

Lukhamen leads the procession out of the sanctuary and into the courtyard, where the invited guests wait to receive him. Simon stands by one of the magnificent columns that he helped restore. He feels good today, happy even. Alia had let him stay with her, and she had soothed his brow. Maybe things would work out, after all. Maybe stealing grain from the Romans was enough for now. Maybe the high priest was right about joining forces. Maybe Alia would marry him.

Flush with hope, Simon smiles at the new high priest as he passes and lingers until the crowd has filed out of the courtyard. He will soon be a guest in the house of the high priest! He will go to Alia afterwards and regale her with stories of the women's clothes and jewels.

He looks up at the clear blue sky. A burst of sunlight breaks through the columns, blinding him and obliterating the shadow behind him. A garrote is slipped around his neck. Simon falls to his knees, astonished, clawing at the metal wire that is sinking into his neck, severing his carotid artery and breaking his windpipe. He struggles with all his might, but at last slips into darkness.

The assassin walks calmly down the empty corridor, through the pylons, and onto the river road. He can see the crowd in the distance, ahead of him. He turns down the side street that leads to the tavern where he is to meet Antonious later, to be paid in full.

---

Antonious, sweating and panting, is driving a run-down chariot at breakneck speed. At the spot just beyond the ditch, he reins in a mottled, exhausted horse, picks his way through the carnage and over to the woman who is still clutching her son. "Madam?" he says, ever so gently.

She starts and looks up, her eyes insane with terror. She tries to scream, but no sound comes.

"Do not fear, Madam. I am a Roman."

She looks at him, uncomprehending, then breaks down in relief.

"I shall take you to the governor." He examines the boy, and seeing that he is still alive, says, "I will put the young master over my horse. Do not worry. He is gentle." The trembling woman gives him her hand. He helps her to rise, lifts her into the chariot, then carefully drapes the boy over the horse. Antonious climbs into the chariot, turns to the woman, and says, "You are safe now, My Lady."

He takes the horse slowly, as it bears a precious burden. Still, she holds onto his arm with an iron grip. When they reach the governor's mansion, she has to be pried loose.

Marcus stares down at his son, now sedated by Sechmetna. The old man, accompanied by Alenna's youngest son, Aahmes, has examined the boy carefully and announced that besides a few broken ribs and a blow to the head that does not seem serious, young Marcus is undamaged. The Roman guard who fell upon him undoubtedly saved his life.

Marcus touches his son's hand, then traces the fingers, which are smaller replicas of his own. Something in him swells, and his heart begins to know something besides pain. He smoothes the boy's hair. This boy, whom he has not seen since his infancy, is his—his to teach, to love, to protect. *At last*, he thinks, with tears in his eyes, *someone belongs to me.*

When he comes to her, Petronia is in bed, awake. She is the same shrill woman he remembers, only fear and outrage are now added to the list of things she hates him for.

"Thank you," he says to her. "Thank you for my son, Petronia."

"And what are you going to do to protect me and your son?" she hisses. "I came to this hateful land against my will. I came because my son needed a father. I left the safety of Rome to reside among savages! What happened is exactly what I expected."

Her voice is a shriek. "Why were we not given better protection? What are you going to do now to find and punish the assassins who nearly murdered your wife and son? Tell me, Marcus!"

"I shall take care of you now, Petronia—and my son," he answers.

"And how? How, Marcus?" she screams.

"They will be found and punished."

"See to it, Marcus, or all of Rome shall come down about your head."

Marcus turns to leave.

"And one more thing. I want Antonious to be my personal bodyguard."

"Very well then, Petronia. You shall have him."

He smiles bitterly, and turns back to her.

"You shall have your own residence, Petronia, and you may do with it what you will, and house in it whomever you will. But Antonious will never live in this house, and he will never come near my son."

⸙

Later, Marcus sits in his room, seeking refuge in solitude and strong, black beer. *Petronia bedamned. But this attack on Roman soldiers and on my son must be dealt with.* For years there has been peace; and he has assimilated, gotten lost in the beauty of Egypt, intoxicated by its people, blinded by his love. *Have I forgotten duty? My training as a soldier?*

He puts down the glass. *That is over.* But what, he wonders, provoked this act of violence? Have insurgents sensed that he has loosened his grip on the reins? Whatever the cause of the attack, it will not happen again.

He walks onto the balcony. The moon's reflection has turned the Nile to liquid silver. He closes his eyes and sees Alenna's face. After tomorrow, she will hate him forever.

# CHAPTER 45

†

"This could not have come at a worse time," says the high priest.

Lukhamen sits beside his father's wheeled chair. They are in the garden, cloaked in silvery moonlight. Whiffs of jasmine drift over them, but the small flower's perfume is no match for the odor of doom that hangs low and heavy over all of Luxor.

The reception following Lukhamen's ordination had ended early, interrupted by news of the attack on the governor's family, followed by the equally incredulous news of Simon's assassination inside the temple walls. They had listened to the breathless reporter in silence, while the servants huddled together in the hallway. Lukhamen could feel the air grow heavy as fear rippled through the house.

"The attack on the Roman guard...what does it mean, Father?"

"It means that the government will come down upon us. Marcus will be forced to take retaliatory measures."

"But surely not against his friends."

"Marcus has no friends now, Lukhamen. He is the emperor's representative, the governor of this province, and we are at his mercy." A bird sings a clear, lilting melody at the moon, oblivious of the dread that has enveloped the night.

"Losing Simon...that is devastating. It is true he vowed to kill Antonious, but for all his talk, he was not a murderer. He was the only link between us, the

Christians, and the insurgents. He was the one thread that ran through us all, our one hope of unity. There is no one to replace him, except for one."

"And who is that, Father?"

"It is you, Lukhamen."

"Me, Father?"

"Hear me out. Tomorrow morning I shall go to see the governor. Someone must speak for the Egyptian people. I do not know what his mood is, or how he intends to deal with the situation."

A servant appears with wine, pours two glasses from a silver pitcher. The dark red liquid shimmers in the moonlight.

"No one knows how far Marcus will have to go to save face. Rome will be watching him. I must try to stave off an overzealous show of force."

"Shall I come with you, Father?"

"I have another mission for you. I want you to be my emissary to the Christian clergy. Go to them at first light, let them know who you are, tell them that we are seeking closer ties with them. You can do this, my son. You are young, and have a clean page upon which to write. Let them know we seek reconciliation, that we seek an alliance. It is the only way we will survive. Unification is our only hope. You must convince them, Lukhamen."

"Yes, Father."

The wine sits, untouched.

---

It is still dark when the high priest arrives at the governor's mansion. The guard looks at Manut, who is lifting the wheeled chair from the sedan, and raises his hand, signaling him to stop.

"The governor is occupied, Your Excellency. There is no need to disembark."

"I am here on a matter of extreme importance," says the high priest.

"Everything is of extreme importance today, Your Excellency."

"I will not take more than a minute of the governor's time."

"He is not here."

"Where is he, then?"

"I cannot say, Sire."

"When will he return?"

"I cannot say, Sire."

"Please tell the governor that I was here."

———— ∞ ————

The high priest opens the curtains of his sedan chair as it bumps back along the river road. The sky is beginning to lighten, and across the river he can see the Valley of the Kings emerging from night's shadows. In the sky above the hills is a ribbon of violet, and he can see it now, set high into the side of a cliff: the place where twenty-six high priests of the Sa'at family are entombed. He lowers his gaze to the valley floor, where, in lovingly decorated tombs, sleep the ancients. A heavy weight is upon him.

*O Blessed Ones,* he prays, *abide with us, for before this day is over, your people will cry out to you in anguish.* He closes the curtains, covers his face with his hands, and weeps.

———— ∞ ————

The dawn's pink light and sand drifting on the air cloak the Christian Quarter in illusion, turning it into a dusty jewel, but all too soon the sun will lift the rose-colored veil and reveal its squalor and sorrow.

The streets are empty. It is quiet. Not a donkey brays, not a baby cries. The little church is shuttered. Lukhamen walks through the deserted labyrinth, ill at ease.

Out of nowhere, a figure runs toward him, stumbling and panicked. A ragged, bone-thin man falls, scrambles to his feet, runs past him, turns a corner, and is gone. In his wake are two Roman soldiers, swords drawn. They stop at each doorway, push aside ragged curtains with their swords, and peer inside. When they reach Lukhamen, they take in his clean linen robe, his hair, his demeanor, and pass him by. He is not whom they seek. They continue down the deserted street, methodically searching the hovels, one by one.

Lukhamen reaches the end of the narrow lane and steps into the open, where the grain fields begin. The sun blazes into his eyes, blinding him. He shuts them tight, and when he opens them again, he sees them.

They stand in measured rows like a macabre crop of scarecrows. At first, his mind does not grasp the scene before him: a hundred men hanging in agony, their faces contorted, their eyes wild with fear and pain. His legs take him toward them, closer and closer, until he is in the crowd at the edge of the field, held back by a string of Roman soldiers. He cannot take his eyes away from the hands and feet dripping blood, the red puddles forming on the blackened earth.

The air is hot and putrid. A strange humming noise emanates from the field. At first he thinks it is the wind, or locusts, but soon realizes it is coming from the crosses: a low, droning chorus of moans. Nausea overwhelms him.

A woman near him whispers, "Jesus Christ, have mercy," then falls against him. He catches her before she slides to the ground.

"Here, brother, let me help."

A young Christian priest bends down to lift her, and together he and Lukhamen carry her to the shade of a tree nearby, where other women are waiting with water to revive the fallen.

"Thank you, brother," says the priest. He looks at Lukhamen, his robe, his hair. "Are you a stranger here, then?"

"Yes, a stranger."

"Thank you for your help."

Lukhamen's gaze is drawn again to the field of crosses.

"They were arrested in the middle of the night by soldiers and taken to the prison," the young priest says in a low voice, "where they were accused of attacking a Roman caravan. They were dragged from their beds, condemned without a trial, and by dawn, they were crucified." His voice breaks. "They are only farmers, simple farmers."

"But why?" asks Lukhamen.

"They were the easiest to capture."

"But..."

"Do not try to understand. We are little more than prey here."

Lukhamen looks again at the crosses, then back to the young priest.

"Are you a priest of Jesus?" asks Lukhamen.

"Yes. And you, stranger?"

"I am Lukhamen, son of the High Priest of the Temple of Luxor."

The young man is startled.

"And a priest as well," Lukhamen adds.

The young priest finds his voice and stammers, "I…am Abba Philip."

"I came here to find you. I did not know about…this…"

"You came to find me?"

"Yes."

"It must be then, Lukhamen, son of the High Priest of the Temple of Luxor, that God has sent you here for a reason. Stay with us today. When the sun reaches its zenith, our people will die. We will have to bury them, and help their families. Stay with us. Help us."

The young man's eyes fill with tears. *Our people*, he had said. He takes Lukhamen by the arm and they walk back to stand with the crowd in the white-hot sun. Philip sinks to his knees and prays softly. As the sun climbs overhead, Lukhamen, who has never seen death, will come to know it intimately, at the feet of a hundred crosses.

Well away from Luxor, Lucenkep lays her head on the neck of the little donkey that is plodding along the river bank. Her eyes are red and stinging. Her throat aches. No matter how Mahda pleads with her, she cannot swallow anything but a little water.

She had held onto her mother's skirts and pleaded, but to no avail.

"Please do not send me away," she had begged.

"When you were but a babe," Mahda had told her, "I had dreams. It was the time of nightmares, just after your father died. Every time I closed my eyes, I would see men hanging from crosses. I knew this day would come. Christians are no longer safe here, Lucenkep. You must go down country, with my family."

"But what about you, Mother?" the girl had pleaded.

"I will stay with you for a while, then go back to Luxor and live with Alia in the rich woman's house. Alia has arranged for me to cook for her. No Roman will harm a member of Haraa's household." The girl did not understand and Mahda did not explain.

"And someone must take care of the lepers, Lucenkep."

———— ∞∞ ————

Lucenkep sways on the little donkey and falls in a delirium to the ground. Mahda lays her under a tree, hurries to the river, fills a jar with water, then bathes the girl's face, which is flushed with fever.

By nightfall, the fever is gone, and Mahda falls into a deep sleep. The little donkey stands guard while Lucenkep, awake and despairing, stares at the stars. A night bird sings, breaking her heart.

———— ∞∞ ————

She had waited in the crowd to see him pass, the new high priest, the one whom she saw for the first time on the barge, the one who would possess her heart forever. But at the moment her mother was to lift her into the tree, a man had come up, out of breath. The procession was approaching, and the crowd was noisy, and she could not hear what he was saying. She saw the look of horror on Alia's face, and turned to look at her mother. The same horror was in her mother's eyes, and she heard her say, "Come, Lucenkep. We must go home. Now!"

"Wait, Mother," she had answered. "Lift me up. He is coming!" But her mother was dragging her through the crowd, even as Simon's body was being dragged from the temple courtyard.

They travel all the next day until they reach a tiny village that has neither a well nor papyrus scrolls for Lucenkep to read.

———— ∞∞ ————

The wind moans behind the high hills, awakens the sleeping desert, lifts the sand and tosses it in turbulent, angry waves upon the air, blocking the sun and turning the last rays of the day into sudden night. Bending against the wind and biting sand, his face covered, Lukhamen fights his way home. At last, he falls against the door.

It is Aahmes who opens it and helps to steady him.

"Lukhamen!"

Alenna runs into the great hall.

"Lukhamen! Your father and I have been so worried!"

She spies his filthy clothes and turns to Manut, who has followed her.

"Manut! Prepare a bath. Make the water hot!"

She turns to him. "Go with Manut, Lukhamen. I will tell Father you are safe. Manut, dispose of these clothes." She puts a hand to Lukhamen's forehead. "You look ill. I shall call Sechmetna. What have you...?"

Then she sees the faraway stare. It sends a chill through her body.

"Where is Father?" His voice is hoarse.

"He is in his chamber. Have a bath first, and..."

"Excuse me, Mother." He walks past her.

---

In the high priest's chamber, sand beats against the shutters. Lanterns are lit against the darkness. He has not moved for two days, ever since the message came that Lukhamen would stay in the Christian Quarter until all who had been executed were buried.

Lukhamen enters and sinks onto the floor, at his father's feet.

Alenna, whose alarm is growing, kneels down beside him. "Lukhamen."

"I will take care of him, Alenna."

"He needs a bath."

"He needs wine, Alenna."

"But he may be ill, and he...*smells*."

"*Wine*, Alenna. Now!" His voice softens. "Please."

She leaves abruptly. Aahmes stands in the doorway.

"May I stay, Father?"

"Get a basin of water, Aahmes, and fetch a clean robe."

"Yes, Father."

Lukhamen's eyes are haunted, his face gaunt. A servant brings wine. The high priest pours it himself and hands it to Lukhamen.

"Drink."

Lukhamen drains his goblet, and the high priest fills it a second time.

"Again."

Aided by the brother whose hands are already gentle with the gift of healing, Lukhamen cleans himself of the worst of the blood and grime.

"One more drink, then you will lie in my bed. I shall watch over you tonight."

"Father…"

"Never mind, Lukhamen. There is time."

Lukhamen staggers to the bed. "Father…"

"Sleep, Lukhamen. It is time to sleep."

Lukhamen lies down and is at once unconscious.

"May I stay, Father?" Aahmes whispers.

The high priest nods, and the boy sits on the chaise longue, next to his father.

"Where has he been, Father?"

"Where none of us has ever been."

"Will he be all right?"

"Yes. He will be fine in the morning."

"The storm is awful tonight, is it not, Father?"

"Yes."

"Father?"

"Yes, Aahmes."

"When I am a doctor, I will heal your legs. I swear it." He moves closer to his father.

The high priest puts his arm around the boy, who falls asleep with his head on his father's chest. Lukhamen flails about on the bed, his hands covering his ears so as not to hear the mournful cries of the crucified that have followed him into his dream.

―◦◦◦―

Alenna, rigid with fury, sits in the tub that had been prepared for Lukhamen. Sand beats against the shutters.

"Cursed sand!"

With a wide arc of her arm, she lashes out and sweeps every bottle of oil and perfume from the table. The crash brings a servant girl running.

"Leave it!" Alenna barks.

The girl backs out of the room.

*Am I not mistress of my own house, then? By the gods, he is still my son!*

Her anger rises to a sharp crescendo. He has changed. He is autocratic now, self-possessed. In the early days, after the accident, the high priest had wanted to talk to her, touch her. She was at his side when the pain made him cry out, when it sent him reeling into the black tunnel. She had gone without sleep for days at a time. He had needed her. His eyes had held hers as if she were the source of life itself. Now that the pain is gone, he is distant, detached, and commanding. And now, even Aahmes is allowed to sleep at his side.

*Damn him, damn him, damn him!*

She thinks of Marcus.

*And damn you too, Marcus! How could you have done such a thing? Why? How stupid men are, how mean, arrogant, and stupid!* She climbs out of the tub, slips on the oil that has spilled on the floor, and falls. A sliver of glass lodges itself into her side.

"Semnut!"

The old woman appears with the servant girl, who immediately begins to pick up pieces of glass and wipe the oil from the floor. Semnut carefully removes the glass from Alenna's side and holds a towel to the wound. Then she holds her as she did when she was a baby.

"Quiet, now...it is all right, my lovely."

Alenna buries her face in the old woman's robe. They sit thus, on the floor, for a long time, Alenna holding onto her, Semnut cradling her head. Deep, throaty sobs convulse her. By the time Semnut dresses her wound and helps her to bed, Alenna's anger has all but exhausted itself. In its place is a dull ache and feeling of doom that creeps slowly into every quiet corner of her being.

# CHAPTER 46

*I looked into their crucified eyes. I felt their ventricles flood, then pulsate! And when they departed the earth, their life flowed back into me, and I began to see, and hear! I was aware of the sun's heat on the jasmine, insects so small as to be invisible, flitting on the surface of the glassy river, the brush of crepe flowers, lighter than air, on my face. That is what death had given me.*

It is barely dawn, but Lukhamen is bathed and dressed. One servant is stirring in the kitchen. Lukhamen retrieves a small pot of coffee, then quietly enters his father's room. The high priest is asleep on the chaise longue.

He walks softly through the chamber, into the garden, and makes his way along the tiled path. The gnarled trunks of the bougainvillea are thick with age. Their branches climb and cling to garden walls and hang over trellises that shade the walk. A breeze blows through the garden. A curtain of bright fuchsia rains down around him. Blossoms tumble along the ground and over a faded wooden soldier that was tossed onto the path by the night's storm. He picks it up and traces it with his fingers.

"How long have you been here?" he whispers to the little soldier.

Holding it in his hand, he continues to the birdcage at the center of the garden. It is just as he left it years ago, when he was still a child, a center of pastel-colored fury. The little birds are hungry as usual; they pick and peck at each other with furious little jabs.

"No one has changed, I see." They jump at the sound of his voice, and Lukahmen laughs out loud.

He closes his eyes, feels the sun rise into the garden, warming his face, then makes his way to the small couch at the far end, sets the coffee pot on the ground, and forgets it. Locusts awake and whirr softly, keeping him company. He closes his eyes and listens to the stridulating of tiny legs against wings. *How marvelous.*

"Sire." The servant has appeared magically, without sound. "Your father requests your presence."

Lukhamen rises slowly, not wanting to end the moment.

⎯⎯ ∞ ⎯⎯

"Good morning, Father."

"Lukhamen..."

"The garden is so beautiful this morning. You should see it, Father." Lukhamen bears no sign of the fatigue that crippled him the night before. He looks closely at his father, who is sitting in his wheeled chair.

"You are dressed, then, Father."

"I have been for some time."

"How long was I in the garden?"

"I believe the sun was not yet in the sky, Lukhamen." Lukhamen turns to gaze at the garden again, longingly.

"Lukhamen?"

"Yes, Father?"

"Is all well?"

"Yes, Father."

"Where is your mother?"

"Still sleeping, I imagine. And Aahmes is long gone, with Sechmetna. There is an outbreak of a rash among the children in the city. Some of them are quite ill, he said, with fevers."

"Will you come to the temple with me today?"

"Of course, Father."

"I thought you would be more...*tired*, Lukhamen."

"I slept deeply, Father."

"Did you sleep at all while you were at the Christian Quarter?"

"An hour or two here and there, like the rest of them. I slept in Philip's room."

"Philip?"

"The priest of Jesus."

"Tell me about him, Lukhamen."

"He is about my age."

"And what else?"

"He sleeps in a small room with a dirt floor."

"Go on..."

"He is strangely remarkable."

"How so...?"

"For his energy."

"Energy?"

"Yes. He was inexhaustible. I don't think he slept at all."

"Get my chair, Lukhamen. We will go to the temple. I want you to tell me everything on the way."

---

"May we stop here for a moment, please, Father?" Lukhamen turns his father's wheeled chair toward the river. The Valley of the Kings spreads before them on the other side. They are silent for a moment. "I was there once, Father."

"There, where the ancients sleep?"

"Yes, when I was a child. Khenti took me in a temple boat. It was when you were very ill. He told me he went there at times to be closer to *them*, the ones who sleep. It comforted him. He said he could feel their presence."

"And how did *you* feel there, Lukhamen?"

"Alone."

They are enveloped by the quiet. A small fishing boat comes into view. Its sail catches the wind. The little boat lists to the right and rides the river swiftly upstream. Lukhamen is loath to leave, but his father prevails. They press on.

"What was it like, Lukhamen, being among the Christians?"

"It is a place…where death is ever present, in every corner, a part of every thought and deed."

"It must be like living in a nightmare."

"There is also something beautiful about it."

"Beautiful?"

"It is difficult to explain. One feels Roman oppression there, Father, surely. But there is something else as well, something I can't describe."

"Go on."

"The Romans are …it's different there, Father. The people are treated like cattle. The Romans' cruelty is cold, detached, efficient. I have never seen anything like it. The worst of it is, the people the Romans crucified were innocent. The Christians say that those who attacked the Roman army escort were mercenaries from the desert. The men pulled from their homes in the middle of the night and crucified were simple farmers."

The high priest stares ahead at the temple coming into view.

"Amon, deliver us," he whispers into the wind.

---

Marcus, astride a white Arabian steed, inspects his troops. His son, dressed in a plain linen robe, rides behind him. The boy sits straight on his horse, as if he were born to it. They had dined together the night before, and Marcus had taken delight in his son's every aspect. He found the boy well-educated and conversant in Roman politics. That was to be expected, as the boy had grown up in the company of Petronia's father and other members of the Roman Senate, including his own father.

Marcus divined the boy's lack of interest in the depressing circumstances of his mother's life, and that her dismal personality and self-pity discouraged her son from wholeheartedly loving her. The boy is, however, uncommonly happy to be in his father's company. He is eager to learn, eager to become his father's son. Later, they sit in Marcus' office in the governor's mansion.

"There are two ways to become a soldier, Marcus," the governor says. "One graduates from a military academy, or one learns his profession in the field. How would you consider a career in the military?"

The boy is exultant. "It would be a dream come true, Father."

Marcus is not yet used to being called *Father*. It warms something inside of him. He smiles.

"Very well, then. You shall begin today."

The governor calls a centurion to him—a seasoned man in whom he has great trust—and places his son under his tutelage.

"The high priest is here, Your Excellency." A military aide has replaced the governor's Egyptian secretary.

"Show him in, please."

The high priest is wheeled into the room. The governor comes forward to greet him. "We shall have tea," the governor says, nodding toward his aide, who turns sharply on his heel and disappears. They wait in awkward silence until the tea is served and they are alone.

"Lukhamen, I—"

"This is difficult for us both, Marcus."

"I never thought it would come to this."

"Nor did I."

"I am sorry that I was not here to receive you on the day... you came."

"As am I, Marcus."

"Where shall we begin then?"

"You killed the wrong people, Marcus." The high priest places his tea on a nearby table.

"I see we shall not waste time on niceties. But then, we are in terrible times." Marcus turns, places his cup on his desk, turns again to look at the high priest. "There is always risk associated with the…containment of insurrection, Lukhamen. You know that."

"It was a precipitous act, Marcus, not well thought out."

"Are you to tell me how to *govern*, then?"

"I know something about these people, Marcus."

Marcus walks to the window and looks out, his back to the high priest. "You are no closer to *these people* than I am, Lukhamen."

"You insult me, Marcus."

Marcus turns abruptly. "Is this all you have to offer me, then?"

"What I have to offer you is this: The men who attacked the Roman entourage were not Egyptians. They were Arabian mercenaries, and if you had looked hard enough, you would have found them and the weapons they stole. You crucified innocent *farmers,* Marcus!"

"And you know this *how*, Lukhamen?"

"I know it. That is enough."

"No!" Marcus says in a loud voice, "That is *not* enough."

"Am I a *liar*, then, Marcus?"

"If what you say is true, those bold enough to try will think again before they attack my army, will they not, Lukhamen?"

"You killed a hundred innocent men to make *examples* of them?" The high priest's voice booms against the wall.

Anger echoes in the air now and makes the room closer, stifling. The governor steps back to the window.

"And now must I consult with a *priest* to decide what Rome shall do and what it shall not do?" His tone is menacing.

"I am more than a *priest*, Marcus, and you are forgetting something."

Marcus turns to face him. "And what is that?"

"The wheat, Marcus, the grain that feeds Rome and its armies. Without that, without the farmers to grow it, things…fall apart."

The governor smiles bitterly. "Are you *threatening* me, Lukhamen?"

"I am simply making a point."

"And that is…?"

"It is not wise to kill *your labor force*, Marcus."

"I cannot, I *will* not tolerate attacks upon soldiers of the Roman Empire, my wife, and my *son*, Lukhamen."

Now it is over. Marcus calls for the aide, who wheels the high priest to the door.

"Marcus?" he says at the threshold.

"Yes?"

"I am glad your wife and your son are safe."

"Thank you," says the governor.

The governor walks to his balcony and watches as Manut lifts the high priest from his chair and places him in the sedan. The old familiar pain fills his chest, tightens his jaw. He had loved this man's wife, he was sure he knew it, and yet he had been his friend.

Marcus sits down and puts his head in his hands. There had been no other course of action, no other choice. The Roman response to insurrection was prescribed long ago. He would ascribe to it or be recalled. He walks to the wall and pounds his fist into it, making a hole the size of a melon. When he has recovered his composure, he summons his aide.

"By tomorrow night I want my wife installed in a residence. See to it that it is proper, secured, and at some distance from the governor's mansion. And have the centurion report to me at once."

*There is only Marcus now. He is all that is left to me.*

Petronia watches bitterly from an upstairs window as her things are loaded onto a military conveyance drawn by two black horses, their manes shining in the sun. The conversation with her husband concerning her living quarters had been brief. He had offered the excuse that since the crucifixions, the governor's mansion was a target for reprisals, and no longer safe. It was to be a fort, not suitable for civilian occupation. She had not believed him for an instant.

The news travels quickly. Haraa is dining alone when a servant whispers it into her ear. She smiles a bitter little smile, and replenishes her glass of wine.

# CHAPTER 47

—⊗⊗⊗—

MY FRIEND JOHN CALLS ME one day, out of the blue. "Helen," he says, "the National Institute of Standards and Technology is creating a new post that will be part of the Foreign Commercial Service. It will put a standards expert inside the United States Mission to the European Union in Brussels. You'd be perfect for it."

"Me?"

"Sure," he says. "You're a standards expert, you're on top of the new European Union standards policies, and you're an independent agent. You'll qualify without question."

"John," I say, "This is really exciting. Let me talk it over with Bill and get back to you."

"Tell Bill you'll have diplomatic status, and a diplomatic title. He'll be able to come with you, of course."

"Okay," I say. "Thank you, John, for thinking of me."

If I take this post, I will be the first American in my field to be so honored.

Technical standards, long considered a marginal issue by politicians and trade officials, are now, after years of effort by everyone in my field, finally recognized as a crucial element of international trade. This new post is a sign of the times, and it sends a message to our most powerful trading partner, the European Union.

I'm stunned.

—⊗⊗⊗—

"This is the opportunity of a lifetime," Bill says. "It will change your career in ways you can't imagine."

I move cautiously to the next step, with one thing always on my mind—my mother, whose Alzheimer's disease is full blown.

"Come in for an interview," John says. "It's not a commitment."

"We're looking at a few other candidates," the Commerce Department official—my third interviewer— is saying, "but you are definitely on the short list. This is an important position. No one understands yet how the European Union's new standards system is going to affect American exports. You would be our person on the ground. You would also be an adviser to the Ambassador and the other mission staff."

The thought of serving my country fills me with enormous pride, but in the back of my head is always my mother. *Would they let her come with me?*

———— ⚬⚬⚬ ————

I had to learn once more that there is a divine order to things, and that Bill and I, whether we wanted to or not, would have to turn our wills and our lives over to the care of God.

Bill, who had a history of polyps on his colon, was undergoing a routine rectal examination when he heard the doctor say, "Oh, oh." He told me when he came home that day and added, "This can't be good."

I didn't dare think about it until it was time to go back for the results of the biopsy.

———— ⚬⚬⚬ ————

The doctor is quick and to the point.

"I'm sorry, but it's colorectal cancer."

We sit stone-still in the office that has suddenly become unnaturally bright and airless.

"I'll leave you two alone for a moment," he says, and walks out. We sit there, staring at his empty chair.

Finally, I look at Bill and manage to say the only thing that comes into my mind: "What do you want?"

"I want you to take that job in Brussels," he says. "If I'm going to die, I'd like to see Europe."

"Okay," I say.

And then he smiles. "And if I'm going to live, I want to see Europe."

"Okay," I say.

Bill gathers his children around him and involves them in the strategy of his treatment. It is the beginning of a long summer.

———— ❦ ————

In a few weeks, John calls. "Congratulations," he says. "You've got the job. You should be ready to leave for Europe sometime this fall. By that time, Bill should be fine."

"Thank you, John," I say, surprised at how quickly the embassy appointment has lost its gloss. So much more is at stake now.

———— ❦ ————

The summer is filled with Bill's chemotherapy, radiation, and my mother's decline. And work. I must finish all my projects so that I can shut down my consulting business.

Bill sleeps long hours after chemotherapy, but suffers from the burns of radiation. We go to cancer support meetings, where patients and caregivers teach me not to nag Bill about eating candy. "But he needs good food to build up his strength," I protest. "Back off," they tell me. "He'll eat better when he's ready."

———— ❦ ————

The FBI begins an investigative process that will hopefully result in a top secret clearance for me, a prerequisite for working in the embassy. Agents interview members of my family, my colleagues, my neighbors, and Bill. They show up unannounced on my doorstep one morning and politely ask me to leave the house while they interview him. If I am an enemy of the state, my husband has the right to inform them in privacy.

I must also appear in person at the State Department to undergo an interview concerning the state of my sobriety. I keep my alcoholism and recovery out of my professional life. I believe in the principle of anonymity and I see no need to burden my clients with information they don't need or want. But this is the FBI. They've asked and I've answered truthfully.

My interview goes well. I have been sober for fifteen years, and the interviewer, who is in recovery himself, is aloof until I tell him I'm married to Bill, whom he has known for twenty-four years in our recovery program. No other reference is needed.

The medical clearance does not go so well. The State Department doctor looks at the results of my blood tests and says," What's going on in your life?"

"Pardon me?" I say.

"What's going on in your life that's got you so stressed?"

"Well, my husband has cancer, my mother has Alzheimer's disease, and I'm working overtime to shut down my business to move overseas. Other than that, everything's fine." I am trying to be funny. She isn't.

She says, "Well, your cholesterol is over 300 and you're about to have a stroke."

"What?"

"I want you to see a cardiologist right away. In the meantime, I'm going to give you a prescription to see if we can't get that cholesterol down. But you're not going overseas until this improves."

I try to make an appointment with a cardiologist, but since I am not having a heart attack, it will be three weeks before I can see him—or anybody. A friend recommends an acupuncturist—a Chinese doctor named Dr. Shu, who has an office in Georgetown.

Dr. Shu is tiny, elfin, and magical. She walks with a marked limp—a childhood accident, she tells me. The failure to repair her leg was her motivation for becoming a doctor. In China, she practiced at the equivalent of the National

Institutes of Health. She talks to me for a full hour, exploring my lifestyle and explaining the techniques and benefits of acupuncture. High cholesterol like mine, related to stress, is imminently treatable, she says.

She is gentle and comforting. I lie down on her table with some trepidation, but I'm motivated. According to the State Department doctor, I'm in considerable peril. She inserts tiny needles into my skin that are over certain meridian points in my body. I expect it to hurt, but it doesn't. In one or two places, though, I feel a tiny electric shock as she twirls the needle into the skin. This is supposed to release my *qi,* or energy, and allow it to flow through my body. When she is finished, she turns down the lights and leaves the room, telling me she will return in a few minutes. I sink immediately into the deepest sleep I've had in months. I get up from the table feeling like I've been on vacation.

In a few weeks, the acupuncture and the statin drug have my cholesterol down and finally, a cardiologist gives me the okay to go abroad.

I stay with the acupuncture because it helps my anxiety. Underlying everything in my life is fear. I am afraid that Bill's treatment will not be successful, that he is going to die. I am afraid to leave my mother, afraid she will die before I can come back to see her. I am afraid to enter the world of diplomacy, a field with skills I know nothing about. I am afraid of everything.

---

My mother reaches another low. Staying alone now is too frightening for her, and she cannot sleep at night. I bring her home with me and make a bed for her in the sunroom. During the day, she sits in a winged back chair in my living room, a blanket covering her knees. Her conversations have all but ceased. She answers direct questions, but that is the extent of my communication with her. I hire a caregiver to stay with her when I take Bill to chemotherapy and radiation, but she is frightened of strangers, and I hate leaving her. Finally, she takes to her bed and stays there most of the time. She must be bathed and taken up a flight of stairs to the bathroom, a harrowing experience for both of us.

My house is a center of crisis management. I try to devise meals to tempt Bill and my mother, neither of whom can eat heartily. Bill's chemotherapy and radiation treatments are sad and frightening. He never complains, but he is so sick. My mother's doctor appointments are disheartening. She is paranoid and difficult to maneuver, and there is no optimistic outlook for her.

The things Bill used to do, like paying the bills, or the laundry, and the grocery shopping, I now do alone. I miss his company, his hope. And my level of exhaustion is increasing.

———— ✺ ————

One night, after a particularly harrowing day, Bill and Mama are at the dining room table, waiting for dinner. They're both weak and would prefer to be lying down, but they're there to make things easier for me.

I look down at what I've served them. It's awful: beans out of a can over rice. It looks dry and unappetizing. They sit there, looking at it and saying nothing. I feel terrible. I open my mouth to say something, but Bill beats me to it.

Looking at my mother he says, "Don't make her mad, Mama. She's all we've got."

We look around at each other and burst into laughter. We laugh and laugh and laugh. Tears are running down my mother's face. I haven't seen her laugh like this in a long time.

I know that I'm worn out, but I look at these two and realize what a gift they are to me, what a privilege it is to be with them now, at this time in their lives.

Later, we eat our delivery pizza, enjoying each other's company, and I thank the Universe for this moment, which will never come again.

———— ✺ ————

I have long talks with my brothers, Eddie and Johnny, and my aunt, my mother's sister. They, too, are proud that I will be in my country's service and they are willing to help me. Take the job, they say to me. You take care of Bill. We'll take care of Mama.

But this is my mother. I can't let go of her.

———∞∞∞———

I struggle through my days, while the machinery of government grinds slowly, but inexorably forward. I am notified that I have been granted a top secret clearance. A mountain of paperwork has been completed at the Department of Commerce and at the Department of State. The mission in Brussels is waiting for me.

I have finished all my projects and notified my clients that I am going abroad and that I can accept no more work. And once again, the Universe moves its own way.

I am notified that there has been a government-wide freeze on hiring. I cannot assume my post, and I cannot accept any more clients. I am neither there nor here, and I have lost all income. There is a budget crisis, and my fate is in the hands of the United States Congress.

In the confusion and anxiety of it all, I lose sight of what I know is true: that there is a reason for everything. In hindsight, I can see now how that time was needed. Bill had time to complete his chemotherapy and radiation, and my mother had time to sink into a world of dreams.

# CHAPTER 48

WHEN I AM AT THE end of my savings, the government, now replete with funds, lifts the freeze. I am notified that I am an employee of the federal government. I am ordered to the State Department's Foreign Service Institute for a crash course, and after that, I am to report to the United States Mission to the European Union in Brussels.

All I can think about is my mother, and the days before she went into a nursing home.

"I don't think I'm going to make it." My mother is in my sunroom on the first floor, curled up in a fetal position on my foldout couch.

"Yes, you will, Mama," I say to her.

I put my hand on her forehead, as she did for me when I was a child and sick with measles. "You're going to be all right." She lets me have my lie.

She changes every day; her light is going out in small spurts. My daughter Niki comes to visit and gives her a massage. Niki is patient, gentle, and sweet with her. Mama is docile, unresisting.

I can't lift her any more, and I can't get her to the only bathroom in my house, which is on the second floor. She's miserable and I'm exhausted. I cry at night.

Sitting in my wingback chair, a blanket over her knees, looking up at me with eyes that are bright like a bird's, she says the unthinkable one day: "It's all right if I have to go to a nursing home."

I am sick at heart that she has said this, and that she has had to tolerate my unskilled, awkward care. It's been so difficult for her. And now, in a rare moment of lucidity, my mother is her old self again, the comforter, telling me not to be afraid of the dark.

---

The supervisor of the nursing home leads me through a maze, promising me that my mother will be happy in her clean, bland version of hell. When the day comes, I am choked with tears and remorse. But my mother seems relieved. She knows she is sick, and it seems like a hospital to her, where she will have her own room, her own bathroom, and a staff to look after her. Her acceptance breaks my heart. The staff does not let me linger.

I sit in my sunroom, on the couch that is now folded up. I wonder if she is cold, if someone has covered her with a blanket. The night is long and I cannot stop weeping.

I cannot wait to see her the next day. I am greeted by two round, ebony women in brightly colored smocks. They have bathed her and fed her and are now adjusting her pillow, talking to her in sweet, lilting Caribbean accents. They are doing for her what I cannot. I see that now. It doesn't help.

One day, a fever sends her to the hospital. I sit by her bed, coaxing her to eat. All of a sudden, she sits up higher in bed and stares at the chair in the corner.

"Who is that man over there?" she asks.

"What man, Mama?"

"Oh, that's my brother, John!" she says, as if I should have known. She settles back on her pillow, satisfied. I turn to look at the empty chair. Uncle John has been gone for many years. Mama's spirits have come to comfort her. But I don't want to give her to them.

---

"Mama, do you know who I am?" I say. She is sitting in a chair in her nursing home room. She is small, like a doll. She does not look directly at me.

"You are Helen Jean," she says, saying both my names.

My brother Eddie and I stay with her a long time, talking mostly to each other, trying to stave off my goodbye. Mama is not interested in our conversation. At last, I have to go. I can't think of what to say.

"Of all the Tindal girls, Mama," I blurt out, speaking of her sisters, "you were the prettiest one."

My brother's eyes are bright with tears.

There was a deep rivalry among those five young, beautiful Southern belles. Mama was the oldest, and always said she never felt pretty beside them. She gives no indication she has heard. One of her sisters is left. She and my brothers will look after her.

"I have to go now," I say, "but I'll be back." She stares ahead. I touch her hair as I walk by. I know that I will never see her again. Not on this side.

She was always there for me. She sat by me and held my hand at Eddie's funeral, and I fainted onto her shoulder. I loved her beyond all measure, and she loved me more. And I was leaving her. I told myself that she didn't understand that I was leaving, but that changed nothing. I left her in her final days, and guilt would follow me all the rest of mine.

The next day, Bill, still weak and pale from chemotherapy and radiation, held the Bible as I was sworn in.

———— ∞ ————

The phone call came four months after my arrival in Brussels. "You need to come home now," my brother said. The State Department cut through the red tape and put me on the next plane leaving Brussels. My mother died as I was somewhere over the Atlantic.

Like my father, she slipped away when I wasn't there. When I saw her at the funeral home, she was dressed in the beautiful pink silk dress I had chosen for her. Her hair and makeup were elegant and flawless. She really was the prettiest of them all.

———— ∞ ————

Back in Brussels, the pressure of embassy life and the endless work pushes my grief and guilt into the background. Rene, a colleague, and I are the only ones working one cold, dark night as I stepped out of my office to let the cleaning crew do its job. Ten minutes later, walking back, I notice a sweet, overpowering aroma.

"My goodness," I say, walking by Rene's office, "the cleaning people must be using something different."

"Yes," he says, "It's really strong."

I walk into my office and I don't see it at first: a large plant, which I'd inherited from the previous occupant, is blooming. I was vaguely aware of several bulb-like protrusions forming when I returned from my mother's funeral, and I'd thought nothing of them. But here in my office, the plant is flowering in February, in cold, dark, rainy Brussels, at nine o'clock at night, smelling like summertime in South Carolina.

"It's coming from in here," I call out to Rene.

"What is it?" he says.

"It's my mother," I say. "It's my mother," I whisper.

When my mother was a child in South Carolina, the neighbors would gather on my grandmother's porch to watch her night-blooming cereus give forth one large, white flower, which it did one night a year, close to Christmas. The Southerners called the plant "Christ in the Cradle." When my grandmother died, the night-blooming cereus came to Philadelphia with my mother, and I grew up with it. The ancient plant was mine now. When I moved to Brussels, I left it in Virginia, in my brother's keeping. It had not bloomed since it left South Carolina.

I look again at the plant in my office. I do not know its name, but against the dark window, it is bright with blossoms, white and fragrant in the winter night, a gift from my mother. She had found a way to let me know that she was happy and safe. In the days that follow, the blossoms fade away. She is still my mother, still loving me and wanting me to be happy.

# CHAPTER 49

&#10086;

☥

IN THE DARKENED SANCTUARY, LUKHAMEN kneels before the great god Amon. Shadows flicker on the highly polished black granite statue, reflecting flames from the altar lamp that burns perpetually. The god of heaven and earth gazes ahead, in pleated kilt, Usekh collar, and a feathered crown. One foot is slightly in front of the other. The statue is largely intact, as it was when it fell over his father, shielding him from falling stones and certain death.

He has come to pray, but thoughts of the past few days come unbidden. He has stood at the foot of one hundred crosses; he has looked into the face of death. He has been among the grieving, has held them in his arms as they wept. And yet, he was uplifted.

He raises his eyes to the impassive face above. *Lord of Creation, God of Light and Darkness, hear the prayer of your servant. Lord of Heaven and Earth, Lord of Life, look down upon me; hear my supplication. Sanctify me, Lord Amon, fill me with your light.*

When the field of horror was at last quiet, the Romans had taken down the crosses, removed the nails from blood-caked hands and feet, and left the Egyptians with their dead. When the digging was finished, the families placed their dead in fetal positions in a mass grave and covered them with earth, then gathered near the well in the square.

They had shared their meager meal with him, making sure his bowl had tiny pieces of meat floating in the thin gruel, while they went without. They would not eat at all until he had had enough. He had to stop himself, because the thin gruel could not satisfy his hunger.

He sat with them in the waning light, and they touched his arm or took his hand when they spoke to him. They looked deeply into his eyes and smiled at him through their tears. A child leaned against him, then laid a little head in his lap. They spoke softly, heads inclined toward one another, so as not to be overheard by Roman soldiers who patrolled the darkening streets. Often, they were silent and still.

*Lord God Amon, God of all Creation, God of Light and Life, hear my prayer. Hear my supplication, Lord of Light, Lord of Heaven and Earth.*

And he had touched them. He had wiped their tears, cradled their children. He had held old women who wept for their sons, put his arm around the shoulders of young boys who would never again know a father's embrace. Some had taken to their beds, and he entered their hovels, and put his hands on their fevered brows.

"Excuse me, Your Excellency." Khenti says from behind him. Your father wishes to speak with you."

In the courtyard, the high priest sits in the shade of one of the great statues of Ramses.

"Ah, Lukhamen."

"Yes, Father."

"Tell me. Who will plant the fields in the place of the men who died?"

"The women and children. It has been decreed that they will produce the same share as before."

"But that is impossible. Women and children cannot produce the same share."

"Certainly not if they are hungry, Father."

"Gods of Egypt! How did we become so distant from our people?" The high priest looks at his son, and as if he has read his mind, he asks, "What must we do?"

"I would like your permission, Father, to give them the sacrificial animals we bury."

"We are not allowed to eat them, Lukhamen."

"*We* are not allowed to eat them, Father, but surely we can give them to hungry women and children."

"You are right. What else?"

"Let me go back."

Khenti opens his mouth to speak, then thinks better of it.

"Very well, Lukhamen. Go. Do what you can. They are our people, even though they follow this Christian God. How did we did not comprehend the magnitude, the invasiveness of this religion of the poor? We kept to ourselves and our temples and they were lost to us. When the Romans left us alone, the better to appease them…oh gods of Egypt, as if it mattered, as if it made their lives easier, we forgot about them. We have meant so little to them. We have done so little for them. But we must change all that now. They are Egyptians, and we are all under the hard hand of Rome. Build a bridge to them."

"Yes, Father."

---

The tent is crowded, hot, musty, reeking with the rancid odor of men who have ridden their horses to lather. They are hard men, dangerous men, lone men who know nothing of the gentle comfort of family and friends. They are scarred, dulled men, wanted criminals, renegades who live on the edges of civilization and roam the desert like wolves. When there are no victims upon whom to prey, they prey upon one another. They kill without motive or premeditation. Killing for them is the feral, mindless response to rage, the rage of the powerless and oppressed.

"Do you think we are *women*?" roars the largest of them.

"No," Antonious whimpers. "I am simply telling you that with the grain we can buy more weapons."

"You think we are *merchants*, then?"

"No, no. I will arrange to have it sold. I just want you to take it."

A roar of laughter fills the ragged tent.

"Listen, men! Antonious wants us to steal grain from women and children."

Another roar of laughter, and a skin of wine is passed around, to celebrate this cowardly, idiotic thought.

"The plan is to discredit the governor, and if we decrease the grain supply, the Romans…"

"What do we care of Romans?" The big one raises his goblet in the air and passes it over the heads of the others. "What do we care of the governor? If we want weapons, we *take* them. We care nothing for Romans."

This inspires another roar of laughter.

"You must not think the governor will not take reprisals against those who attack his army," says Antonious. "You must stay low for a while. No more attacks. But stealing grain is another matter. He will blame the Christians," says Antonious, with a weak smile that fails to hide his fear.

"He has already blamed the Christians, Antonious, or haven't you heard?"

The laughter rings out again, this time more raucously.

"I must go. The governor's wife does not like to be left alone."

"Just let us know when and where we strike next, Antonious."

The big one inches close to his face. Antonious feels sick to his stomach. He is overcome by the smell of sweat, sour wine, and danger.

The man grabs Antonious's robe and pulls him closer. The bloodshot eyes narrow.

"That's all you have to do, Antonious. Just tell us when and where."

"I've got to go."

Antonious feels the sweat trickle down his back. The big one releases him, and Antonious stumbles backwards.

"I must go," he whispers again, and backs out of the tent.

Outside, a ways from the tent, he hears the raucous laughter again, and feels his stomach lurch.

He rides his horse hard, beating him unmercifully. *Stupid, stupid idiots! Idiots!* He needs a drink. Badly.

———⊗———

"*Lepers?* Did you say *lepers?*"

"Yes, Madam."

Antonious has foregone drink for a bath, and is seated at Petronia's table. In Rome, she would not have allowed a bodyguard to sit at her table, but in this godforsaken outpost there is no protocol, and her choices are to have dinner with him or dine alone. She has dined alone far too many times in her life.

"He allows them in the city?"

"Actually, they live in their own compound, on the edge of this...city, if you can call it that."

A servant starts to pour wine into Antonious's goblet, but he stops him.

"No wine, Antonious? It is Roman."

"Thank you, Madam. I never drink on duty."

"But you are not on duty now, Antonious."

"I am always on duty, Madam."

She smiles a quick little smile.

"So. The lepers are confined to their quarter."

"Well, not exactly, Madam."

"Not exactly?"

"I mean they are not quarantined until their leprosy is...advanced."

"Ugh..." She shudders.

Antonious reaches for a second helping of grilled lamb. "Yes, one has to be on one's guard every moment in this...place, Madam. One can pass a leper in the marketplace and not even know it."

"But the governor is responsible for conditions in the city, is he not?"

"Yes, Madam, but the governor can only do what he can do."

"Meaning what?"

"The governor is law here, Madam, but he is not always in control, if you know what I mean."

"No, I don't know what you mean, Antonious."

"The previous governor was murdered. He was a wonderful man."

"There were rumors in Rome..."

"He was murdered, Madam."

"No one is safe here, are they?"

"There is no need for *you* to worry, my lady. I will stand between you and anyone who tries to harm you. You have my pledge."

"Thank you, Antonious."

He lets a moment pass. "The governor was the last to see him alive, you know."

"Marcus?"

"Yes. It is a wonder he was not murdered, too."

"You say my husband was the last to see him alive?"

"Yes, Madam."

They eat in silence for a while.

"What kind of a governor is my husband, Antonious?"

"A fine governor, Madam. A fine governor." A servant heaps more rice onto Antonious' plate. "Only…"

"Only what?"

"Oh, it is nothing."

"*What*, Antonious?"

"There are people who say he is too close to the Egyptians, that before you came he was too lenient…too… *friendly* with them."

Antonious opens a pomegranate with his knife.

"*Friendly?*"

"The previous governor kept to himself. He was strictly Roman in every respect, and nothing untoward ever happened in those days." Antonious heaves a deep sigh. "And his wife, a lovely woman, was always at his side. Until she died, that is."

"What do you mean by *friendly*, Antonious?"

"Perhaps that was a bad choice of words, Madam."

"Does he sleep with Egyptian women?"

Antonious chokes on a mouthful of pomegranate seeds.

"I have known him a long time, Antonious. There is no need to be delicate."

"Oh, no, Madam. Just one. I mean——" Antonious stammers.

"So, he has had a servant woman?"

"No, Madam. She is quite rich."

"*Rich?*"

"My apologies, Madam. I have said far too much."

"He allows them to be *rich?*"

"I am sorry. It has not been our policy to confiscate the property of the upper class. They help keep the others in control. They have had quite a proud..."

"I don't care *what* they have had, Antonious. That is *outrageous!*"

Antonious lets it all sink in; then, wiping his mouth with his sleeve, he stands.

"Thank you, Madam, for a lovely dinner. If you will excuse me, I will see to your night guards. We shall post two outside your bedroom door and two at the entrance to the residence. I shall be in the room next to yours. You have nothing to fear, Madam."

She is too possessed by fury to answer him. It keeps her from sleep. Finally, in the hours before daybreak, she writes a letter to her father.

# CHAPTER 50

He had stayed with them in the square until the moon rose. He had drunk their watery tea and sat, enthralled, as they whispered the secrets of their Living God into the silvery night air. The stories were strange and wonderful, but it was the rapture that caught him—the look in their eyes, the gentleness of their speech, when they spoke of…Him. It was the joy in the face of unspeakable poverty and death that moved him. It was incongruent; yet he felt the joy, understood the paradox.

His mother was waiting for him.

"Lukhamen."

"Good evening, Mother."

"Have you eaten, then?"

"Yes, Mother."

"And what did you have for your dinner, my love?"

"Soup, Mother."

"Come. We will sit together."

They sat at the dining table in the great hall. A servant brought him lamb and vegetables, cheese, and sweet cakes. In spite of himself, he ate it all. Afterwards, they sat over coffee.

"What is it like where you go, Lukhamen?"

"The people are poor, Mother."

"And what do you do there?"

"Today I brought them food and carried them a message from Father. I told them he interceded for them with the governor."

"Your father went to see Marcus?"

"Yes, Mother."

"Marcus is a barbarian," she says acidly.

Lukhamen holds his silence.

"More coffee, my love?"

"Thank you, Mother."

"We must talk, Lukhamen, about your wedding."

He has not expected this.

"Haraa and I have decided that we do not have to wait two years until Femi is fifteen. You can be married now and wait until she is fifteen to consummate the marriage."

Lukhamen is caught off-guard.

"Why now, Mother?"

She takes a sip of coffee, places the cup on the table. "There are any number of reasons. For one, we should like to consolidate the fortunes of our families. Our relationship with the governor has changed drastically, and Haraa no longer feels that her fortune is safe. Incorporated into that of the Sa'at family, it is less likely to be confiscated by the Romans. I agree."

"Oh."

"Haraa will provide a house for you, and a staff, and a chaperone for Femi, until she comes of age. It will be a cheerful household, Lukhamen, a household of young people. You will be able to act your age, enjoy a social life. This can be a gloomy house, sometimes. Ask your brother. He spends almost every waking moment in Haraa's house."

Lukhamen is silent for a while. "And Father? What does he think?"

Alenna's eyes flash, and her cheeks color, but she holds herself in check and her voice is steady and cool when she replies. "I do not burden your Father with household matters or wedding plans, Lukhamen. He has enough responsibility as it is."

"What is it you would like me to do, Mother?"

"Tomorrow night we shall dine with Haraa and Femi. It is time you got to know them a little better."

"But Mother—"

"We need to do this, Lukhamen."

"Yes, Mother."

She stands and kisses him on the top of his head.

"Goodnight, my love."

"Goodnight, Mother."

Lukhamen walks into the garden from the kitchen so as not to disturb his father, who is sleeping in the next room. He stands in the moonlight, watching the shadows it casts on the tiled pathways, and thinks of the pitifully thin boy standing next to the well, holding his precious bowl of soup—a thick broth with bits of temple lamb floating on top. Before he lifted the bowl to his mouth, the boy had smiled at him. He remembers the movement in his heart at that smile, the first sign of inner stirrings since he left Luxor and his childhood.

"I have never known hunger," he whispers to himself in the moonlight, "and they have never known anything else." Something in him awakens, reaches out to them. The loneliness in his heart dissipates. It floats away, like a cloud.

—————⚬∞⚬—————

"Alenna!"

The voice of her husband reverberates throughout the house.

"What is it?" She enters, breathless. "You have not touched your breakfast, Lukhamen. Are you ill?"

"Alenna, sit down, please."

"What is it, my love?" She comes closer, alarmed.

"I am...*disturbed*, Alenna."

"What is it that disturbs you?" Her voice is cold. He knows.

His face is flushed. His hands grip the arms of his rolling chair.

"Alenna." He struggles for composure. "Alenna, I should like to talk to you about the timing of Lukhamen's wedding."

"You need not worry about it, my love. I shall take care of everything."

"Alenna," he begins again, gathering all his patience. "We are living in very difficult times."

"Yes, my love, I know," she answers. "That is exactly why I do not trouble you with domestic matters."

He clears his throat. "Lukhamen is not a *domestic matter*, Alenna. He is a member of my temple, my successor, and at present, my emissary to our less fortunate brothers."

"And what, may I ask," her voice has lost all its lightness, "does that have to do with his wedding?"

"What does it have to do with his *wedding?*" he thunders.

"You do not have to raise your voice, Lukhamen," she says quietly.

"I'll tell you what it has to do with his *wedding*, Alenna."

She stands and turns her back to him. "I shall come back when you are in control of yourself."

She is in the corridor leading to the kitchen when she hears him call her. She walks back slowly, enters regally, sits down, and faces him.

"You are right. I had no cause to raise my voice."

"Thank you." She settles comfortably into the chair.

He takes a deep breath. "As I said, Alenna, we are living in difficult times, perhaps the most difficult of our generation."

"I know that, Lukhamen. That is precisely why we need a little happiness in this family."

"What I am trying to tell you is that what happens to our people now, to us, depends greatly on how we handle the situation. I need him, Alenna. I need him to be my right hand, to be my legs, to be my eyes. He is my emissary. His job is difficult and will require all his courage and strength."

"But a wife, a home, would only help him. It would take nothing from you, Lukhamen."

"It would take him out of my house."

"You took him out of *my* house when it suited you."

A curtain of icy silence drops between them.

Finally, he speaks.

"I will have all of Haraa's assets transferred to the temple. She will not own anything legally, not even the house in which she lives. She will be allotted funds as she requests them, from her own account, managed for her by the temple. I will protect her, Alenna. There is no need to wed our children before their time. By the mercy of Almighty Amon, our crisis will be over at some point and Lukhamen can settle into a normal life. I want him to be married, just not now."

She stands, filled with rage. Her eyes brim with tears, and her voice quavers.

"When he was nine, you took him from me. He was sent into exile for twelve years—twelve long, precious years. I missed every year, every hour of his childhood. My little boy left and never returned. You gave him to your priests! I was not there to hold him, to soothe his brow when he was sick. I was not there when he cried for me in the night." She is crying openly now.

"I lost him, Lukhamen. A man was returned to me; my little boy was gone forever. Now you send him into the company of squatters, slaves who live in filth—vulgar people, filled with every manner of disease. You endanger his life and dictate his every thought." Her voice rises.

"You took my *son* from me, Lukhamen. It broke my heart. His life among the loveless priests you sent him to made him a loveless child, a loveless man. If I do not help him, he will become like *you*, Lukhamen—loveless, bitter, and cold. But hear me, this will not happen! I will not permit it!"

She is standing at her full height before him, fists clenched, shaking with rage, tears pouring down her face. The only sound in the room for a long time is of her muffled weeping.

"I took your son *and* your husband, Alenna." His words stop her, and she looks at him. "Many nights I have lain awake, wondering when you would leave me, or when you would go to the arms of another man."

"Lukhamen."

"I know you have not, Alenna. I cannot fathom *why* you have not."

"I…"

"I would not have blamed you. How tragic, how unfair is it that the most beautiful woman in all of Luxor sleeps alone in the prime of her life? What a travesty!" He turns his chair around to face the garden so that she does not see his tears.

"Lukhamen, I did not mean…"

"I suppose I have grown hard. I needed to find a way to survive. In the end, though, I could not have lived without you." His voice is a whisper. "I *would* not have lived without you."

She goes to him. He wraps his arms around her waist and buries his face in her robe. She strokes his hair.

"I shall not deprive him of love, Alenna," he whispers. "In the end, it may be all that we shall have."

---

The priests from the temples of Karnak, Philae, and Edfu are gathered in the inner courtyard of the Temple of Amon. Karnak, the larger of Luxor's temples, is watched more closely. It is more open, and easier for Roman ears to hear their discourses. The high priest is the first to speak.

"The governor has declared a curfew on the citizens of Luxor," he begins. "No one is allowed on the streets after sunset, except those on official business. The taverns are closed, and military guards patrolling the streets have been doubled. The atmosphere here is one of tension and suspicion. Privacy is difficult to come by, practically impossible, even here in this courtyard. I therefore suggest that we depart from the tradition of holding our convocation in Luxor and move, with caution and in small groups, to the Temple at Edfu, where we may speak more freely."

A murmur of approval emanates from the crowd.

"We must decide our future, the future of our families. We are now living in a new era, a frightening era, and we must form a reasonable, unified position to present to the governor. We are descendants of royalty and are, after all, still a force to be reckoned with. This governor is well aware that our presence is a stabilizing force among the people; we are the last visible remnants of Egypt's greatness. In spite of his ill-advised and cruel act of reprisal, we must see to it that he is not in danger of being replaced by a…less…*informed* administrator. We are in a delicate position, my brothers. Every move we make must be the right one."

Speaker after speaker follows his train of thought, and in the end, they have reached a consensus. They will move the convocation to a more remote location.

That night, the first small boat, containing six priests, leaves from the dock of the Temple of Luxor.

The high priest, accompanied by his eldest son, is on the second boat to Edfu when the edict arrives from Rome. It is written under the seal of Petronia's father, the most powerful Roman senator. It orders the immediate confiscation of all Egyptian property and contains a mild rebuke to the governor. Within the hour, Marcus also receives a letter from his wife, saying the residence he has provided for her is not adequate and that she has selected another—one more suitable to the wife of the Governor of Luxor and Thebes. It is Haraa's house. But it is to Alenna that Marcus goes.

She is sitting in the garden when Manut announces him. She is about to say that she will not receive him when he appears before her. She stands. He has not seen her for a long time. He drinks in the dark hair, the eyes that seem to see his soul.

"Alenna."

She does not answer, nor does she ask for tea to be brought.

"Please leave us," he says to Manut.

Manut looks to Alenna and she nods. He leaves and they are alone.

"I must speak with you, Alenna. Please do not refuse me."

"And what is the nature of your call, Your Excellency?" Her voice is like ice.

"I have been told that Lukhamen is away."

"Yes. He is holding his convocation in a...safer place."

"He has never been in danger, Alenna. Nor have you. I would protect you with my life." His voice breaks. "You know that."

She does not reply.

"I must get a message to him."

His tone alarms her and breaks down the wall between them.

"What is it, Marcus?"

She has said his name, and he feels lighter, relieved.

"I need to speak with Lukhamen, Alenna."

The urgency in his eyes frightens her. "Sit down," she says.

She indicates a chair, but he sits next to her on the small sofa. She can feel heat radiating from his body.

"Alenna..."

"Yes?"

"I do not know where to begin."

"Begin anywhere you wish, Marcus."

He pauses a moment, listening again to the sound of his name, then speaks. "The governorship was thrust upon me by a dying man, Alenna, whom I could not refuse. For years I hoped that someone would relieve me. When no one came, I did the best I could..." He pauses, "...for a man not suited to the job."

His voice is hoarse. "I never expected to, but I came to love this place. I love it now because it is where you are. It is the ground you walk upon, the air you breathe."

She opens her mouth to speak, but he holds up his hand.

"Please. Hear me out. I may never have another chance." She looks away, but he turns her face back to him.

"There are two people for whom I would lay down my life, Alenna: my son, and you. While I live, no harm shall come to you, or to anyone you love."

"You are frightening me, Marcus."

He takes her hand. "I have received orders from Rome that I am to confiscate all Egyptian property. I have no choice but to obey."

She stands; he stands with her. She searches his eyes, trying to understand. Then it is clear. She removes her hand. "You are going to take my home from me."

"I would never take your home from you, Alenna."

"But you said..."

"I still have some authority as to who may live in this house, Alenna, even though it officially belongs to Rome, and I decree that you and your family shall live here. Do you understand?"

"Oh, gods of Egypt!" Her knees give way, but he catches her.

He is the Roman governor who has killed a hundred of her countrymen, who will take everything from her, and she stays in his arms because he is Marcus, who loves her beyond all reason, Marcus, who will lay down his life for her, Marcus, whose arms are drawing her closer, Marcus, whose desire has kept her from becoming empty and sere, and the weeping comes from deep and far away, from down the years that she has been alone.

She cannot tell him that she cries because he trembles, because he has loved her so hopelessly, because she is *alive*, because she has wanted him since he touched her in Haraa's garden, because he is Marcus. She closes her eyes and he kisses her tears, tasting their salt. His mouth finds hers, and it is as if she has known this kiss all her life, as if he has kissed her in this very garden, long, long ago. She wants to say, *yes, yes, I know you. I have always known you.*

At last, he steps away from her and the world is with them again, coming into focus, becoming earth and sky.

"Alenna..."

She is breathing deeply.

"The executions..."

"Marcus..."

"They would have recalled me if I had done otherwise."

She looks into the clear brown eyes that are brimming with his old, hopeless love.

"I could not leave you to another governor. I would trust no one with your safety. I *will not* trust anyone else with your safety. Send word to Lukhamen that he is to end the convocation and come home and occupy his house."

He touches her face, kisses her again, and is gone. She sinks onto the sofa, still feeling his arms around her, his kiss on her mouth. Her head feels as if it is going to spin out of control.

---

Marcus thunders into the room. "You shall not have it, Petronia!"

"I shall have any house I want, Marcus, and you will give it to me!"

He strides up to her, comes too close. She takes a step backward. "You have made a tactical error, Petronia. You used all your resources in one precipitous little letter. I am surprised."

He takes another step forward. She takes one backward.

"Let me explain your situation to you, Petronia. Your father responded to the first letter, but a second, coming so soon upon the heels of the first, will be regarded as petty. If you cry that I will not give you the house you want, you will betray yourself as the whining, self-centered shrew you really are. If, on the other hand, you behave yourself and quiet down, I shall allow you to stay here and be near your son. But if you lift your voice against me again, you will be on the road to Rome in the time it takes to give the order."

Petronia stiffens with anger, but Marcus goes on.

"When I return to my office, I shall write a letter. It will sit in my desk, waiting for the smallest misstep from you. It will inform your father that I have uncovered a plot to kidnap you and that to save your life, I am returning you, under heavy guard, to Rome at once."

She digs her fingernails into the palms of her hands and trembles with rage.

"From this day forward, you will be acquiescent, the perfect wife. All correspondence from you shall carry my seal or it shall not go forward. That means I will read your every letter from Luxor. Personally. You shall stay in *this* house, Petronia, the one I have provided for you, with a snake and a traitor for company. Antonious shall be your only companion. My personal guards will replace his, so you will be watched. You will see your son when I send him to you, and you will not interfere in any way with the life of any Egyptian person. And that, Petronia, is your situation."

She reaches back to strike him, but he catches her wrist. He holds it above her head and speaks close to her face.

"Of course, you are free to leave Luxor of your own accord when it becomes too...*uncomfortable* for you here." He smiles bitterly. "It gets very hot in the summertime, you know. Almost unbearable."

He drops her arm and strides from the room, passing Antonious in the hall-way. "See to your mistress, Antonious. She is…distraught."

As Antonious enters the room, a vase crashes against the wall, narrowly missing his head. He turns and leaves quickly, before the next piece of expensive pottery is hurled.

# CHAPTER 51

―――∞∞∞―――

MY DAUGHTER DEBBIE AND MY granddaughter Céline live in Paris—a three-hour drive from Brussels. On rare weekends, I can be with them and, for a little while, relieve the homesickness that has come upon me.

Bill is doing well. He has joined an English-language theater group and, because he is friendly and outgoing, has made himself known to lots of people, including our Belgian postman and the man from whom he buys the Herald Tribune every day at the *Librarie*, the corner newsstand.

He also has lively, cheerful cousins in Ireland, whom he visits regularly. He is never morosely affected by this northern climate that boasts more than two hundred days of rain a year. He enjoys what the Irish call "a soft, warm day" but what I call damp, dank, and chilly. But it is the darkness that gets to me. I go to work in the dark and come home in the dark. Bill, God bless him, walks me to the metro stop every morning. It's the small kind things, sometimes, that get us through. I don't think I could do this without him.

My feet are perpetually wet from stepping into pools that lie under the loosened, gray paving stones. All of my shoes are spotted with mud. My chilly clothes smell of wet wool. I walk through the streets under a blanket of gray, dreaming of the red brick sidewalks of Bethesda dappled with the sunlight that filters through its green, leafy trees.

There is a photo on my dresser. In the photo, my brother Eddie is holding Elenni. She is about four years old, and she is wearing red cowboy boots. I look at the photo every morning and fight back the tears. I miss Debbie and Céline even though they are just a few hours away. I miss my family back in the States. I miss my daughters, Michaela and Niki. I miss home.

It may be that I am just tired. We are working twelve, sometimes fourteen hours a day. An embassy is a twenty-four-hour-seven-day-week microcosm of the federal government. The Ambassador represents the President, and the rest of the staff acts for the State Department and other agencies with Foreign Service functions, such as mine, the Commerce Department.

Everybody is bright; everybody works impossible hours. I am working alongside career diplomats—dedicated, competent, ambitious, and tough. It is no place for the faint of heart.

Despite the homesickness, the rain, and the long hours, I'm there to do a job. And I love it. The Ambassador is a man of staggering intelligence who sleeps four hours a night, a brilliant lawyer who reads every word of every memo I send him, and who returns them with thoughtful questions in the margins. He has come to understand the fine points of standardization like no "outsider" I have ever met. And, unlike most "outsiders" who think of standards as too technical or too tedious a subject to broach, he is able to see the challenges the new European standardization system can present to American exports. I have his ear, therefore, and his support, something everyone in the embassy is striving for.

Every evening—morning in the United States—I talk on the telephone with small business owners from every State in the Union, hard-working, innovative Americans who call because they need the new European Union market. Everything about it is new—new rules, new laws, new institutions, new people in charge. These Americans are my clients, the people who create products and jobs, and I'm their source of information, their eyes and ears; I'm their advocate. Working for them is a privilege and I know it. They're why I get up every morning.

It never occurs to me that I might be in Brussels for another reason.

---

Two years into my three-year term, I get a phone call from Washington. I am asked to come home, as Foreign Service Officers are required to do after a certain period, to touch base with the mother ship. I am overjoyed. After two years abroad, home will replenish my soul, even if for a little while.

I am there a week. The day before I fly back to Brussels, I have lunch with Belinda, my agency sponsor. It is an Indian summer day in October.

"Want to sit outside?" she says.

"Oh my God, yes," I reply.

We carry our cafeteria trays to a table that is near a group of red and golden maple trees that is spotted with evergreens and an oak in the middle that has turned bright orange. Heaps of white fluffy clouds float above us. I'm happy in the warmth, sun, and the array of colors. I try not to think about leaving.

"So how are *you* doing?" I ask Belinda.

"I'm swamped," she says. "And on top of everything else, I have to go to Egypt to give a speech." Her remark hangs there in the bright blue air. The hair on the back of my neck stands up. "I really wish I didn't have to go."

*Say something.* "Let me give it for you," I croak. "I'm in Brussels—halfway there already."

"I wish you could," she says, seeming not to notice that my voice has gone awry, "but the director wants me to go, put a face on the agency."

I breathe out and my voice comes back. "Okay," I say, "but if anything changes, let me know."

On the plane back to Brussels, I can't stop thinking about it. *Egypt.* I try to put it out of my mind, but it will not go away. Two weeks later, Belinda calls.

---

"My father has had a heart attack," she says. "Does your offer to go to Egypt for me still stand? I can send you the material. You know a lot of this stuff already."

My heart is beating so loudly I can hear it.

"Are you there?"

"I'm here," I say.

"Think you can do it?"

"I'll see if my boss will let me go," I tell her, "and I'll get right back to you. I hope your father gets better soon."

"Thanks," she says.

I must do something quickly, before this goes away. I run. The head of our section is staring at his computer. My heart is pounding and I'm out of breath. I rush through my request. "I'll go," he says without looking up, casually invoking his right to outrank me.

I stand there, dumfounded.

"I've always wanted to go to Riga." *He hasn't heard me.*

"Not Riga," I say, *"Egypt."*

"Oh, *Egypt.* I thought you said Riga. Sure. Go ahead."

I run back to my office before he can change his mind, call Belinda, and then Bill. "Bill!" I scream into the phone, "We're going to Egypt!"

"What?"

"We're going to Egypt!"

———

That night, I cannot sleep. I find myself smiling into the darkness. *Lukhamen,* I whisper to him, *I am coming to Egypt!* And then it hits me. *You knew, didn't you?*

———

I wash my musty summer clothes, memorize Belinda's presentation, and arrange for some leave time. Before I know it, Bill and I are on a plane, bound for Cairo. I am a boiling mixture of excitement and anxiety. *What am I supposed to see? Did I live there in another life? Is that why I'm going? Suppose nothing happens? Suppose I imagined everything? Suppose it's all nothing?*

I have such little faith.

———

The Cairo International Airport is swarming with people. As we head toward the exit, a crush of taxi drivers surrounds us, hawking their services. It is all noise and confusion, and I have turned into a statue, a deaf, mute statue. I look to Bill, who is in control of himself. He chooses a driver and we are out of the airport and driving like mad toward Cairo, the largest city in the Arab world and Africa.

⸎

We swerve in and out of hit-and-miss traffic and come perilously close to other cars.

Our driver looks in the rearview mirror and laughs. "Don't worry," he says, trilling English, "Sometimes our cars kiss each other. It's not so serious." He blows his horn at a car that is inches away. I'm not worried. I am not in Egypt to die in a taxicab.

Cairo is a kaleidoscope, a whirling mass of seventeen million people. We careen through its crowded streets, down wide boulevards, past modern high-rise buildings. We squeeze through narrow alleyways, coming within a hair's breadth of crumbling structures with half-hanging shutters and tattered awnings. In one such alleyway, which I am sure is off our route, the taxi driver stops in front of a man holding a camel.

"My cousin," he says. "He will take you to the pyramids." The cousin smiles broadly. The driver hands us his business card. "Call me. He is the best guide. I will arrange everything." Sand floats in on the wind and hides the guide and his camel behind a dusty, golden veil. We continue on, to a busy section of Cairo that houses our hotel.

⸎

Our room overlooks the Nile, where barges carrying cargo are leaving small ripples in their wake. Bill and I stand on the balcony and stare out at the City of a Thousand Minarets. It is sunset, and a wailing call to prayer sounds over loud-speakers, echoing through the city. A thrill runs through me. Of all the places I could be in the world, I am in *Egypt.*

Our dinner is lamb and perfumed rice in the hotel courtyard. The moon is full and the air is fragrant with night-blooming jasmine. I am not in Luxor but I am in Egypt, and I feel at home and peaceful, content to breathe in the night air, gaze at the moon, and sit in the courtyard, as if it were the most natural thing in the world.

---

There is a saying that Egyptians are born with a smile on their face. Our Egyptian hosts are warm and friendly, and lend credence to the claim. Bill makes friends immediately.

My presentation comes on the second day of the conference. There is a dinner that night.

At the reception, Bill chats with his new friends. We are waiting for the director of the Egyptian government's standards agency. At length he appears, with an entourage. He is obviously a man of some importance; the other Egyptians defer to him. I am seated on his right, as I represent the United States agency that is most like his own.

He is stunningly handsome, with bronzed skin stretched tight over sculpted cheekbones, and dark, liquid eyes. *The high priest might have looked like this.* I can hear Haraa, as she sees him on Lukhamen's ordination day, thinking to herself...*By all the gods, he's beautiful enough*...

He is courtly and charming. He steers the conversation to the new, technologically advanced paint standards that have recently been introduced by the United States. I return the polite flattery by paying homage to the paint on the walls of underground Egyptian tombs that have retained their vibrancy and colors for centuries.

"What paint standards *they* must have had," I say.

"Yes," he says, "But of course the walls were not exposed to light and other degrading elements. In any case, that knowledge is gone, and Egypt uses other paint standards today."

What he means is that Egypt must now use standards that come from more developed countries.

We change the subject. He introduces me to his beautiful daughter, who is sitting across the table, next to Bill.

I look at Bill. We smile at each other. *We're here. We're in Egypt!* He winks at me.

When the director rises to leave, so do the guests. He says good night. The business part of my trip is over.

———⊂≋≋⊃———

Now. Now I am here.

We spend most of our one day in Cairo in the Egyptian Museum. It is practically empty; we have it mostly to ourselves. My footsteps echo on the stone floors as I walk into Egypt's glorious past. So much is here—gods, sacred animals, coffins, furniture and jewelry, the treasured remnants of a civilization that was the light of the world thousands of years before I was born. In the mummy chamber, I stare at a pharaoh, Ramses VI, who lies in regal preservation, his arms folded across his chest. I cannot take my eyes away.

It is not the first time I have seen Egyptian antiquities in a museum, but here it is different. This is where they belong.

*Alenna wore hanging earrings and delicate bracelets like these...I know these colored glass vials. They were in her bath. You could see sunlight through them. They held oils that smelled of oranges and cardamom.*

Everything reminds me of *them*. How much of this, I wonder, did *they* see? What artifacts do my eyes see that theirs might have lingered on as well?

We come upon a small statuette of the god Amon in a glass case. The guide book notes that "*numerous are the Kings whose names incorporate in the composition the name of Amon, and the New Kingdom Kings never failed to add to their titles the epithet "beloved of Amon...At the end of the New Kingdom, it is his High Priest who takes over the royal power."*

And the name! Lukh-amen, Lukh-amon, Beloved of Amon. The spelling is different, but the name is unmistakable. I feel a chill. That is what the high priest called him upon his ordination. *Beloved of Amon.*

"Helen," Bill says gently, "We have to leave if we want to see the pyramids."

———⊂≋≋⊃———

We go not by camel, but by embassy car to Giza. The pyramids are not in the middle of the desert as they appear in photographs, but are perilously close to the encroaching metropolis of Cairo. *Never mind. They are here. I am here. I am at the ancient wonders, the great hallowed tombs, and I will probably do this only once in my life.*

Tomorrow we will go to Luxor.

# CHAPTER 52

———

THROUGH THE WINDOW OF THE plane I can see the great Sahara, a sea of sand that stretches to the horizon. This is *his* desert, his home.

The Nile appears in the distance, a sparkling ribbon of water. I feel suspended, as if in a timeless capsule. I feel nothing; I have no thoughts. The air is holding its breath.

Our plane touches down.

———

We collect our bags and step out into the sun. It is calmer here. I follow Bill into a taxi.

The driver is pleasant and chatty. He is the driver for a famous American singer who owns a house here, he says proudly.

The drive is four miles of wonder. I drink in the land: palm trees, wheat fields, a small stream, a donkey tethered to a post. The Nile Valley is lush with bright green grasses and irrigation ditches that sparkle in the sun. The land shimmers with light.

———

Our small hotel is just off the river road. In our room, Bill looks at me and I look at him.

"I want to walk the river road," I say.

We leave our bags unpacked. I must see the river road, the place where I saw the high priest for the first time—walking swiftly, a breeze blowing against his robe, his back to me. We walk to the end of the hotel driveway. I turn to the right and step into my dream.

I feel my feet touch the sandy road. Here and there, a sycamore tree shelters us from the sun. The river is on my left. I know exactly where I am. I am in place; I am centered. Lukhamen's words resonate in my heart:

*"Egypt. Beloved of my heart, my soul. Even now I can hear her people's cries, smell the desert blossom perfumes, and feel the hot streams of sunlight burning my back."*

I am comfortable, at ease, as if I have dropped into the proper cosmic slot. There is no need to hurry. We walk on.

Something stops me. I look to my left, to the river and beyond, to the far hills on the other side. *There lies the Valley of the Kings, the crescent in the hills of Thebes, where the ancients sleep.*

I look to my right, back toward the land. A grand old British-era hotel, The Winter Palace, stands before me.

"That is where his house was," I tell Bill. I stand there, staring.

"Let's go in," he says, shocking me into the present.

"No."

"Come on," Bill insists.

"I don't want to."

Bill is going in, with or without me. *What am I resisting?* I follow him, trepidation dogging my every step.

I tread lightly as I follow Bill into the lobby.

A smiling young man in a red coat welcomes us and invites us to have a cup of tea in the lobby. I sit down carefully. The furnishings are old and unpretentious. The lobby is spacious, dignified, and quiet.

*I don't belong here.* I can't shake the feeling. The young man brings us tea. He is smiling as he pours. The tea is red.

"Have you never had a tea like this before?" he says. I shake my head no. "It is hibiscus tea. You will like it."

*Hibiscus tea. That's what it was! Alenna's red tea.* I sip the tea. It's a little bitter. *Alenna used honey in hers.* "May I have some honey?" I say to the young man.

"Certainly, Madam," he says.

I try to relax into the slow, easy tempo of the grand old lobby, but I can't. I am on the edge of my seat, irritated by the hotel guests in their shirts and shorts and pink sunburns, walking about as if they owned the place. *There was a house here that was once somebody's home!*

Bill brings me back to the present. "Let's take a walk out back," he says.

"Okay," I say, trying to shake off my ill-tempered thoughts, glad to get up and move away, where I cannot see *these intruders*. We walk down the broad flight of back stairs leading to the garden.

————— ⊗☙⊗ —————

And I am there. The garden is just as I saw it years ago, as I first wrote it— the tiled paths, bougainvillea everywhere, brushing the ground, swaying in the breeze, its petals beneath our feet. In the center is a birdcage. I walk to it and touch it. It is old and rusted, but it can't be the same one. It had been full of parakeets. Lukhamen would feed them, held aloft by Semnut, the old nurse.

*"You see, Mother," I hear him say as the little birds scramble over the seeds, "they have waited entirely too long for breakfast." I hear her laugh.*

I stoop to pick up a petal from a bougainvillea blossom.

*There was a couch there, against a back wall. Red cushions. Red tea under the tree. But there is no wall. Even the locusts are gone.*

I am suddenly overwhelmed and tired.

"Let's go," I say to Bill.

We walk back to our hotel. I have to go to our room and lie down.

————— ⊗☙⊗ —————

The next morning, we have breakfast in our hotel dining room. I am recovered and anxious. I have to walk the river road again.

I look away as we pass The Winter Palace. I am on my way to the temple. Bill is looking at a map, but I walk on ahead. I know where it is.

Ahead! Still standing! I walk slowly along the side wall, my heart beating quickly. I examine it, drink it in. Parts of the wall are missing. The stones are the color of sand and age, and rounded at the corners.

*They used to sit perfectly upon one another. Never mind. I am here. It is here.*

We continue to the end of the wall and round the corner. Ahead, at the entrance, are two massive statues of Ramses II, sitting straight-backed on thrones, staring ahead. We walk around to face them.

On their foreheads are *Uraeuses*, rearing cobras, symbols of divine authority, and on their heads, the double crowns of Egypt. Their hands rest serenely, palms down, on their laps. We come closer. The faces are partly worn away.

On the left side of the statues is one dusty pink granite obelisk. Its twin is in the center of the Place de la Concorde in Paris, a gift to the French people by the viceroy of Egypt in 1829. I have seen it many times, standing in the spot where once the guillotine reigned supreme. I have stared at it from afar many times, never realizing it was from *this* temple. *Our temple.*

*Why would he give it away? Why not something of lesser importance?*

I remember the Egyptian obelisk in St. Peter's Square in Rome, transported there by the Romans. I remember other Egyptian obelisks in London and New York. It makes my heart sick.

My gaze shifts to the great pylons and down the long corridor, to a statue of Ramses II in the distance, sitting in the courtyard. *Waiting.*

"It looks like a Cecil B. De Mille set," my actor husband says, in awe.

In truth, it does not look real. But this is the Temple of Luxor—worn, parts of it crumbling, but standing still, dusty with the sands of three thousand years, its colors gone, but still grand, glorious, and heart-stopping. A breeze lifts sand into the air. Ramses is waiting for us in the distance.

I walk slowly toward him. Guides block us at the entrance; Bill engages one to take us through.

*It will be cool in the shade of the pylons.*

We walk through to the courtyard. Our guide regales Bill with a lecture on the architecture of Egyptian temples. I scan the perimeter of the courtyard, gazing into the blank eyes of eleven likenesses of the great Pharaoh, Ramses II. I half-expect Khenti to step out from behind one of them.

The guide rattles on. "The statues out front are fifty-one feet high. Some say forty-six, I say fifty-one. This temple is almost thirty-five hundred years old..."

I bend down, fill my hand with sand, let it sift through my fingers. I have dreamed of this courtyard. I want to stay longer, but the guide moves us steadily forward, into a forest of papyrus-shaped columns, carved with hieroglyphics and scenes from ancient battles. I touch the indentations in the ancient stone lightly, reverently.

"And these columns are fifty-two feet high...Of this I am sure." *He's going too quickly.* High above us, a bird flits from column to column. I stare up, up, up into the forest. *The columns were painted up there. Red, blue, and gold.*

"Come ahead," the guide says.

We are through the forest, the hypostyle hall, and I look to my right.

*That is where the bath was.* There is no longer a room there, only the outside wall, with its missing stones. Sunlight slips through the openings, casting pale yellow light onto the dirt floor.

*But there was a sunken tub there once, and a tile floor, and Khenti in a white robe, gathering towels and soap, acolyte boys assisting him, incense rising to the ceiling, Khenti kneeling in back of the high priest, massaging his temples, saying, "It is not seemly, Sire, that you should walk among common people and lepers."* I can almost see them, moving about.

We walk through the second, smaller courtyard. Ahead of us is where the sanctuary would have been, the holy of holies, the innermost room of the temple. "And this is where the sanctuary would be..." *He doesn't know what happened here.*

We are at the far end of the temple, and there is no sanctuary, only a crumbling wall, with rocks on the floor of the holy place. *The wall fell here. It almost killed the high priest.* I am tempted to tell him this, but I don't. *There was a great statue of Amon at the far end that stood over the altar. Lukhamen was ordained here, as was his father before him, and his father's father.*

I hear the faraway echoes of their voices. *"You should ride the river road, Your Excellency. The sun is far too brutal this time of year." "The people expect to see us, my friend," says the high priest to Khenti, "especially now. No, now is not the time to hide behind the curtains of a sedan chair."* They are gone and I am here, beneath these pillars. Tears rise in my eyes. I miss them.

"Of course, this isn't the largest temple. You must go to see Karnak." The guide turns us back; we retrace our steps, and just before we reach the pylons again, I look to the right.

*The small antechamber was here, where Sechmetna, the physician, brought the high priest after he was lifted from the rubble. That is where they laid his broken body; that is where Lukhamen stayed with his father, day and night.*

There is nothing there now, no small, dark room. Only space. The guide passes it wordlessly, oblivious to what happened here.

How empty it feels! I am here and they are gone, and strangers walk through the holy places with guides who know only what they have read in books.

That night, Bill and I go to the sound and light show at the grand Temple of Karnak. It is exquisite, moving. My eyes fill with tears at the music, the narrated history, the unspeakable beauty of the carved walls and statues so artfully lit under the dark Egyptian night. But even as I sit in the splendor of the great temple, my heart is drawn down the long avenue lined with ram-head sphinxes, the corridor that connects Karnak with the Temple of Luxor, and down the river road where, at its dark, quiet end, there was once a house.

# CHAPTER 53

———— ✐✐✐ ————

IT IS THE THIRD DAY, and we are in the Thomas Cook Travel Office. Bill is making arrangements for us to visit the Valley of the Kings. The young man taking care of us has a small tattoo on the inside of his wrist: a cross.

*A Christian. The old governor's servant girl had one just like it. "So the girl is a Christian, he had said to himself. "I wonder how the high priest feels about the growing number of Christians here."*

"Let's go to the Christian Quarter," I say to Bill. "We have time."

"Okay," he says.

"This way," I say, turning to the right.

Bill never asks if I know where I am going. There is a compass inside me, unerring and true, driving me, guiding me to places I have never been and have known for a long time.

———— ✐✐✐ ————

We make our way downriver, away from the center of town. A group of school-children in uniforms calls out to us: "Welcome in Egypt! Welcome in Egypt!" they chant, making us smile. There are no tourists here. At length, an older boy approaches us.

"Do you need a guide, sir?" he says to Bill. "I can take you anywhere you want."

"Can you take us to the Old Christian Quarter?" says Bill. The boy looks at him in surprise.

"But you are already there, sir," he says.

We walk the few paces to a church that looks like a small European cathedral. It is not the domed mud structure upon which Simon and John placed a wooden cross, the day Antonious ran down one of its builders with his chariot, the day Simon vowed to kill him. I am disappointed. *Why did I think it would still be here?*

"Would you like to go in?" says Bill.

"No," I say.

"Come in, come in!" A rotund, smiling priest is standing in the doorway, beckoning to us.

"I am Father Michael," he says, beaming.

*It was Abba Michael who baptized Lucenkep, Mahda's daughter.*

I shrug off the coincidence and we follow him into the darkened church. The interior is as unremarkable as I thought it would be, but Father Michael is proud of it.

As we are getting ready to leave, Bill gives him a donation.

"Thank you, thank you," he says.

"Goodbye," I say to him, walking toward the slant of sunshine coming in through the open door, anxious to get out.

"Of course," says Father Michael, "This is not the original church."

*I know that.*

"Would you like to see it?" I stop in my tracks.

"Yes," Bill says.

"Come with me," Father Michael says, leading us back inside, toward a side door.

He opens it and leads us into a mud structure no bigger than a room. I look up. *There it is: the dome.*

He is telling Bill something about the early Christians, but I am not listening. Here it is— cradled inside a present day Coptic Church.

*It was so small.*

"We try to take care of it as best we can," I hear Father Michael saying. I put a few more dollars into his hand. It's all I have with me.

Bill and I are silent on the way back. He has read everything I have written. I'm wondering how he feels. Neither of us can find words just now.

As we walk the river road back toward the city, I look out at the river, calm and serene under a clear blue sky. A small felucca is listing slightly under a gentle breeze. I stop for a minute to gaze at it as it languidly makes its way upriver, and then I am aware of something: *The governor's mansion was here.*

I turn inland. There is nothing there, only an empty field. But I can see it: *a white columned structure, with balconies around the upper story.* The wind rustles the tall dry grass. No one comes here anymore.

*Marcus. Poor Marcus. He was so handsome.*

We board a small, flat boat, filled with tourists, bound across the Nile, to the Valley of the Kings. I turn back to see Luxor receding in the distance. From here the temple does not look so worn, so *incomplete.* To the right I see The Winter Palace, its cupcake architecture marring the ancient shoreline.

I am brought back to the present by the voice of the guide as we approach the shore. He is preparing us for the tombs we are about to see, the mysteries and treasures that have lain beneath this hallowed ground. Bill and I are squeezed in among people with sunglasses and absurd hats. I try to ignore their *inane comments.* I'm irritable again.

We approach the immense crescent bowl, a rough terrain of sand and rocks, surrounded by high cliffs. The sun is blazing and blinding. There is no shade, no shelter. We walk behind our guide, Mustafa, a scholar. His lecture is informative, erudite, and respectful.

*He is worth listening to.*

We stand in the sun in long lines to enter the tombs. At last, we descend into the earth, where it is cool, where the tombs, long emptied by robbers, are still wondrous to behold, the walls and ceilings replete with paintings and decorative tributes to ancient royalty, the colors still vibrant. *They were laid here with such loving care.*

Not once does Mustafa mention that high priests are buried in this valley.

Before I step onto the boat to cross the Nile again, I look high up onto one of the cliffs, searching for the place where the Sa'at high priests are entombed. I see no sign of a great stone engraved with the name *Sa'at*. Time has hidden it, probably forever.

*But I know it is there.*

A few years later, while browsing the magazine of the American-Egyptian Society in Washington, D.C., I will read of the discovery of an underground tomb in the Valley of the Kings containing the remains of a high priest. But I know there is another—up high, carved into the side of a cliff.

---

I must go back to the temple before we leave. I want to be there alone, in the courtyard, before the sun sets. *It is the only thing left that is as it was.*

In the waning daylight, I sit on a stone step, surrounded by the statues of Ramses II. There are no tourists about, and the guides are gone. The sun casts the courtyard in an orange glow.

*I am here, Lukhamen*, I whisper. *I am here, Eddie.* They do not answer. The sun is almost gone. I must return to the hotel.

---

That evening, the sky blackens and the wind howls. From our hotel window nothing is visible, only great, dark vortexes of sand. *There was a sand storm like this after the crucifixions.*

The hotel manager informs us that the airport may be closed tomorrow if the storm doesn't lift. I hope it will not open, that we will be able to stay another day. But in the morning the sky is clear.

On the way to the airport, I drink in the land again, savoring each moment, each sight. We pass the same little donkey, tethered to a pole, grazing in the bright, green grass. In my purse is a small plastic bag. In it is a handful of sand from the temple courtyard.

I turn to look out the back window of the taxi and watch as Luxor recedes into the distance. I feel as if I am leaving home.

---

There is a theory called *Occam's razor* that states that among competing hypotheses, the hypothesis with the fewest assumptions should be selected. In other words, the simplest explanation is most likely the correct one. For me, it was the tear.

On the plane, a tear dropped onto my hand, glistened briefly, then fell away. And then I understood. I took out the small plastic bag and looked at the sand from the floor of the temple. My heart swelled at the sight of it. I closed my eyes and remembered the empty bird cage. My little boy, gone. All of them gone. Another tear fell, and then another. I came home and they were gone.

# CHAPTER 54

—◦◦◦—

*L*

*BEHOLD THE RIVER AFTER THE storm, Beloved. How dark and fathomless, how silent and peaceful in the darkness, how sweet its secret kisses upon the shore. But look, now! The moon has crested and the river is liquid light. Oh, sweet loveliness!*

*The conquerors are gone, but the moon still lights the river and roams through the temple. It slips into the courtyards, across the pillars. It moves along the tops of papyrus columns, and sends its silvery shaft even into the sanctuary, and they, they who sleep across the river, awake and behold it!*

*They walk with me in the moonlight. It lights my way as I pass through the courtyards and out of the temple, as I walk the river road to my mother's garden. It is still there! The conquerors are gone, and the moonlight is still in our garden! The bougainvillea still drops its petals onto the tile floor, and the royal palms still sway in the midnight breeze. Ah, look. See how the moon has forced the night jasmine to burst. Its perfume spills onto the ground, making it sweet!*

# PART THREE

---

*"For those who believe, no proof is necessary.*
*For those who do not believe, no proof is possible."*
~ *Stuart Chase*

# CHAPTER 55

---

♀

THERE IS SCANT RAINFALL IN the forests of Africa, and for the first time in many years, the river does not rise. The farmers plant grain in the winter as they have always done, but the tiny shoots struggle through the dry soil and wilt under the springtime sun. Panic strikes the Christian Quarter. The governor inspects the fields, rations grain from the stores, and distributes it to the poor.

In time, the vegetables die, as do the young trees and animals. From time to time, a bold crocodile slithers up a riverbank to drag a braying, emaciated donkey into his muddy lair. Ragged little boats sail further and further upriver, looking for fish that have gone down into Africa.

Eager, greedy merchants with caravans of provisions begin to arrive from Turkey and Greece. They trade first with the Romans but soon, unwashed and reeking of cheap perfume, they sit in the homes of wealthy Egyptians, bartering food for jewels, finely crafted furniture, and works of art. The governor, whose edict declared that all such things were the property of Rome, looks the other way.

Haraa's name is known to many of the tradesmen, because of her husband. She knows their tricks and makes use of the secrets imparted to her over the years by the braggadocio of her faithless husband. She is more talented than he, she discovers to her delight, and enjoys the thrill of risk. She completes any number of advantageous sales for herself and for Alenna, after which she is invited to accompany a large caravan to the Greek Isles, where Egyptian treasures are to be sold. She is promised a handsome commission by the leader, a coarse but charismatic Turk who cannot keep his eyes away from her breasts.

She moves her daughter Femi into Alenna's household and bids her goodbye.

On the way out of town, Haraa rides a handsome white steed past the governor's house. She is dressed in a silk magenta tunic that is belted at the waist, matching pants, and fine leather boots. A scarf of the same material, anchored by a ring of dangling gold coins, covers her head.

Marcus stands at the window of the governor's house, watching the procession. As she passes, he bows his head toward her. Haraa pauses, returns his bow, then turns in her saddle and fixes her eyes ahead, where lie the blue-green waters of the Ionian Sea.

---

"They are here again, Your Excellency," says Khenti.

"Then we must find bread for them," replies Lukhamen.

Khenti's back is bent, his step slow and faltering, and he is alarmingly thin. His eyes, once like black fire, are white with cataracts. Even sightless, he knows every inch of the temple and walks through its corridors alone and with confidence.

"There is only enough bread for the priests, Your Excellency."

"Then the priests shall share their bread with the people."

Lukhamen is thinner too, like everyone else, and his robe is coarse, like Khenti's. The silk robes in every color of the rainbow are now in Haraa's care, bound together and strapped to the back of a horse.

"But your father..."

"He will approve, Khenti."

"Yes, Your Excellency."

They are waiting for him—ragged children, hollow-eyed mothers, old men and women, and men and women old before their time. They stand quietly while the priests put small pieces of bread into unsteady hands. An old woman lays a trembling hand on Lukhamen's arm.

"The Living God will bless you, my son."
*The Living God had better feed us before we die,* he thinks.

———⊷———

*Ah, yes. The Ancients, the Divine Ones. All they ever wanted, all they ever asked of us, was to remember who we were, to remember from whence we came! And when we could not remember, we bowed down to the oppressor, and in its grief our river did not rise, and our grain died in the sere ground. We could not remember, and we bowed down and gave them our homes, and our children. Because we could not remember, we accepted their lie, the lie that gave them the right to our land, and our grain, and our temples.*

*They were who they were. I do not blame them now.*

# CHAPTER 56

$\varphi$

THE ENVOYS FROM ROME ARE waiting in Marcus's office. They stand when he enters. One steps forward, his helmet under his arm.

"I am Linus, Sire, Auditor General and Inspector. I represent the emperor."

"Welcome, Linus. Be seated, all of you."

"Thank you, Sire. It looks very much the same as when I was here before, with a few notable exceptions, of course."

"So this is not your first time in Egypt, Auditor General?"

"No, Sire. It was my pleasure to meet your predecessor."

Marcus is surprised.

"Unlike yourself, Sire, the previous governor *requested* our audit." Linus smiles an unfriendly, toothy smile.

"The previous governor was an exceptional man," says Marcus, "and my mentor. No doubt he had reasons of his own to make use of your..." Marcus looks him up and down "... services."

The governor's tone has placed Linus squarely in his rank. The Auditor General straightens his already straight back.

"Yes, Sire."

"Now. Let us get to the business at hand, Linus."

"Yes, Sire."

It crosses Linus's mind that this man is a centurion, a governor, the son of a Roman senator, and that he recently crucified a hundred men. He decides to forego the game of intimidation.

"We have a problem here, Linus, and I want you to take a full report back to Rome. Do you understand?"

"Yes, Sire."

"Life here depends on the river, and the river has failed us."

"Yes, Sire."

"There is a sophisticated irrigation system in this valley, installed when pharaohs ruled. For centuries it has worked with miraculous efficiency, turning this desert valley into one lush, fertile field of grain. But now there is no water to run through it. It is a simple problem, but one we cannot solve with aqueducts or other irrigation devices. It is a problem imposed upon us by Nature, and we shall have to wait it out until the rains in lower Africa fill the river. Do you understand?"

"Yes, Sire."

"In the meantime, Linus, please report that I am feeding the people from the stores. I must keep them alive through this season so that they can plant again when the river rises. There is not enough to send to Rome. What little there is I have reserved for the maintenance of the work force. It is not pleasant news, Linus, but there it is."

"Yes, Sire." Linus is writing furiously.

"And there is the matter of accounts."

"Yes, Sire."

"We have had to buy provisions from the caravans to feed the army. Our records are straightforward. You may review whatever you feel is necessary to complete your report."

"Yes, Sire."

Linus finishes scribbling and looks up. The governor is standing, looking down at him.

"Will that be all, Sire?"

"Is there mail, Linus?"

Linus snaps his fingers, and an aide jumps to his feet, handing Marcus a leather pouch.

"Thank you," says Marcus without looking at the aide.

Linus, sensing the meeting is over, stands at attention.

"My aide is just outside the door. He will see to your housing and provisions, humble though they may be."

Linus raises his hand in salute. "Hail to the emperor!" he says.

"To the emperor," says Marcus.

When they are gone, Marcus opens the leather pouch. Inside are two letters, one from his father and one for Petronia from her father. Both letters are sealed.

⚬⚬⚬

In her bed chamber, Petronia breaks the seal on her letter.

*My Beloved Daughter,* it reads.

*I have received a letter from your companion and guardian, Antonious, and I am much disturbed by it. I understand now why I have received no correspondence from you for such a long time. Dearest Petronia, do not be afraid, and do not despair. Rome is still the center of the known world. Your husband has no authority unless Rome dispenses it. Of this you may be sure. I have dispatched my agent, who is traveling as an aide to the auditor general, to Luxor. They are there supposedly to investigate the lack of grain caused by the drought. You may expect him to call on you shortly. Prepare now to return to Rome with him.*

*I am sending for Antonious as well. I believe he can enlighten us considerably on the situation there. It has been overlooked for far too long, in my opinion. In that regard, you may have done us all a service by being there, Petronia. Your suffering, therefore, will not have been in vain. You will have done a great service to the empire, to the emperor, and of course to your...*

*Loving Father*

Petronia reads the letter over and over. Finally, she folds it carefully and puts it in a trunk with some of the Egyptian pottery she plans to take back to Rome with her. She extinguishes the lamp, climbs into her bed, and sleeps well for the first time since coming to Luxor.

⚬⚬⚬

Priests from all over the region have gathered in the Temple of Luxor to discuss the edict that has made every Egyptian temple the property of the Emperor of Rome. They have also come to discuss the hunger raging throughout the land. The High Priest of the Temple of Luxor is not at home, therefore, on the night his wife leaves home.

It is long after moonrise. The streets are empty. Miraculously, no Roman patrol sees her as she walks unhindered, all the way to the governor's mansion. At the entrance, she is stopped by an incredulous guard. She tells him in imperious tones that she is a personal friend of the governor's and demands to see him. Her manner is convincingly bold, her face convincingly beautiful. The guard decides to awaken Marcus.

"Alenna! What is it? Why have you come all this way alone, and at this hour?"

She is shivering. He dismisses the guard and leads her into a receiving room, off the grand entrance. He takes off his night cloak and wraps her in it, helps her to a sofa, and sits beside her.

"Alenna, has something happened?"

She smiles at him in a way he has not seen before. It is a childlike smile, expectant and innocent, as if she were about to be given a sweet.

"Alenna! What is it?"

"Hello, Marcus."

"Alenna, what is wrong?"

"Wrong? There is nothing wrong."

"Then why are you here in the middle of the night, shivering?"

He looks down at her bare feet. Her gown is a nightdress.

"It was a long walk, Marcus. And cold."

"Alenna, Alenna."

He holds her, wraps the cloak more tightly around her.

"I passed the temple. My husband is there with the priests from all over. No one saw me."

"Alenna. Sit here for a moment. I will have tea brought for us. Will you stay?"

She laughs. "Of course I will stay. I never refuse tea."

Marcus rouses the kitchen maid and returns quickly to the receiving room. "Tea will be here shortly."

She looks around the room. "This could be a very nice room, Marcus, if you had someone to decorate it properly for you."

The maid arrives with tea, and Alenna claps her hands. She sips it delicately, her gaze drifting to the sheer curtains that adorn the windows. "I do like the windows, though, Marcus. I approve."

He does not know what to say, and so when she puts her cup down he takes her hands. They are cold. She looks down at his hands covering hers, then into his eyes. Her face crumbles, and she begins to cry.

"What is it, Alenna? What is wrong?"

"It is too soon for me to die."

"Of course it is too soon for you to die. What are you talking about?"

"I feel it, Marcus. I feel as if I am about to die."

"Oh, my love." He holds her, and she clings to him. "You are not going to die, Alenna. I will die first. I will not let anything harm you."

"You can't help it, Marcus. No one can help it. It is just going to happen."

She is crying like a child. He caresses her hair and holds her to him.

"I love you, Alenna. You are not going to die."

"I love you, too, I do."

She has whispered it, but it resounds like thunder through him.

She raises her face to him, and when he kisses her, they are in a world where all is safe, all is well. She was afraid and came to him. She passed the temple where her husband lay sleeping, and came to him. It is the only thought his mind can hold, and he gives himself to it. He closes his eyes and breathes in the scent of orange blossoms. For the first time in his life, he feels completely happy. He lifts Alenna into his arms and carries her up the wide staircase.

———— ◦◦◦ ————

The high priest opens his eyes.

"Alenna!" he calls out.

After a long, frightening moment, he realizes he is in his small cell in the temple, covered in sweat. The nightmare has left his heart pounding, and he is breathing heavily. He dreamed she had fallen into a river, greater and deeper, blacker than any river he had ever seen. He tried to run, to rescue her, but his legs would not move. *Lukhamen, Lukhamen*, she had called out, over and over. *Alenna*, he had cried to her, *Alenna!* It was when she disappeared into the swirling depths that he had awakened in fear and dread.

He is still awake when the sun rises and a young priest comes to help him into his bath.

---

Semnut answers the knock upon the door. She is still in her nightdress. The sky is violet except for a small line of orange at the horizon, signaling the sunrise. A few stars are still visible. The old nurse is frightened when she sees the Roman guard and the sedan chair. She stands there agape as the governor steps down, then helps Alenna alight.

Alenna floats forward, looking at her with sweet delight, as though seeing her for the first time.

"Good morning!" sings Alenna.

"Good morning, mistress."

Alenna walks past her into the entrance hall. Marcus follows. Alenna looks around the spacious, elegant foyer, and turns to him.

"You see, Marcus. This is what I mean. Your receiving room should have more appointments—sofas, cushions, tables. Like this."

Marcus turns to Semnut.

"Leave us, please."

Semnut looks to Alenna.

"Please tell the kitchen maid that we will have tea."

Semnut bows out, and disappears like a shadow.

"I cannot stay, Alenna."

She pouts, then shakes her finger at him.

"It is not nice to refuse tea, Marcus."

He takes her face in his hands and kisses her.

"Alenna, I want you to remember something."

"Yes?"

"I want you to remember that I shall love you all of my life." She smiles the childlike smile at him.

"Of course I will remember, Marcus. I'm not a child, you know."

"And I shall always be where you need me to be."

"You shall always be where I need you to be."

He kisses her again, turns quickly, and is gone. A maid appears with tea, followed by Semnut. Alenna turns to the nurse.

"It is time for my bath, is it not?"

"Yes, mistress. Will you have tea first?"

"Tea?"

"Yes, mistress."

"Must I?"

"No, mistress. Only if you wish it."

"Very well, then. Bring it along."

Semnut takes her by the hand and they walk up the stairs together. She helps her off with her clothes and into the tub, which has been filled with warm water. The servant girl sits the tea tray on a small side table, and Semnut pours a cup and hands it to Alenna. She looks at it, then at Semnut, then around the room.

"Where am I? What is this place?" she says in a strained voice.

"You are in your tub, mistress," says Semnut.

"Where am I?" she says again, in a voice grown louder and more agitated.

"You are at home, Alenna," says Semnut quietly.

"This is not my home."

Semnut moves closer. Alenna hurls the cup at her but the old woman moves quickly, and the cup shatters against the wall.

"You tell me where I am this instant, old woman!" Alenna is screaming now.

"Alenna, little one, you are at home. You are safe." Semnut is frightened.

"No, I am not!" Alenna screams. "I shall have you beaten if you do not tell me!" Alenna begins to shake violently.

"Oh, gods of Egypt," Semnut whispers. The old nurse begins to sing a little song, a lullaby she had sung to Alenna as a child. Alenna looks at Semnut and starts to cry. The nurse lifts her mistress from the tub, still singing, and wraps her in a towel.

Later, Semnut will bring a cup of warm wine mixed with a little powder of poppies, and Alenna will sleep all day.

---

Lukhamen is the first to find him. Khenti has fallen from his cot and lies on the stone floor, clutching his chest and gasping for breath. He lifts the old man onto his cot.

"Rest easy, Khenti. I shall send for Sechmetna."

Khenti smiles. "There is no need to summon a physician." He struggles for breath. "I should like you to call the high priest, if you do not mind."

"He is here in the temple, Khenti. I shan't be long."

---

The high priest wheels himself up to the little cot. "Khenti," he whispers, "Khenti, my friend."

The old man opens his eyes. "It is time, Your Excellency. I must ask you to pray for me."

"Oh, my dear old Khenti. Will you not call me Lukhamen, even now?"

Khenti smiles. "When your son was a boy, he asked me to call him Lukhamen, too. I have never been comfortable with such...informality."

"Whatever you wish, my friend." The high priest's voice breaks.

"I should like a grand funeral."

"You shall have a pharaoh's funeral. And you shall sleep in the mountain with my family."

The old man smiles. A moment passes, and neither speaks. "Your Excellency." Khenti's breathing is labored.

"Yes, my friend."

"Do not lose hope."

The high priest lets the tears come freely down his face.

"It may seem as if all is lost, but it is not." Khenti squeezes the high priest's hand tightly. "It is never all lost."

The old man sighs deeply and breathes no more.

—————∞∞∞—————

Khenti's body lies in the sanctuary for two days, with priests to guard it by day and by night. There is little incense to burn, but every bit that remains in the temple is used in the funereal ceremony. The high priest and his eldest son wear the purple robes of their office, the only silk robes that have not been sold.

A coffin has been fashioned from papyrus reeds by the priests, and painted with decorations so intricate and delicate that only by the absence of gold would one know that it was not that of a pharaoh. The inscriptions tell the story of Khenti's life—an exemplary life marked by service to Amon, God of Life and Breath, and to his temple in Luxor. A cartouche on the lid spells out *Khenti, Chief Priest of the Temple of Luxor.*

The boat that takes his body across the river is not draped in white, nor does it carry baskets of food, or statues, or jars of beer, or accoutrements of any kind, as it would have in better times. No jewelry adorns the body, and within the lovely encasement, Khenti lies wrapped in coarse linen, his eyes lined with kohl, a small amulet in his hands, placed there by the high priest.

The chanting echoes up and down the river as the small boat is oared slowly across the low waters. The high priest sits next to the makeshift coffin, his hand resting upon it. Khenti has asked him not to lose hope, but he can feel it ebb, like the waters that are almost too low to sail upon.

—————∞∞∞—————

The girl Lucenkep hears the chanting from the bank, looks to the river, and sees the boat. Even from this distance, and although she can only see the back of his head, she knows that it is he, the one who took possession of her heart before she left for the south country, sent there by her mother after the crucifixions.

*I am home, Lukhamen*, she whispers to him. *I am home.*

# CHAPTER 57

THE HIGH PRIEST SITS AT the edge of the dock, watching the boat as it heads up-river, back to Philae. He lifts his hand in salute to the priests who are aboard. Khenti's funeral has ended the convocation.

"Let us go home, my son. I am weary."

"As well you should be, Father."

"Lukhamen?"

"Yes, Father?"

"I've changed my mind. I should like to go across the river."

Lukhamen and two priests help the high priest into the small temple boat, and within minutes they are away. A gentle breeze comes from downriver, and a cloud moves over the sun. Instinctively, they all look skyward, and in each one's heart there is the same desperate hope: rain.

"Leave me," the high priest says to the others as they disembark. "I will go on alone."

He wheels himself over the rocky valley floor. At the foot of the mountain, he looks up. The boulder has been replaced, but the entrance to the tomb is clearly visible.

"Khenti, my friend," he whispers, "Will you hear me?"

The breeze quickens into a light wind and lifts the dust in small circles around his feet. The sky darkens, but he does not notice.

"I have lost the support of the high priests," he says toward the mountain. "I want to change everything and they want everything to stay the same. As long as they feel safe, they will not move." He tightens his fists. "We are starving and the Romans have tightened their vise! They are taxed in Philae until they bleed, their temple is stripped bare, and still they refuse to listen. And the people! They have forgotten who they are! Am I the only one who remembers, then?" His voice carries upon the wind. *AM I THE ONLY ONE?* A clap of thunder sounds overhead.

Rain begins as a drop here and there in the sand, then becomes large plops of water, splattering and disappearing into the dry dust, falling faster and faster, until they beat down upon his head. He looks up, and the rain pours onto his face. He wipes the rain from his eyes. Lukhamen is running toward him.

"Come, Father." He is out of breath. "Let us get you back to the boat."

"Rain, Lukhamen!"

"Yes, Father."

Lukhamen is wheeling him down to the river, faster and faster.

"I have not seen it rain like this since the night Aahmes was born!"

"Yes, Father."

"A sign, Lukhamen! It is surely a sign!"

Drops explode on the river's surface. They cross in the little boat, their vision obscured by the driving rain. It soaks their clothes and drips from their hair. It covers the floor of the boat and is ankle-deep by the time they reach the temple dock.

"Let us get you inside the temple, Father, where you can be warmed and change into dry clothes."

"No, Lukhamen. We will go home."

"But Father—"

"I have not been home in two weeks. I will go home. Now."

By the time they reach home, chilled to the bone and shivering, the high priest is in the throes of a fever. Aahmes prepares a bitter-tasting tea. The high priest sinks into a fitful sleep.

Sometime during the night, he is aware of Alenna by his bedside, singing softly. He opens his eyes. She is sitting on the edge of his bed, brushing her hair, singing a tune she used to sing to the boys when they were little.

"Alenna."

She looks at him, startled.

"My love," he says. "I did not mean to startle you." She does not reply. She is preoccupied—brushing, brushing. "Alenna?"

She turns away, then back to him. "Oh, you did not startle me," she says coyly, then resumes the brushing and singing.

"Alenna?"

She takes a deep breath, as if exasperated. "Yes?"

"Alenna, is something wrong?"

"Wrong?"

"Yes. Are you all right?"

"Why would I not be all right?" Fear shines in her eyes.

He reaches out to touch her, and she pulls away, looking at him suspiciously.

"Why did you ask me if something is wrong?"

"Because, Alenna, you are sitting here in the middle of the night, brushing your hair and singing, and you will not talk to me."

"I am talking to you."

"Alenna! What is wrong?"

"Why are you shouting at me?"

"I am not shouting at you, Alenna."

"But you are, you are, you are! You are always shouting at me!" Little whimpering sounds come from the back of her throat. She puts her hands over her mouth, muffling the pitiful cries, leaving only the eyes to look at him, eyes that are like the eyes of a trapped animal. He feels a chill.

"Alenna, I am sorry," he says.

The eyes soften a bit.

"You are?"

"Yes, my love. I am sorry."

She uncovers her mouth and smiles at him. Then, as quickly, her face crumples, her lip quivers, and she begins to cry.

"I am going to die anyway."

"Die? Alenna, what are you talking about?"

"I am going to die anyway," she whispers.

"Alenna, my love. You are not going to die."

"Yes, I am," she cries, "and there is nothing you can do about it."

He reaches for her.

"Alenna. Come closer to me." She lays her head on his chest. He strokes her hair. A pain begins somewhere in his throat.

"I feel it," she whispers into his chest, "I feel it. I am dying now. Little bits and pieces of me are dying now. I can feel it."

"I won't let you die, Alenna."

"You won't?"

She lifts her head to look at him, sees the tears fall from his eyes.

"Why are you crying, then?"

"I am happy to be home."

She takes a deep breath, smiles brightly, lifts her head, looks around the room, then down at her gown.

"Do you like my gown?"

"It is beautiful."

"It is one of my old ones. I had lots of gowns once, but they are all gone now."

She looks around the room again. "Do you remember Haraa?"

"Yes, Alenna."

"She was my friend, but now she is gone."

"She will be back soon."

"No, she will not."

"Why do you say that?"

"Because she is dead."

"Dead?"

"Yes. Dead, like all the rest."

"Like who, Alenna?"

"Like all of them."

"Who?"

"All of them. Marcus, Lukhamen. All dead. Dead and gone."

She strokes his forehead and hums her little tune again.

And so they are thus, through the night—talking, crying together, sometimes laughing. And he remembers the days after the accident, when they had done the same, the nights when pain made sleep impossible, when she would sit by his side and stave off the darkness of his despair. But now it is she who lives in the dark. He enfolds her in his arms as he would a child, and weeps.

---

*My Dear Son,*

*This letter is written in some haste, as I must get it to the delegation that is coming to you. There is trouble afoot here, Marcus. I know not what lies in back of it, but I have gotten wind of an inquiry that is to be made into matters of state in the province of Luxor. I must only suspect, since Petronia's father has initiated this "inquiry," that it has something to do with her disenchantment with the situation there. I shall try my best to become party to the inquiry, if only to keep things on a more balanced scale.*

*In any case, I would advise you to be extremely careful. See to it that all matters of state are adhered to strictly and according to policy. Above all, be mindful of the party that comes to you. One of the "auditors" is a member of the senator's staff.*

*I am indeed sorry to be the bearer of ill tidings. You and young Marcus are always in my thoughts.*

*Your Loving Father*

The governor sets the letter aside and looks up to find Linus standing before him.

"I shall take my leave of you, sire. We have found all in order, and a copy of my report is with your aide."

"Thank you, Linus. Where are your auditors?"

"Assisting your wife at the moment. She is preparing to join our party on the return trip to Rome."

"Yes, I know."

Only the day before, Petronia had asked permission to leave Egypt, and Marcus had granted it. Antonious was given leave to accompany her.

"We found the rain a remarkable occurrence, Sire. I only hope it portends well for you."

"Thank you, Linus."

"Goodbye, Sire."

"Goodbye. Safe journey."

"Thank you, Sire."

"Oh, and Linus?"

"Yes?"

"Please give the senator my best when you see him."

"Your father, sire?"

"No. Petronia's father."

Linus blanches.

"Yes, Sire."

Linus stumbles over the doorstop on the way out.

---

It is a small party of twelve: three auditors, the wife of the governor, her companion, Antonious, and seven of the governor's own imperial guards. They are a day's ride north of Luxor when they are struck. A band of twenty renegades attacks swiftly from behind, appearing out of nowhere.

The guards are killed first in a short, fierce contest. The auditors look on in disbelief, unable to move. Finally, the marauders close in around them, laughing and taunting, some wearing helmets taken from the governor's bravest and best. Linus is brought down first, then Petronia from her horse, screaming shrilly. She continues thus throughout the debate on whether she should be raped before being killed. A large, hairy man with protruding teeth settles the argument by slitting her throat neatly, in one swipe.

Antonious sits calmly upon his steed, surveying the bloody scene, his lips twisted into a crooked smile. After a few minutes, he turns his horse in the direction of Alexandria, where he will board a ship bound for Rome.

# CHAPTER 58

IN A FEW DAYS, COMPLETELY recovered from the fever, the high priest sits alone at breakfast, reading the governor's letter. Standing in the entrance hall, a sentry awaits his reply.

"Manut," says the high priest to the steward, "tell the sentry that I will return with him to the governor's residence."

When they arrive, Marcus is waiting. There are dark circles around his eyes.

"Marcus. Your letter sounded urgent."

"Thank you for coming so promptly, Lukhamen."

"What is it?"

"My wife and her entire party were killed on the road to Alexandria." The high priest gasps. "They were discovered yesterday by a patrol. Their bodies have been returned to Luxor. Today they shall be cremated."

They stare at each other for a long moment, each becoming more aware of the darkening circumstances that surround them.

"Marcus, I—"

"I know the assassins were not Egyptian, Lukhamen." The high priest's sigh is audible.

"Nevertheless," he continues, "she was the daughter of Rome's most powerful senator, and there will be a reckoning. At this moment, I can only guess what that might be."

"Holiest of gods! We shall all pay for it, Marcus."

"Yes. We shall all pay." They look into one another's eyes and feel the danger that singes the air.

"There is one who was not counted among the dead," says Marcus: "Antonious. He is now on his way to Rome. He was counted among those on a ship out of Alexandria. I have long suspected it was he who masterminded the first attack upon my troops. His escape confirms my suspicions."

"His presence in Rome means, then..."

It means that I am in imminent danger. That is why I have asked you here."

"Gods of Egypt."

A guard brings tea and sets it before them. Marcus pours. "I have always loved hibiscus tea. My predecessor taught me to drink it."

"There is none like it in the world."

The men savor their tea. Neither speaks. A white river bird soars past the window, circles widely, then comes to rest on the windowsill. Marcus smiles.

"Lovely, these birds. They appear at the most interesting times."

"What are we to do, Marcus?"

"I want you to protect my son, Lukhamen."

The high priest is taken aback. "But he is a citizen of Rome! Surely they will not harm him."

"If I am found guilty of treason, they will not allow him to live."

"Treason!"

"Antonious will accuse me of treason."

"But this is preposterous..."

"Lukhamen, listen to me. My wife came to believe that I killed the governor."

"What?"

"Antonious planted the seed very carefully, then wrote shadowy, accusatory letters to the senator on behalf of his daughter. Now, with Antonious at his ear to embellish the lie, he will believe I killed her to prevent her coming to Rome. Miraculously, he will tell the senator, he escaped to bring him the truth."

"Then you must go to Rome as well, Marcus."

"I am not permitted to leave my post without permission from Rome. Antonious will see to it that it is denied."

Lukhamen looks at the governor, the weight of realization on his face. "What will you do?"

"I do not know. I only know that I must keep my son out of their reach. I want you to take him, Lukhamen, disguise him as one of your priests, send him to the temple at Edfu, or Philae—it matters not where. Take him, and do not tell me where he has gone." Marcus's voice breaks.

The high priest is quiet for a long time. "Send him to me, Marcus. They will have to destroy every temple in Egypt to find him."

Marcus turns away from the high priest and walks toward the window. The bird, surprised, flutters its wings and soars up and away, toward the river. Marcus regains his voice at last.

"There is something else I must tell you, Lukhamen."

"It is not necessary." The high priest breathes quickly, his chest moving up and down in shallow waves. He wants to know no more. *Marcus, just let it be.*

"It is important."

"Very well, then." The high priest braces himself for what he does not want to hear.

"Alenna should be taken away from Luxor as well."

This is not what he expected.

"Surely you do not think she is in danger?"

"We are all in danger now, Lukhamen. Send her away with my son, if you choose. He will look after her. I shall instruct him to protect her with his life."

"Marcus..."

"Roman rule in Egypt has been gentle in your time, Lukhamen, no matter what you may think. But you must know it was not always that way. I believe they mean to restore a hard order. Egyptian women, especially of the noble class, will be...at risk."

The high priest is suddenly filled with fear. "Marcus..."

"She must be kept safe, especially now..." His voice breaks again. "I implore you, Lukhamen, send her away."

"I know that you love her, Marcus. I have always known it."

Marcus turns to him with the same pained eyes that have followed her every step, measured her every gesture, memorized her every move, followed her around every room, the pained eyes that have always betrayed him.

"She has lived in my heart from the moment I saw her. It was when you were lying in the temple, after the wall collapsed. She visited you. I was in charge of the renovations."

"Marcus..."

"I would lay down my life for her."

"I know."

"I wish it had not been so, Lukhamen. It has only brought me pain." The tears are flowing now, streaking his face. "And now," he continues, "she is...different, crushed by cruelties. Crushed by Rome. By me." A great sob racks him. "I would give my life if it were not so!"

"As would I," whispers Lukhamen.

"When you were in the temple with the convocation, she walked here in the cold and dead of night, frightened and alone. I could not send her away. She told me that she was going to die. It broke my heart. Forgive me, Lukhamen."

"I cannot condemn you, Marcus, for loving her, for protecting her."

"She was...not herself, Lukhamen. Losing her house, the crucifixions, the drought, all of this...was just too much for her to bear."

"You are not the only one who is to blame for Alenna's...*state*, Marcus. I was the one who turned away from her when she was alone and frightened. I turned away from her long ago. I offered her no comfort, not even the little I was capable of."

The white bird returns to the windowsill. They are quiet for a long while, watching his stillness. Marcus breaks the silence.

"There is one thing I must do now, Lukhamen."

"What is that, Marcus?"

"I do not know when Roman authorities will come for me, but it will be soon, and my son must not be found here. May I bring him to you this evening? It will be better to travel after sunset, with night to cover us."

"We shall await you. And him."

"Let us have a meal together. A banquet." Marcus smiles.

"A what?"

"A banquet. Tonight. You, me, Alenna, our sons, Haraa's daughter. My mother died when I was young, Lukhamen. After her death, my father threw himself into the business of the Senate. It became his life. I grew up with my grandfather. Besides him, you are the only family I have ever had."

Lukhamen reaches out and touches Marcus's hand. "Our rations are meager, Marcus, but we shall—"

"I shall send a lamb, Lukhamen—a lamb and perfumed rice, and wine. The army has eaten well enough. There is food in our stores. Enough for us and for your servants."

They look at each other and smile through their tears. Lukhamen turns his chair to go, then turns back.

"She shall be safe with me, Marcus. I will not turn away from her again."

Marcus walks over to him. "One last thing, Lukhamen."

"Yes?"

"The crucifixions…"

"Please…"

"If I had not carried out the emperor's policy, they would have removed me. I had a choice to make. I had to make it quickly. I made it and I do not regret it. I took a hundred lives. I would have taken a thousand to protect her. If there is a God, I would hope he would forgive me, but I could not risk being replaced by someone as cruel as Antonious. Ironic, is it not? Antonious will probably be governor anyway. It was all for nothing."

"Not for nothing, Marcus. It was for you."

"For me?"

"It was for you to see us as people, to understand suffering, to know Egypt as you know it now." He takes his hand. "You may yet be our voice in Rome."

He turns his chair and is gone.

---

It is high noon, and the sun beats down upon the woman, burning through her thin robe. A veil covers her face. Only the eyes show, desperate and afraid. She lowers her bucket into the well, and when it is heavy with water, she begins to pull the rope, but she is too weak to bring it up. A strong hand grasps it and brings it to the surface.

"May I carry it for you?"

She looks up into the handsome face smiling down at her. He is dressed in a plain linen robe, but she recognizes him. The son of the high priest lifts the bucket of water, and together they walk down a small, dusty lane.

"I am Lukhamen."

"My name is Alia," she whispers. "My house is just here."

"I will bring it inside for you."

"No!" She realizes she has said it too loudly. "No, thank you," she says in a normal voice. It is just fine here by the door."

"There is no need to be afraid."

"It will be just fine here."

"Very well, Alia."

She is bent, but looks up at him sideways to see the beautiful face once more, when her legs give way. She slides to the ground, and as he is about to help her rise, she shouts at him.

"Do not touch me!"

"It is all right, Alia, I am just going to help you."

"No! No! Do not touch me!"

"I am not afraid, Alia," he says softly. "Lean on me. Put your hands on my sleeve. I will not touch you." She begins to cry.

"Please, please, go away."

"It is all right. I will tell no one."

He picks her up in his arms, takes her inside the little hovel, and lays her on the tiny cot. He brings the bucket inside, and holds a cup of water to her lips. She sips a little, then hands it back to him.

"Please. You must go away. I try to go to the well when the sun is high, when there is no one there. Why were you there?"

"I suppose I am too stupid to stay out of the sun," he says, still smiling. "I come here sometimes with my brother, Aahmes. He is studying with the great Sechmetna. He wants to be a doctor."

"No doctor can help me."

"My brother thinks he can do anything. He's stupid, too."

"No. Please."

"I shall see you tomorrow, Alia."

*Stupid boy! Jesus, protect him.*

Alia's prayer echoes through her soul. It is the purest request of her life, issued with every ounce of desire she can call forth. And it goes forth, truly and swiftly into the universe, where it is heard and made manifest.

Marcus opens the gate quietly. He and young Marcus walk their horses through, tether them to a tree, then walk across the courtyard to the doorway, which is framed by vines of night blooming jasmine. Marcus stops a moment to take in their fragrance and remembers the first time he entered this house. He had escorted the high priest from the temple, where he had lain after being crushed by a collapsing wall. When Alenna opened the door, he had stood there, dumfounded, speechless. He had expected a servant and the time to compose himself before seeing her.

*Shall we get him out of the sun?* she had said.

He knocks. The door opens. It is Manut, the head steward. He leads them into the reception hall, where the high priest is waiting. It is empty, hollow. All of Alenna's fine furnishings are gone, sold to buy food. Marcus remembers the quiet elegance of this great room. *I sat on a couch with her, just there.*

"Welcome, Marcus," the high priest says.

"Your Excellency, may I present my son, Marcus Aurelius."

"Welcome young Marcus, welcome."

"Sire," the boy responds.

"Please. Follow me. We shall dine on the terrace tonight."

The boy is fascinated by the rolling chair, which the high priest wheels expertly before them. They must pass through his chamber, which was the dining room before the accident, and through its archways, to the garden. The boy notes the shelves of scrolls that line the walls. It has not occurred to him that among other things, the high priest is a scholar.

Marcus has apprised him of his situation, and the boy has taken it surprisingly well. He is still young and hopeful.

Femi comes through the archways from the garden to greet them. "Governor," she says, still blushing at the sight of him.

"Hello, Femi. You are still as beautiful as ever. I trust your mother is well?" Haraa flits across his mind, her face streaked with tears on the day he moved out of her house and back into the governor's mansion.

"She is doing quite well, Governor. I received a letter from her just yesterday."

"Let me introduce my son, Marcus."

"Welcome, Marcus."

Like his father, young Marcus is capable of losing his speech at the sight of a beautiful Egyptian girl. He manages a weak smile.

"Come," she says. "Mother Alenna is waiting."

Femi leads them through the archways that lead to the garden, to where a table has been set on the terrace. Femi has brought Turkish Lilies from her mother's garden and placed them in bronze bowls down the center of the table. Lanterns are lit along the tiled paths and hung from the trees. Alenna sits quietly at the table in the lamplights' glow. She looks up as they enter, and gives them a dazzling smile. Marcus's heart stops.

She is dressed in her finest silk robe. It is fuchsia, the same as the bougainvillea on the far garden wall, and worn, ever so slightly. Her hair has been burnished to a high sheen by Femi's stiff brushes, and she is wearing a milky white opal set in a silver bracelet—the only piece of her jewelry that has not been given to Haraa to sell.

"This is my son, Alenna," says Marcus.

"Welcome, young Marcus. We have been expecting you. These are my sons, Lukhamen and Aahmes." They rise to meet him and soon all are seated, the high priest and the governor on either side of Alenna, who is at the head of the table.

*She seems...*well *this evening,* thinks Marcus, as the servants enter bearing lamb and perfumed rice that had been sent earlier in the day by his courier.

He looks contentedly at the young people, who are lively, chattering and exuberant, except for the high priest's son, Lukhamen, who surveys them with cool, but not unfriendly, detachment. His son's eyes have not left Femi's face, and he notices at once that Aahmes is jealously protective of her. But it is to Lukhamen that she will be wed. *Please,* he prays to no one in particular, *spare my son the misery of love.*

His eyes turn to Alenna, who is playful and delighted by everything. She claps her hands when a new dish is brought to the table, and eats heartily. Her eyes are bright with anticipation, like those of a child at a birthday party. She speaks only to comment on this dish or that, but never directly to Marcus or to the high priest.

The high priest is lost in his own thoughts. He is remembering another time—when servants stood in the corners of the great hall, waving large palm fans, sending trails of perfume from the garden into the air, while on a raised platform, musicians plucked and strummed gilded harps. It was before Lukhamen's first ordination. He was nine years old and Alenna was in her chamber above, with a new baby.

He looks back through the archways and into the dark beyond where, on that great occasion, the tables in the great hall were draped in white linen and piled high with food from the coastal markets of the Mediterranean, where servants wearing white linen loincloths and braided wigs walked among the guests, replenishing silver goblets with plum colored wine, tiny bells on ankle bracelets tinkling as they walked. The great room was vibrant, noisy with laughter and festivity. Kitchen servants carried in great plates of smoked silver fish arranged with the heads pointing outwards, lamb marinated in olive oil and rosemary, rice, fragrant with raisins and nuts and cumin, while mounds of figs, goat cheeses piled high, and pomegranates split open and blood red, weighed down the side table. In the center of each table sat a whole roasted peacock, decorated with its own tail feathers.

He sees himself strolling splendidly among the guests, a goblet of wine in his hand, a servant following him, replenishing it often. "Next year, next year," he hears himself saying, "Next year, Lukhamen will enter the temple. We will teach him to read here at home and in a year or so he will take his place beside the other novices." That was before the wall crushed him and he lost his son to the priests at Philae too soon. Alenna would have had time to adjust, to accept Lukhamen's future.

"More wine, sire?" says Manut, drawing him back into the present.

"Thank you, Manut," he says.

His eyes meet Marcus's: *it is time.*

"Femi," says the high priest, "Will you take mother to her chamber? It has been a long night, and she is tired."

"Alenna?" he says.

"Yes?" she answers.

"Good night, my love."

"Good night." She rises from her chair, walks around in back of Marcus, places a hand on his shoulder and says, "Good night, Marcus."

It is the first time she has spoken to him directly. He stands to face her, drink in her eyes, her hair. "Goodbye, Alenna," he says. *Goodbye, my love.*

Her face crumbles as if she had heard his unspoken words. Quickly, she smiles, turns, and lets Femi lead her from the room. Marcus stares after her until the house swallows her in darkness.

Marcus, the high priest, and their sons remain at the table until it is cleared and the servants retire to the kitchen. Not once has young Marcus made mention of his mother, whose funeral took place earlier in the day. He does not miss her; he does not mourn her. He is relieved to be in the company of warmth and obvious affection. And Femi.

Within the hour, the high priest and the governor have fully informed their sons of the situation in Rome and reviewed the plan for young Marcus to be taken to a temple in a location unknown to all present except the high priest. It is well past midnight when the governor leaves to return to his residence. Alone.

Manut unties young Marcus's horse and tethers it to a tree some distance from the house, where it will stay the night.

# CHAPTER 59

"Shall we abandon our temples, then? Shall we surrender our land, and all that we possess, or shall we rally the priesthood, the poor, become soldiers, and fight? Shall we die in shame or in battle?"

The young priest stands before them on the highest ground in Philae, in the temple courtyard. Behind him, the monumental figure of Isis—carved into the pylon, her face turned aside, looks out onto the sparkling river.

"Please, my brother," says the High Priest of the Temple of Luxor, "let us speak as reasonable men. Insurrection is suicide. We have no weapons; our people are weak from starvation."

"If I may, Father," says Lukhamen. All eyes turn to the young man. It is Lukhamen's first time to speak in convocation.

"My fellow priests: We are reduced in every way. In Luxor, crucifixions, starvation, and leprosy have greatly diminished the people. All resistance, all desire for resistance, all memories of freedom are gone. The people are engaged in one thing only—survival. We are only dim reminders of a past that no longer exists for them."

The crowd comes alive with an angry buzz.

"Young man," an older priest shouts, "for shame! And you, the son of the High Priest of Luxor! We are from royal lines! Descended from pharaohs! The Romans would not dare harm us!"

"They have already taken our temples," Lukhamen answers quietly. A hush washes over them, but it is only temporary.

"Your Excellency!" An older man addresses the high priest. "Is this how you have raised your son?"

"I have sent him among the Christians, Your Excellency, and he is merely reporting what he has seen and heard."

"The Christians? You have sent him among the Christians?"

"I have."

A roar of disapproval arises like dust in the heat of the day.

"Sire," the younger Lukhamen says, "I meant no disrespect. Only a few days ago, my father permitted me to enter the tomb of the Sa'ats, where I touched the burial boxes of my forefathers. When I succeed my father, I will be the twenty-eighth in an unbroken line of high priests of Amon. I know, Sire, who I am."

"Then what is this talk about 'dim reminders'?"

"I am merely saying, Sire, that the people are too tired to feel anything, too sick to remember anything except the pain in their bellies. They are slaves, hungry and exhausted."

"They are Christians. What would you expect? They are rabble—meek, cowardly rabble."

"They are Egyptians, Sire," Lukhamen says quietly.

"They used to be Egyptians," says the older man, feeling the approval of those around him.

The high priest leans closer to his son. "Leave it, Lukhamen," he whispers, "It is useless."

"We will make our peace with the new governor, whoever he is," says the older man. "We will continue as we always have. It is as simple as that."

"And the hungry?" Lukhamen says.

"The Romans will feed them, as they always have," says the older priest.

On the voyage back to Luxor they are quiet, each lost in thought. As the mountains of Thebes come into view, Lukhamen breaks the silence.

"Father."

"Yes, Lukhamen."

"There is something I have never told you."

"And you wish to tell me now."

"Yes."

"Very well. It seems it is a time for unburdening."

"It is something I have kept secret since I was a child. Khenti is the only person who ever knew."

"What is it?"

"I have heard a voice, Father."

"A voice?"

"It comes to me, particularly in times of great stress."

"And this voice…what does it say?"

"It is like a whisper. It is…reassuring."

The high priest touches his son's hand.

"There is a great power, Lukhamen. It dwells in another world; it is a power we cannot see or touch—a power greater than our pain. It is the power I called on when I took my great journey into the world of spirit. Do you remember that night?"

"Vaguely, Father. I remember I sat up all night. Khenti was with us."

"I told you my spirit would journey forth, across the sacred river. I have never told you what I discovered there."

"What did you discover, Father?"

"I saw my father there, Lukhamen, radiant and more beautiful than he ever was in life. He transformed my broken body into another body—a spirit body, a reflection of who I really am—a being of light and beauty that has life in both worlds. I went to that place to answer my father's call, to seek relief from physical pain, or barring that, death. But my father and the other ones I met there gave me much more. I am not quite sure I understand it completely, but I have tried, ever since then, to know who I am, to know that I am more than I appear to be. I believe that the voice you hear emanates from that spirit world. It speaks to the beauty within you, your true self. It is there to guide you as you serve our people."

"I have tried, Father, to have faith, but I do not have a faith like yours."

They are quiet for a while, floating easily on the river.

"Do not worry, Lukhamen. Life, and the experiences it brings, will strengthen your faith. Faith is nothing more than the belief that we are not alone—that every burden is not borne alone."

"Father—"

"Yes, Lukhamen?"

"My Voice told me that I was not alone."

Their boat approaches the dock of the temple. Three boy priests run out to meet them. At this moment, deep in the forests of faraway Africa, rain clouds burst open, drenching the forest floor. The air fills with steam, rising in clouds from the earth. Water will rise in the streams and slide toward the great falls, racing and tumbling until it falls once again into the Nile.

Lukhamen looks upriver and feels it, smells it in the wind. The time of famine is over.

As he watches the boys lift his father from the boat and place him in his chair, a small white river bird that has flown from across the river settles on his shoulder. It stays there until he brushes it off.

The high priest sits in the sanctuary, before the great granite statue of Amon, in the center of the Holy of Holies. In the darkness, he closes his eyes, gives himself up to the deep silence. To his mind comes the image of the place in the mountain where they sleep. And he sees the fathers, one by one, arise from their tombs and come to him, holding out their arms, embracing him with their light.

At the moment of Marcus's arrest, the high priest feels a shift, as if the ground has moved beneath him. Roman troops surround Marcus and bind his hands. Antonious, the new governor, reads the charges against him in a loud, rancorous voice. The high priest closes his eyes more tightly. The sweet aroma of incense encircles him, and fills his nostrils. It wraps the room in a mist, and climbs up and around the head of Amon—up, up, into the ceiling of the sanctuary.

———⊗⊗⊗———

Marcus is, after all, a Roman citizen, and a former governor. As such he is extended the courtesy of house arrest. In two days, he will be sent to Rome to be tried for treason. Antonious institutes an immediate search for young Marcus, but he is nowhere to be found.

"A sure sign of your guilt, Marcus," Antonious sneers at him.

Marcus stands bound before the new governor. Antonious is seated at his new dining table in the governor's mansion, stuffing himself with grilled lamb and figs and drinking noisily from an exquisitely blown wine glass. Swaying and drunk, he points a greasy finger at his enemy.

"A sign of your guilt, to hide the boy from me, Marcus. But never mind. We will find him."

He slams the glass onto the table. It shatters. A servant girl hurries to pick up the pieces. In her haste, she cuts her finger.

"Stupid cow!" Antonious roars.

The girl runs quickly from the room.

"You will make a fine governor, Antonious," says Marcus, his voice thick with sarcasm.

"I will make a fine *Roman* governor—unlike you," sneers Antonious. "You were never anything but a soldier. The job was always above you." He belches loudly. "You were soft, and stupid. You slept with Egyptian whores and treated them like they were Roman ladies. It was a big mistake."

The girl returns with another glass. As she places it on the table, Antonious grabs her wrist.

"You see, Marcus? They are barely human. You shouldn't treat them as if they are. You should *use* them...copulate with them like a shepherd boy with sheep."

The girl starts to cry. She breaks loose and runs from the room.

"I'll tend to her later," he slurs, smiling a crooked smile at Marcus. He empties his glass and fills it again.

"Oh, yes, Marcus. I am a Roman Governor. And these animals are going to discover exactly what it is to be ruled by a Roman Governor. And you, Marcus? Because you were playing in a game that was far beyond your capabilities, you are going to Rome, where you will be tried and sentenced to death."

Marcus is silent.

"What—no reaction? No insults? Come, come, Marcus. Come, come!" His speech is slurred. "And when you are dead, Marcus, I will take your fine Egyptian women. I will strip them naked, and parade them in the streets." He is reeling in his seat. "Especially that priest's wife, Marcus, the one you like so much."

He reels one last time and falls from his seat onto the floor. Marcus looks to the centurion standing at the door.

"Take the governor to his bed, centurion."

"Yes, Sire."

In a few moments, the centurion returns and leads Marcus to the room to which he is confined, in the servants' quarters in the back of the mansion.

---

At midnight, Marcus feels a hand over his mouth. A blindfold is placed over his eyes. He is taken from his bed and led to a back entrance. He feels the ropes being cut from his wrists. A voice whispers in his ear.

"There is a horse outside, sire. He is swift and sure. He is strong and can ride all the night."

Marcus removes the blindfold. "Do not do this, centurion…"

"The blame, Sire, will fall ultimately upon him."

"You too will be punished."

"Yes, Sire."

"Why are you doing this?"

"Because you are one of us—a soldier, Sire."

Marcus starts to speak, but the centurion continues. "There are sentries all the way to Libya. They will be notified. A horseman will ride ahead of you. He has already begun his journey."

"There is something you must know."

"Yes, Sire."

"I did not murder the governor."

"We know."

The centurion leads Marcus to the door and disappears into the darkness of the mansion.

Marcus mounts the sleek black horse and rides slowly and quietly away. A short distance out, he leaves the steed tethered to a tree and returns to the governor's mansion on foot. He enters by the door through which he left, slips past a sleeping guard, climbs the stairs to the governor's bedroom, and strangles Antonious in his sleep. He then comes down the stairs and wakes the guard, who jumps to his feet.

Luxor has no governor when the high priest presents himself and asks for an audience with Marcus. The guard, uncertain whether to grant the request or deny it, goes to the only authority he knows: Marcus himself.

He escorts Marcus into a reception room, where the high priest is waiting.

"Marcus."

"Lukhamen."

"How are you?"

"I am well, Lukhamen."

They look at each other, not knowing what to say.

Marcus smiles. "Antonious was furious that he could not find young Marcus."

"He is quite safe—and bored, I am told."

"I've been thinking, Lukhamen."

"Yes?"

"I still feel proud to have served Rome, even though I cannot condone all of its actions. I went to the finest military academy in all the known world. My grandfather was a great general and served a great emperor, Marcus Aurelius, for whom I am named. My father is a senator. Rome has done things others have only dreamed of, and I have been part of it. That is what is in my mind now, even as Rome prepares to execute me. Do you not think that is odd?"

"We are who we are, Marcus."

Marcus smiles.

"A little of the glory of our ancestors rubs off on us, burnishes our faded spots, adds light to our darkness. I know such pride well, Marcus. Egyptians built the greatest civilization in the known world. Science, art, medicine, architecture, beauty beyond belief—all were expressed right here. It is still all here, all around us."

"However did we become friends?"

"Life thrust us together. We could have made of it anything we wished. We chose friendship."

A soldier brings hibiscus tea. "I shall miss this lovely tea, Lukhamen." They sip the sweet crimson beverage, savoring the moment.

Finally the high priest speaks. "Why did you do it, Marcus? Why kill Antonious and assure your own death? You might have been acquitted of the charge of treason."

"Rome has better governors to offer you, Lukhamen."

"It has already given us its best, but he is lost, because he loved us."

Alenna's face flickers in Marcus's mind, and with it the old pain that is sharper now, more insistent.

"I had nothing to lose. I was a condemned man."

"But you were innocent."

"I was never innocent."

A soldier appears at the door. Marcus looks at the man in the wheeled chair. "It is time. They have been more than generous with me."

Lukhamen holds out his arm. Marcus takes it.

"Do not worry, Marcus," says the high priest, his voice breaking. "They shall both be safe with me."

Marcus holds tightly to the arm of his friend, then lets go and walks away without looking back.

———— ∞∞∞ ————

Alone in his room, Marcus holds the short, blunt sword that has been given to him by the centurion. He poises it against his middle. With both hands, he plunges the blade into his body and withdraws it. The sword makes a clattering noise as it drops to the floor.

From the small bed onto which he has fallen, Marcus can see the moon through the window. It has never been so beautiful. Alenna appears in its light, wearing a silver robe. The scent of orange blossoms is in her hair. Loosened and luminous, it falls over her shoulder as she leans over him, placing her hand on his wound.

"Are you in pain, Marcus?" she says softly.

He smiles at her. He tries to speak, but cannot. He wants to tell her that the pain is gone, at last.

# CHAPTER 60

☥

WITHIN THE WEEK, ROME DISPATCHES its new governor—a career administrator who was serving nearby as governor of the Greek province and outlying islands. He is chagrined to learn that the officers under his command have given Marcus a military funeral while Antonious was unceremoniously cremated—his ashes placed in an unadorned urn, which is now standing alone in a corner of the governor's office.

Marcus's grave, which is in the military compound, has been marked with a stone upon which is carved *Marcus Aurelius, Centurion, Roman Army*. The governor orders the stone removed and crushed. On many a night thereafter, a guard in full uniform can be seen standing at attention at the site, while straight-backed soldiers of every rank file by, salute, and empty jars of beer on the unmarked grave.

On the third day after his arrival, the governor posts a notice that a census will be taken of the Egyptian population. Failure to cooperate with the census takers will result in immediate death.

Within five days, all taverns are closed. A raid upon one in particular is an outstanding success, for it yields a large cache of arms and a band of alien outlaws. "No doubt," says the governor, upon inspection of the arms that are easily identified as property of the Roman military, and the feral renegades that sit growling sullenly in their cells, "the raids on Roman troops will now come to a halt." The criminals are sentenced to slavery. Heavily chained, they are set to work digging out the irrigation ditches that have, because of the drought, grown shallow and hard with dried mud.

The governor is appalled at conditions in the Christian Quarter. Each adult citizen is assigned a portion of a large communal plot that he establishes for the cultivation of vegetables and for grazing livestock. Farmers are assigned to specified portions of the great wheat fields, and informed of the quotas they are expected to fill. The river is swollen again, and preparations are underway to plant as soon as the water recedes and leaves its rich silt on the land.

In the meantime, the granaries are emptied. What little is left is distributed among the people, and government funds are authorized to purchase food from the caravans for the general populace. The governor sends a series of detailed reports to Rome, outlining the present conditions, his plans for recovery of the province, and a promise of triple the amount of grain that Rome normally receives per year. The only thing left to deal with is the noble class and its clergy. The High Priests of Karnak and Luxor are summoned to the governor's mansion.

---

"I am Cyrus, Governor of Luxor and Thebes."

He does not ask the High Priest of Karnak to be seated, and takes only slight notice that the High Priest of Luxor is in a wheeled chair.

"This province has been badly managed," he says, "but all of that is in the past. The people will be fed and expected to produce in greater quantities than they have ever done before. You will find that I am neither cruel nor permissive. I have no interests other than to use this province to support the empire, and I shall do so with dispatch and efficiency. I shall not permit any obstacle to stand between me and this objective."

The room is still, the air oppressive. The governor seems not to notice the heat.

"Above all, I am a practical man. Anything and anyone that does not serve the empire is expendable. That is my rule, and you will find that I will implement it to the letter."

An aide hands him a scroll. He opens it and turns to the High Priest of Karnak.

"There are fifteen priests in residence at the Temple of Karnak."

"Yes," says the young high priest.

"They will be given work assignments in the grain fields. They will be expected to produce and fill a quota the same as any other able-bodied man in this province."

"But——" says the priest.

"You will address me as Your Excellency."

"Your Excellency," he begins, "my priests know nothing of farming."

Cyrus looks at him coldly. "They will learn."

"But——"

"Or they will be given something that requires less skill, such as digging irrigation canals or cleaning the latrines behind the military compound."

The young high priest is dumfounded.

"You shall join them, of course. You are young, and from the looks of you, have eaten regularly throughout this drought. I expect you to set them an example." The governor turns to Lukhamen. "You, of course, will not be expected to do anything so…physically demanding." He consults the scroll again. "And how many priests are there in the Temple of Luxor?"

"Nine."

"Does that include your son?"

"Ten."

"Yes, ten. I see that your other son is a student physician. A little young and not a bona fide physician, but we will make use of whatever knowledge he has."

The high priest does not answer.

"He is immediately conscripted to be physician, however inexperienced, to the farm work force. He is to attend them exclusively. In turn, he will be given the food allowance that is accorded every other adult male. Their well-being and fitness for work shall be his only priority. If there is such a time when he is free from his medical duties, he will, of course, work in the fields like anyone else."

The high priest feels something heavy growing in his chest. It spreads throughout his body, and weighs him down. There is no air in the room. There is a pain over his right eye, and he feels light-headed. He struggles to concentrate.

"Your priests, like the others, will join the work force."

Lukhamen looks into the eyes of the governor. There is no light in them. *Let us go on*, the lifeless eyes say.

"All property, as you know, belongs to Rome. However, my census takers have reported that there are certain objects of art, religious icons, and even jewelry still in your possession. These will be confiscated, sold, and used to buy farming implements for your priests."

He smiles coolly.

"We are but at the beginning, the starting point. More is to come. But there is something I want to make clear. Idleness will not be tolerated. Every bit of land and property—every man, woman, and child—will be dedicated to one thing: service to the Roman Empire. There is a great equality about to come to this land. All of your servants shall be conscripted to the fields, and you shall work beside them. There is no privilege here, only the privilege of work. This is a simple concept, easy to understand." He gestures for a guard to see the priests out, "Those who test my resolve will discover the length and breadth of my commitment.

"One more thing. The women of your households will be occupied in preparing food and suitable clothing for the working priests, as their servants will be conscripted to the fields. I am certain that, knowing nothing but lives of luxury, they have neither the strength nor the mental fortitude to lead lives of real labor. A waste."

He snaps his fingers, and the guard comes forward to escort them out. The High Priest of Karnak guides Lukhamen's wheeled chair carefully through the door. When they are on the river road, they stop under a tree. He turns the chair to face the river. A breeze blows gently upon Lukhamen's brow, and he can breathe again.

Neither man speaks for a long while. Finally, Lukhamen finds his voice.

"Behold the river, Your Excellency. It flows today as it did yesterday and as it will tomorrow. Neither he nor the Roman Empire can stop it. It is the river, and this is Egypt, and nothing can change that."

---

"I know how to farm, Father," says Lukhamen, smiling at the high priest. "We grew our food at Philae. I know how to work in the sun, and I am strong. Our people have worked this land for generations, and their blood runs in my veins."

"And I, Father, shall be fine as well," says Aahmes. "I am a doctor—almost a doctor—and my patients are people who are sick, no matter who they are or what they do."

The high priest looks at his sons—so handsome, so filled with the resilience of youth, so anxious to relieve him of worry and despair.

*Lukhamen has never known what it is to be a true priest of Amon*, he thinks to himself. *I have so much yet to teach him!*

---

It is dawn, and Femi has prepared a midday meal of bread, goat cheese, and small smoked fishes for Lukhamen and Aahmes. She hands each a sling pouch of water.

"Now do not forget to drink. It is even more important than eating."

"There she goes, Lukhamen, acting like a mother again," says Aahmes.

"Do as I say, Aahmes, and you will be fine."

"Fine? You are telling me I will be fine? I am a doctor, and you are a girl, and you are telling me I will be fine?"

He makes a clicking noise with his tongue on the roof of his mouth.

"You are nothing more than a boy, and you don't know everything."

Aahmes swats her with a napkin. She ducks and laughs. He chases her around the table.

Lukhamen and the high priest look on in astonishment. The two catch themselves and stand quite still.

"Sorry, Sire," says Femi.

"Yes, sorry, Father," says Aahmes, "Sorry, brother." Femi is, after all, betrothed to Lukhamen.

Lukhamen says nothing. Manut appears with two manservants.

"Ready, I see," says the high priest.

"Yes, Sire."

"Surely, Manut, you are not going with them."

"I am, Sire."

"But you are well beyond the age..."

"I was assured, Sire, by the governor's representative, that I was able-bodied."

"Gods of Egypt!" says the high priest.

Manut looks at him and smiles.

"I will be fine, Sire," he says.

———— ✸ ————

The high priest sits just outside the garden gate, where he can watch them as they walk the river road, toward the fields. Alenna appears at his side.

"Where are they going, Lukhamen?"

"They are going to work, my love."

"All of them?"

"Yes, all of them."

"Is that not Manut?"

"Yes, my love."

"That is odd."

"Indeed it is, Alenna."

"Are you not going as well?"

"There is no work for a man who cannot walk."

"Oh," she says.

Others file past them, on the way to the fields. They nod to the man in the wheeled chair and the beautiful, smiling woman who stands beside him. Her smile seems to comfort them.

"How nice. Everyone nods to us, Lukhamen."

"Perhaps it is because you are so beautiful, Alenna."

She smiles and touches his hair.

"Lukhamen?"

"Yes, my love."

"Your hair is white."

"I suppose it is."

"Not all over, just in front."

She touches his hair again.

"Mine is not."

"So I see."

"That nice young girl hennaed it."

"Femi?"

"Yes, Femi."

She turns around, full circle.

"Do you like it?"

"It is beautiful, Alenna."

Her face clouds, suddenly. "It does not matter anyway."

"I like it, Alenna."

The tears are falling again.

"What it is, my love?"

"So many of them are going to die."

"Alenna…"

"They are going to die where they are going."

"Alenna…"

"They're going to die, just like Marcus."

"Marcus?"

"Yes."

"How do you know about Marcus, Alenna?"

A young woman comes toward them, from the direction of Haraa's house. She stands before them and curtsies to the high priest.

"I am Lucenkep, Sire. My mother, Mahda, who is looking after the Lady Haraa's house, has sent me to be of help."

For a moment, the high priest does not understand.

"She has sent me to you since you are without your servants. I am quite strong, Sire."

"Why, yes…Lucenkep. Please. Come inside. Femi will see to you."

Together the three go inside, Lucenkep taking Alenna's arm.

———— ⌘ ————

Alone in the temple, in the shadow of a great papyrus column, the high priest looks to the small courtyard ahead. He runs his hand over the carvings on the column, lovingly, tenderly, then wheels the chair through the courtyard and into the darkened sanctuary. He looks up at the magnificent, granite statue, the Lord of all Creation in his human form.

"Lord Amon," whispers the high priest.

And then his father stands before him, wearing the high crown, a white linen pleated kilt, fastened by a wide gold belt, and a leopard skin over one shoulder, the tail hanging down his back. His eyelids are lined in kohl. He shimmers in a great light that surrounds him. He extends his arms, and from them great shafts of light illumine the dark sanctuary and descend upon the high priest.

With that light a great energy descends and moves through the high priest's body, electrifying him. He braces himself on the arms of the wheeled chair, lifts his body, stands on trembling legs, and walks. Step after trembling step, he makes his way to the altar. Behind the altar, he removes the stone that covers a niche in the wall.

# CHAPTER 61

⚓

☥

THE AFTERNOON IS COOL; THE golden hour beginning. An old woman makes her way from the leper colony onto the river road. She is covered from head to toe; only her eyes show. She has come to the road to beg for alms.

At the river, she stops to lean against a tree. So it is that she is the first to see the small temple bark, which is adorned fore and aft with small bronze figures. In the center is a small deck cabin that resembles a temple. It is covered with a canopy of purple.

The figure in the small boat oars past her, toward the Island of the Crocodiles. At the island he turns the vessel around, and starts downriver again, toward Luxor.

The leper is struck dumb for a moment. Regaining her senses, she runs back to the compound, calling for them to come see.

"Come! Come see what is on the river! Hurry!"

"What is it?" they cry.

"Come see, quickly!"

The lepers are crowded along the riverbank, huddled together, when he passes them. Slowly, slowly, he pulls the boat with the long oar. Then he puts it down and lets the river carry him on its gentle, undulating current, toward Luxor. They watch him until the river turns slightly and hides him from view. They stand there long after he has passed from sight.

A small boy on the bank, pulling a rope that is attached to an obstinate donkey, watches the boat float gently by in the golden afternoon, his mouth agape.

The sun begins its descent toward the horizon, leaving a pink dusty haze on the mountains across the river. The man has made his way now to the prow, and is standing there, his hand on its upturned end.

Alenna is at her window, gazing at the white birds gathering on the bank, as he approaches. She is blinded at first by the burst of white light reflected off the high conical crown, but then the figure in the boat turns slightly, and she can see what has caught the sun. It is the sacred *uraeus*, the brightly colored poisonous snake that rears on the brow of the crown.

"Lukhamen!" she whispers. "*Lukhamen!*" she cries.

Through her tears she sees the leopard skin over his shoulder, the tail flowing down his back. He is wearing gold bracelets, and a corselet of gold, ivory, and carnelian made of two rectangles, patterned with feathers inlaid into gold, worked in cloisonné, and rows of alternating blue turquoise, lapis lazuli, and red glass beads. On the front are figures of Amon in blue skin and Ramses in gold; on the back, enclosed within a trapezoidal frame of gold, the solar scarab beetle. A pleated kilt covers his loins, belted by a striped frontal tab and streamers that reach down to his calves. In his free hand he holds the hooked *heka* scepter.

"*Lukhamen!*" she screams, running down the stairs and through the great hall.

"Mother!" cries Femi. "What is it?"

Lucenkep runs behind them.

"My husband! He is on the river!"

Alenna is out of the house before they can stop her. In a moment the three are standing on the riverbank, watching the small boat drift away, toward the temple.

"Lukhamen," Alenna whispers.

They stand together in the hush of the early evening and watch the river birds gliding on the warm air, up and down in graceful waves, leading the way upriver, their white wings like sails before the small boat.

"Mother..." says Femi.

The smell of night jasmine floats around them.

"Be still, my daughter. See how straight he stands. Behold Lukhamen, the last High Priest of Amon."

"Mother..."

Alenna takes Femi's hand and smiles, then looks at Lucenkep.

"Come, child, stand by me."

They watch in the orange glow until the boat disappears from their sight.

The group of men walks along the riverbank in the setting sun, bent from their day in the fields, exhausted and hungry, carrying hoes and wooden plough-shares, eyes on the ground. Aahmes is the first to see him.

"Lukhamen, look!"

Lukhamen follows his brother's pointed finger to the river. The sun is behind the mountain now, and the white crown and kilt have turned violet and fluorescent in the oncoming twilight. Whispers run through the crowd.

"Who is it? Who is it?"

"It is the high priest."

"But he is standing."

"It is him, I tell you!"

Lukhamen runs to the bank, the others following.

"Father!" he whispers.

Someone whispers behind him.

"It is Pharaoh."

"It is the high priest, I tell you."

"It is Pharaoh's ghost, come to deliver us."

"Is it not the divine bark? It is Amon himself!"

Something lodges itself in Lukhamen's throat. He stands rooted before the luminous figure passing by. The small wooden boat rocks gently from side to side, making its way further downriver. Lukhamen runs along the bank, trying to follow, Aahmes behind him. The crowd follows until they are stopped by Roman troops.

"Back, back!" shouts one. "Where do you think you are going?"

The soldiers push them back, blocking the road and river bank.

———∞∞———

High on a hill, just across the river, Haraa sits astride a great white horse.

"What is going on over there?" says the large Turk at her side.

Haraa looks down at the troops in the street, the crowd of farmers pushing against them.

"Look, there! On the river!" says the big man.

Haraa draws in a breath.

"What is it?" he says.

Haraa strains her eyes to see. Then they fill with tears. "It is Egypt," says Haraa, "It is Egypt." She turns her steed toward the foot of the hill.

"But where are you going, Haraa?"

"Home," says Haraa. "I am going home."

———∞∞———

The governor stands at the window of his office on the second floor. The twilight is purple now, and the figure passing below is all but invisible, except for the crown and kilt that shine white against the blackness of the river. It passes slowly beneath the window and is swallowed up into the night.

"What a fool!" says the governor, "to flaunt the law like that! The wearing of an Egyptian crown has been forbidden for hundreds of years! Is he begging for execution?"

The centurion who stands beside him says nothing. The governor yawns. "Go get him."

"We will never find him upon the river at night, Your Excellency."

"Don't tell me what you will not do!" the governor says, suddenly awake, suddenly furious. "Get a boat and bring him back! The fool is only drifting!"

"Yes, Your Excellency."

The centurion walks down the wide staircase, slowly. Deliberately.

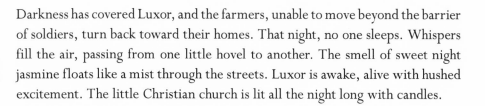

Darkness has covered Luxor, and the farmers, unable to move beyond the barrier of soldiers, turn back toward their homes. That night, no one sleeps. Whispers fill the air, passing from one little hovel to another. The smell of sweet night jasmine floats like a mist through the streets. Luxor is awake, alive with hushed excitement. The little Christian church is lit all the night long with candles.

It is midnight, and the street is all but empty of Roman guards. Lukhamen, still in his work clothes, has made his way carefully to the temple. He walks quietly down the long, deserted black corridor; the pylons loom above him. He makes his way into the darkened courtyard, through the columns, across the second courtyard, and into the sanctuary. One torch bears a flame. Amon, Eldest Lord of the Sky and of Earth, wearing the high feather crown, a plaited beard, a corselet and pleated kilt, bracelets, and a high collar, stands above the altar. At his feet is an empty wheeled chair, turned over on its side.

Something on the altar catches Lukhamen's eye. It is his father's ring, a great amethyst set in gold, the ring each high priest receives upon assuming office. Lukhamen picks it up, holds it in his hand for a moment, then puts it on his finger.

# CHAPTER 62

———— ⌾⌾⌾ ————

THIRTY YEARS HAVE PASSED SINCE I first met Reverend Brown. I see him once a
year, and if I'm lucky, twice. He is nearing retirement and reads mostly now
for members of his chapel and close friends. I'm always glad to be in his company. His once-dark hair is white, as is mine. The blue eyes are the same—like
cornflowers.

He greets me as he always does, with a smile and a funny anecdote.
The laughter brings good energy into the room. As usual, I have been
given a three-by-five card on which I am to write the names of three people who have passed over, and three questions. There is nothing magical
about the number three. It's the way Reverend Brown manages his time
and energy.

The trip to Luxor had been a defining moment for me. There, an internal
compass had guided me to the spot where the high priest's house once stood.
I recognized the garden in back. I walked unerringly to the temple and to the
Christian Quarter, places I had never been. I felt as if I had come home. There
is no doubt in my mind that I lived there, and that I lived there in Lukhamen's
lifetime.

But there is a veil between me and that life in Luxor. I still see it through a
mist. I've never been able to see anyone's face clearly, and I can't place myself
in the story. Lukhamen calls me *Beloved*. I need to know who I was, who I am. I
might know then why the story was given to me.

On the card is my best guess: "Who was I then? Was I Lucenkep or Alenna?"
I fold it tightly and put it in Reverend Brown's hand.

"Say, 'it's a beautiful day.'" He asks me to do this to clear my mind so that my thoughts will not interfere with his. "It's a beautiful day," I say.

He holds the folded card. During a reading he may close his eyes, sit quietly, and nod from time to time. At other times he will turn his head slightly to the side and say quietly, "Yes, I hear you, I hear you." After all these years, it still amazes me.

In the reading, Eddie comes through, and Lukhamen, my mother and father, two aunts and an uncle. He calls them all by name: Precious, John, Butsie (my uncle's nickname), Ida, Hazel. Once, in a reading, he spoke to my mother: "Yes," he whispered at his shoulder, "I know you're precious, but what's your name?" I had to laugh.

They tell me that Spirit is helping to write "the book," that I am on the right track. They are full of love and encouragement.

Reverend Brown does not know what "the book" is about. I doubt that he would remember it if he did; he sees so many people. He has described himself as being like a telephone, an instrument that receives information and transmits it to the person sitting in front of him. He is not interested in the message. He has heard thousands of messages.

He pauses. It seems as if the reading is over. I am disappointed and half out of my seat when he opens his eyes, looks at me and says, quite out of context, "Alenna. You are Alenna." And then, "That's all I have." The reading is over.

Sometimes he asks me if I understand what I am being told. This time he says nothing. Even though I came expecting an answer to my question, I'm shaken, as I often am when I leave him. One can ask a question that is glib, casual, or deadly serious. One can even be reasonably sure of the answer. But to hear it answered from Spirit is still shocking.

---

A long time has passed since death changed the trajectory of my life. I no longer question the messages that are passed on to me from Spirit. I no longer doubt their validity. Age is a softening experience. Love becomes more important than proof, and hope more important than logic.

Through a cosmic keyhole, I witnessed a life in which there was more truth and beauty than any I could have constructed or imagined. I was the beholder of a marvelous view, a priceless glimpse into another time. I saw the end of an era, the sunset of a glorious civilization, and in the end, I saw myself in it. I was there. I was someone's mother. I was Alenna.

By what I can only call Grace, I became privy to Lukhamen's memories, memories that encompassed not just the life of the person known as Alenna, but the lives of those she loved and lived with, memories brought to life and set in a glorious landscape—Luxor on the Nile. Like a beautiful jewel wrapped in silk and enclosed in a lovely story box, Alenna's life was a mirror in which I could see myself reflected in the past.

---

How lovely it is now to turn back the pages to Lukhamen's words at the beginning of the story:

*Oh, to be a child again, and to see my mother. So long, and still I miss her. She was everything that Egypt is, that Egypt was. She painted her eyelids and brows in the style of the ancients; and when she walked, her robes rustled softly, like water rushes in the breeze. She was warm and smelled of oranges and cardamom...*

*I remember the coffee and sweet, pungent odors that came from our kitchen, and I long for the days of my childhood in Luxor. Oh, to feel again the touch of my mother's hand on my brow. Oh, to hear her voice, calling my name!*

---

I have never learned by revelation. My road has always been long and winding. In hindsight, I see that there were signs along the way, always pointing to Alenna.

In Luxor, there were sights, sounds, smells, visceral, sensory reminders that evoked feelings I had not anticipated, such as the resentment and anger that swelled in my chest as I sat in the lobby of the Winter Palace, the colonial-era hotel which sat on the site of Alenna's home, and the sharp relief at finding the garden in back, bougainvillea waving in the breeze, and a birdcage in the center like the one that held Lukhamen's colorful birds.

I was filled with exhilaration at finding the temple still intact, then quickly saddened at its emptiness. So much was felt there! But it was on the plane, amid tears, that the sad realization came fully upon me that I had come home and everybody I loved was gone. I went to Egypt filled with excitement and anticipation, not knowing that what I would find there would be love long gone.

I came to this life rooted in Alenna's traumas. She was married to a damaged husband, a de-sensitized man who left her lonely and loveless, as was I. Her home was taken from her, as was mine. She lived a life subjected to the wants and ambitions of men, as did I. The circumstances of her life left her powerless and filled with rage. She coped with the pain of it by escaping it, as did I. Alenna chose dementia; I chose alcoholism.

But the loss of sons was our bond.

I came to this life richly endowed with Alenna's psychic DNA. It was what I needed to move forward—from despair to hope, from darkness to light.

When Eddie died, I lost hope in everything—in God mostly, but also in life. When, through a spiritual medium, I found evidence that Eddie's spirit still lived, I was glad. But I was not comforted. I accepted the concepts of life after death and of reincarnation. In theory. But grief, I discovered, was more powerful than theories, despair more powerful than concepts. They were forces that could blind the soul.

My despair stemmed from the assumption that life was short and precarious, a meaningless, random prank that could be ended at any moment by the decree of a cruel, detached God. Death meant that the people we loved were lost. The idea is embedded in our lexicon. I said it myself: "I lost my son."

In a last desperate measure before suicide, I asked for help from the only source left—the spirit world. And my son answered.

With the wisdom of a wider perspective, Lukhamen showed me another aspect of life. With a son's love, he gradually and carefully opened my mind to another assumption—that no one was lost. Not even me. The story was not to distract me from suicide as I originally thought; it was to show me the futility of it.

———— ✧ ————

There are dark, rainy days just before winter sets in, when I long for the desert, its heat, and its sun. I have taken to going to Arizona. I love it there. It feels like home. Perhaps Alenna and I are becoming more…integrated. One thing is certain: I have more to learn.

There are days when memories of *this* life rise to the surface of my consciousness and touch my heart, days when I long for the little children who lived with me and gave me such joy, especially the little boy with the big brown eyes and the curls that fell over his forehead, the little boy in whom the joy of life shone like the sun. There are days when I long for *my* mother, and the smell of coffee coming from her kitchen.

But most of my days are lived in the present, where the little girls, my daughters, have grown into women, where my granddaughters have grown into women. I have known happiness with a husband whose love for me was ever patient, and kind, and enduring. I have much to be grateful for.

What happened to me is what happens to many, many souls. At the darkest moment, in the deepest throes of anguish, at the point in time when all seems lost, a gift is imparted, a pinpoint of light shines in the night, the glimmer of a small star reaches a spirit in despair, and gives it hope.

A messenger came to me bearing a story. It was given to me so that I might see myself in it and find within it a secret, a light in the night for all who mourn, the message that death is banished, that life is all there is, and that *love is greater than fire, and wind, and time.*

# EPILOGUE

―――∞∞∞―――

THERE WERE TIMES DURING THE course of writing the story when, in the throes of little faith, I wanted an inkling of proof, some thing or some event to which I could connect what I was experiencing to actual recorded events. Soon after I embarked on what can only be called a timid foray into history, I felt instinctively that I should leave things as they were. When I abandoned the search, the inkling made its appearance.

I had decided to search the Internet for alternative terms of address applied to Roman officers. (The term "sire" had become tiring.) Instead of finding what I was looking for, I stumbled across a list of Roman Governors of Egypt, and there it was:

*Marcus Aurelius Heraclitus, Governor of Egypt, 215-216 AD.*

The years correspond with the time impressed upon me at the beginning of the story—214 AD. I believe Marcus governed Luxor officially, or as an interim governor, longer than one year. Perhaps his governorship was extended to the whole of Egypt for a limited time. But he lived, as did they all.

# ABOUT THE AUTHOR

Helen Delaney is a writer. She is a former diplomat and has worked in the technical standards field for over forty-two years, first as the Washington, D.C. representative for one of the world's largest standards organizations, and later as the head of her own consulting business. She is a mother, and a grandmother, and lives on Maryland's Eastern Shore.